Between Two Women

A Stratford Story

Enjoy

Between Two Women
A Stratford Story

Bruce Alexander Woods

Second Edition

Bramy Books, 167 Fallingbrook Dr.,
Ancaster, Ontario, L9G 1E7

Between Two Women

A Stratford Story

National Library of Canada Cataloging in Publication

Woods, Bruce Alexander 1931-
Between Two Women: A Stratford Story

ISBN 978-0-9784236-0-5

1)Woods, Bruce A. 2) History 3) Humour 4) Memoirs

Second edition, revised and enlarged, November 2008
For more information contact
Bruce A.Woods
Web Page: www.between two women.net

Bramy Books is an imprint of Maracle Press Limited, 1156King Street East, Oshawa, Ontario. L1H 1H8 Toll Free 1-800-558-8604
Bramy Books ISBN 978-0-9784236- Editor: Dorothy Alexander
Design Cover: Jordan Grupe

These stories are true but some names have been changed to protect privacy.

Table of Contents

Tribute:

There are two redeemers in my life. The first, who is my mother, is spelt in this book in lower case; the second, is spelled in capitals. My mother was gifted; she was born beautiful and talented. Unfortunately, she was destined to live a tragic life. Through her sufferings, she gave me the priceless legacy of love and thereby my earthly redemption. I honour her sacrifice on my behalf. She made my life better and therein freed me to live well. I dedicate this book to her memory.

Introduction:

I am a hopelessly unrepentant romantic. I love to look at simpler times, through rose-tinted glasses. This is the tale of a kid who grew up in Stratford, Ontario, and loved every minute of it. I raise an important question; is the story more than it really was? I will let the reader decide that. Nonetheless let it be known that all the facts are at least 97% pure. The fiction part is the humour and where my memory gets fuzzy. Still, the story is basically true and the narrative is real. So to all and sundry let it be known as a lover of life, you can read with confidence and know that this story really happened. I am also an aspiring historian. The only thing that gets in my way is that I am a born optimist. This drives my wife crazy, because as my best literary critic, she keeps saying, "Did that really happen or is that just your imagination?" Truth be told, it's my old girlfriends that get her. She tells me I should have married one of them. I tell her there ought to be a law against making girls as beautiful as she is. The compliment works. It needs to: after more than fifty years, who would have me?

The heart of this tale is the tender and compassionate story of the relationship, between a mother and her son. It is a story of redemption through suffering that both contradicts but also parallels my own happy childhood. My awareness of my mother's sorrows only came gradually because my happiness obscured my understanding of mother's pain. This journey of nostalgia into the past is a compelling story for me, because in my old age, I have decided to look back and interpret the declining health of my emotionally disturbed mother. I honour her for her contribution to my life, but others also contribute to my adventure. There are more than a hundred people in this story. I like to give them the benefit of the doubt except when I laugh at their indiscretions. So I spin my tale through sixteen years of what some historians view as the epoch of the twentieth century. They include the roaring twenties (as told to me by my mother, since that comes from before my times) the great depression, and the climatic events of World War II, and its aftermath. It is a tale of triumph and tragedy. I tell it as I naively perceived it, through the eyes of a growing child.

On a lighter note, I came into this world a mediocre seven pounds and was a sickly baby, so my mother delayed my circumcision until I was two; and as you can imagine I have ever since, 'been scared of growing up'. Amazingly I have achieved that worthy goal and left three score and ten, five years ago. There are advantages to being old; for one thing, I don't have to worry about dying young. Therefore, as an old man, I can relate the story and smile at the things that humiliated me as a child. So, with tongue in cheek, and with malice towards none, I grant you access, to laugh with me at the foibles of my youth. And no I did not keep a diary; I have had to rely on my memory. For this reason when names escaped me I simply invented new ones. Rarely have I tinkered with the facts; however, sometimes I resorted to a composite story. I only did this once with the 'old swimming hole' episode. From time to time, I have resorted to sanctified imagination and research in The Stratford Beacon-Herald and the Perth Archives. The latter two, are indisputable, the former — well, let the reader decide. All of this aside, I therefore once again affirm the details are 97 % pure.

Resource persons whose contributions to this book proved invaluable

Alan MacDonald
Dorothy (Johnston) Landers
Margaret Wade
Rita (Butler) Garvin
Cheryl (Gillatly) Martin
Laverne Heath
Nancy Bacle
Stan Hollowell
Bethany Dekorte
Ronald Amy

The Memories of Bruce A.Woods
and the City that shaped my life

Chapter 1
My Palace

Shortly after the crust of the earth had cooled, (it is alleged) some unknown and now forgotten savages clustered around three intersecting trails in Western Ontario and established a village. In time these three trails became roads. When it was discovered that these roads led to three remarkable lakes, unlike any to be found on earth, by some stroke of genius they were given street names to point weary pioneers to their destinations. Thus, Huron, Ontario and Erie streets were born. When the need for identification of the crossroad itself arose, a homesick Englishman called the place Stratford and dreamed that one day the Garden of Eden might be restored to this pristine location so elegantly favoured by the placid Avon River. Meanwhile the gods of caprice and their ilk attempted to spoil paradise by turning the village into an industrial railroad town. Providence, however, smiled and the factory foundries fell into decay. The Muse takes its cues. The untidy industrial town traded its tools for tomes and became the cultural centre of the universe. This transition coincided with my sixteenth birthday, but now I'm getting ahead of my story, so let us begin with the house where I grew up.

156 Brunswick Street is one of the oldest houses in Stratford. It stands today as it did in 1867, a modest 1½ story brick house painted red. I say painted. The house was originally made of brick that was supposed to be red. Somebody should have painted them white; it would have looked better. Poorly made bricks deteriorate with age and discolour, so Grandpa mortared the worst of them and to preserve the bricks, painted them red. The house itself had been tastefully laid out by some unknown builder who must have had an understanding of what makes for charm. This now forgotten artisan knew the value of a bay window facing south, and a box window facing east, (where Grandma kept all the ferns); this was my palace for 16 years. The house had been enlarged before Grandpa Gillatly

bought the place, with a kitchen extension out the back that included the gas room, and the cellar-way.

What is a cellar-way? Don't ask me. We always called it that. Perhaps it's because it was two steps down and had a cement floor. A common feature of houses built, before the arrival of central heating and electricity, was two

156 Brunswick Street

kitchens. The second kitchen was for summer only and was small. Beside it was the cold room (our cellar-way) for preserves, also quite small. Our house had these two small rooms side by side with doors that opened to the larger wintertime kitchen. The gas room was so called, because the gas stove which dominated the room is where the cooking is done from late spring to early fall. The crowning adornment was the veranda where we sat on hot summer nights listening to the occasional birdcall before the crickets struck up the band.

Friends seemed to call easily in those days without the need of an invitation. I cannot ever recall anyone who complained of loneliness. These were the days when it is common for neighbours to borrow a cup of sugar or two eggs to bake a cake, because they had just run out of the necessities to finish. Conversation occasioned by these commonplace customs makes for entertainment. The radio provides the rest. Fibber McGee and Molly, the Amos and Andy Show, Edgar Bergen and Charlie McCarthy kept us chuckling. The program I liked best was the Jack Benny comedy hour which we heard every Sunday evening. All this material made for plenty of fun when we talked with the neighbours. We knew every family on our street in both directions right up to the sixth or seventh house and were not surprised to be similarly known by them. The advent of television changed all this and banished the special life of the sidewalks indoors, where all reasonable adults veg in silence before the ubiquitous TV set.

When the maples planted out front turn red, and Halloween [my birthday] approaches, the coal stove is lit in the main kitchen. The gas room is now abandoned for six months. I can still remember how cold my boots felt going outside on a winter's day, because boots are always kept in the gas room. The Cellar-way is where Grandma keeps the preserves, with one corner boarded off for newspapers. We always keep a winter's supply of newspapers for lighting fires in the kitchen stove. When I am old enough, one of my jobs is to chop the kindling, so that on cold winter mornings, we can quickly get the fire going, and then add the coal, which keeps the kitchen warm. All day the stove is fed its allotment of coal until it is bedtime when it was slowly allowed to go out.

I can still see the shelves of the cellar-way lined up neatly with the rows of preserves that Grandma puts down every fall. One shelf for peaches. Another shelf for raspberries, that are so delicious, I can still taste them to this day. Another shelf is for pickles and beans. Plums are also preserved, because there are two plum trees in the back yard. One is especially good for climbing. Never will I forget the day I was hanging upside down on the branch of that aging plum tree! It is a few minutes after lunch, and I decide on a little tree climbing before I return to school. Mr. Plum tree is at least forty years old but familiarity deafens my ears. I ignore his creaking warnings, but warnings cannot impact my childish inexperience. The branch on which I am hanging breaks under my weight, and down I fall, flat on my back.

"I will die right here on the ground, and nobody will find me in time!" I am in pain, and I can't breathe. Panic-stricken, I get up and stagger for the kitchen. I think, "I can't breathe, and I am going to die!" And then suddenly it happens; my lungs bursting for air open, and I can breathe again. Sobbing, I tell my Grandma that I will never be the same again. It is amazing how soon a little boy can recover in the arms of a loving Grandma, so by the time mother rushes in, I am healed. My first growing-pains lesson that I remember is learned that day. When you get the wind knocked out of you, you will recover, although it takes a few seconds. At the time, it seemed it was much longer. After I am settled down, I plead for a reprieve from school. Surely suffering like this ought to be compensated with reward.

"I can't go to school this afternoon after this." I cry. Grandmothers can be merciless at times, and mother backs her up. This is not my lucky day; all I get is a note explaining why I am returning to school a few minutes late. That line of preserved plums in the cellar-way has a special meaning for me that I shall never forget. Mr. Plum tree must have forgiven me for my indiscretion, despite his obvious injury: he just kept on producing plums for my insatiable palate as long as I can remember.

Another memory that lingers is the smell of oatmeal cookies. We never have oatmeal cookies in the summer, because the oven in the gas stove doesn't work. Only in the cool weather, when the coal stove heats the built-in oven, do we have cookies. When I could have eaten six cookies freshly baked, I can only have two per meal. It is my job to stack the cookies in little boxes, sixteen per box, — all twenty boxes. Being the connoisseur of cookies common to little boys, when Grandma isn't looking, I get my six cookies anyway. Years later I find out she knew it all along. Week by week the cookies would disappear. Funny how those oatmeal cookies so easy to eat at the beginning lose their appeal after three or four weeks. I guess it is called the law of diminishing returns.

In our house there are four small bedrooms and a bath upstairs, with an eight-inch hole in each of the bedrooms covered by a grate. Imagine, they are still there! These prehistoric creations let the heat escape upwards from the warmer rooms below. The living room has a large circular grate, where the heat from the furnace rises. Ours is a house where you roast by the fire and freeze in the corners. Near the furnace grate, looking like an indoor scarecrow, is the clothes rack for drying the wash. Many of the family activities take place around that grate. On winter mornings, I race downstairs to stand as close as I can near the heat to get dressed for school. Later, when I am old enough, it is my job to stack the furnace with an embankment of coal, so the fire won't go out over night. That is fine in late fall and spring, but I still get a shiver remembering how cold the house was in winter, particularly when we woke up in the mornings.

The luxury of such a furnacc was hard won. When grandpa bought the place there was no furnace or basement to accommodate our house. Creating a cellar after a house is built was Grandpa Alexander's first challenge. He dug it out by hand. I remember mother saying,

"I never saw a man work so hard as my father did when he dug out the cellar with a pick and shovel. Why, he even poured the cement, mixing it all by hand." The cellar was big enough for the furnace and an adjacent room to store coal under the steep stairway that led down to the cramped basement, a true labour of love. Eighty-five years later, nothing has changed except for the new forced air unit that has replaced the old furnace I remember.

My bedroom, like the others, has a sloping ceiling on the one side, where you can bump your head, if you are momentarily distracted. (Expletive deleted). My cuss words are collected and duly repented of at bedtime prayers. You can lie on my bed with your head near the inside wall, and play footsies with the ceiling on the far side. So there is only one way to place the bed, which simplifies the choices, when it comes to furniture arrangements. My window looks south, where I can see the street below. I like our house, and I can never comprehend why mother says,

"Imagine, father a carpenter by trade, buying such a house as this." When I was a child, an old man came by one day to ask a favour. He explained that he had been born in our house at the time of Confederation 1867. He had fond memories of the place, where he had grown up, and wondered if we would mind, if he could look through the old home place. Of course, Grandma and mother agreed. After a few stories and an hour of memories, he left never to be seen again. I understand that unknown stranger. I too have made such a pilgrimage. The present occupants were accommodating. After 59 years, I had the thrill of seeing it all again.

Modernity has changed and upgraded the house a little, but the configuration today is much the same as it was back then. I was able to share with the present occupants a few stories of my own. A house like 156 Brunswick has its own personality. It shaped the elderly stranger that wanted to see it again, back in 1941. To this very day, it continues to shape me, though now only in my memories. Years later, as one who had a hand in creating beautiful buildings (I designed one and helped renovate two more), I can testify to the personality of any building, especially a house. It leaves a mark on your character that moulds your thinking.

I have never seen a kitchen to match the like of ours! There never was a proper foundation for the kitchen, so the slowly deteriorating wooden supports underneath had conveniently sunk creating a saucer affect. This Act of Providence was helpful on wash days, always on a Monday. That's when Grandma would roll out the old wringer washing machine which was stored in the gas room, to do the laundry. The wringer is used to separate the water from the clothing and the buttons from the shirts (hopefully only a few) which Grandma dutifully sews back on after the wash has dried. Small spills conveniently roll to the centre of the floor, and are mopped, when the wash is done. On rainy days or in winter, clothes are hung from ropes strung across the kitchen ceiling or by the grate in the living room. Two wooden chairs that grandpa modified by sawing off the backs support two laundry tubs full of rinse water. They stand side by side with the second tub, suitably doused with the bluing block, to make the white wash look white, instead of tattletale grey. If evening darkness descended before the work was completed, it was banished by a naked lightbulb that hung from the ceiling which was operated by the switch, a black rotating knob at the kitchen door.

The hand pump is in the kitchen corner, and magically produces soft water, when primed by a cup of the same. This wonderfully soft texture is sometimes grey. The cistern eventually fell into disuse when it cracked due to frost. The soft water source was the rainwater collected from the roof, which, although pure at first, was soiled due to the frost-damage. The aging hand pump sat for years ashamed of its diminished glory until in a singular act of mercy we finally laid it to rest. We do have running water from a single tap, which can be heated on the coal stove in the winter, and on the gas stove in the summer. As a child, I have my bath in the kitchen every Saturday night. As I get older, we carry the hot water from the kitchen to the bathtub upstairs. What a celebration we have, when the hot water heater is installed upstairs in the bathroom with a hot water tap to supplement the original in the kitchen!

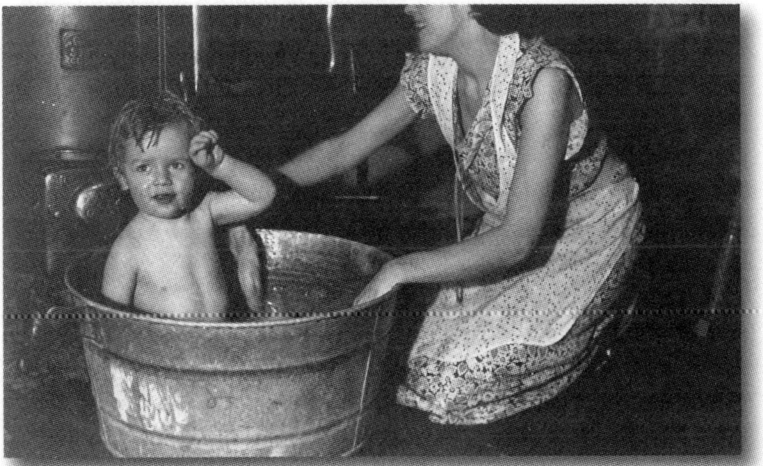

My Saturday night bath in Grandma's rinse tub.

By the age of three, since I had assumed that nothing of real importance had happened before I was born, I conclude that life at Brunswick Street is good. There is me, Grandma and Grandpa, Mother, Uncle Norman and Uncle Gordon. Uncle Frank had left two years before I arrived. I never questioned the absence of a father; the mystery of an absent father never occurred to me until I was ten years old.

My grandfather was a strikingly handsome man who died when I was three, which explains why I have little memory of him. Today's psychologists tell us that a child's personality is pretty well formed by the time he is three and a half. I guess, somewhere in my makeup, there stands a shadow of my grandpa. How often have I looked at his picture, with his pipe between his teeth and me on his knee while he is reading the newspaper. Grandma always said he was irresponsible and lost too much money in the stock market. Then, to escape the shame, he moved from Sarnia to Camrose, Alberta. I would like to have heard grandpa's version but that, of course, isn't going to happen. Then, seven years after grandpa died, miraculously, he spoke (well sort of). Grandma received a lawyer's letter, to confirm that she was indeed grandpa's rightful heir. It seems that some of that worthless stock that grandpa bought had surprisingly increased in value. Grandma searched the records and found the necessary verification. A few weeks later a windfall of $300 was deposited in Grandma's account at the British Mortgage & Trust.

"Well," said mother, "imagine, grandpa actually did make some money on the stock market." If you listened carefully, you could almost hear grandpa chuckling from his grave.

Grandpa's story, as it was told to me, was that grandpa, a carpenter by trade, simply decided to cash in on the 1912 building boom that was taking place in the West and so moved the family to Camrose, Alberta. Grandma hated Camrose, but my mother loved it. Unfortunately those happy days were marred when her best girlfriend died of appendicitis. I used to wonder if mother ever got over the loss. She still talked about it thirty years later, when I was in my teens. I didn't think much about it at the time, but gave it a great deal of thought much later. On the other hand, 156 Brunswick Street, Stratford, was my house, my world, and my unmarred happiness. Every now and again, when I can make the journey to Stratford, I drive by the old place, and marvel at how narrow Brunswick Street has become. Even the house is shrunken in size.

The other institution of importance to me is the candy store. A short walk past the 'Smith house' at the corner of Nile and Brunswick stood an unimposing building, with this sign 'Albert W. Lloyd'. It was a corner grocery store. Such stores were to be found on just about every second corner in Stratford. Two blocks south of Lloyd's was Tom Cruickshank's. One block further south on Douro and Nile was Bannister's. Cross the railroad tracks and there is Allan's, but those were the days before everybody owned a car and supermarkets were non-existent. Albert Lloyd always dressed in his white apron. A diminutive man with a white moustache, he would smile at the kids, who came with their penny and say,

"Now what would you like to buy?" Now that I am an old man, I think Mr. Lloyd had an enviable job. When I was a kid, looking at the glass case that displayed the candy, I would ponder that important decision for a considerable time, and usually decide on blackballs. Three for a penny is good value for the money. I wonder what forbidden substance was in those candies that would turn my tongue black for at least a half an hour.

Our house has large moulded casings on all the doors and oversized baseboards that have survived to this day, including the staircase banister. I especially remember sliding down the grand handrail. The staircase had a second option. As a robust five-year-old, with a soft bottom, the staircase was the other choice. How I love to entertain and impress an audience with the royal bumps. Wherever company arrives, I call out from the top of the stairs,

"Look at me". As soon as I have their attention, from the top step, I give a push, and bounce, at full throttle right to the bottom step, in four seconds flat. While the guests laugh, Grandma, smothering a smile, scolds me saying,

"You'll wear out my stairs that way." Next I show them how I can handle the handrail, from top to bottom in two seconds. Grandma sighs and says,

"I guess I'll never need to polish that banister." I've always appreciated a practical thinker.

The part of the house that intrigues me most is Grandma's secret room where she keeps all her gold and expensive jewellery. I always knew that Grandma was very rich. It's just that she isn't telling anybody, especially me. At least that's what I intuitively have come to understand. That crawl space under the living room floor leads to Grandma's secret room, where all the gold is kept. I am sure of it. I explain all this to my cousin, Billy Gillatly, who being a year older, at the age of six, thinks I am letting my imagination get the best of me.

"Bruce Woods, you're crazy."

"I am not; I know Grandma is rich!"

I can see that Billy is wavering as I tell him about Grandma's treasure room in the cellar. He doesn't believe me yet, but I can see he's getting interested even though he doubts. I persist until Billy becomes a treasure hunter just like me. We fantasize the candy we can buy if we can just get to that room in the cellar where Grandma keeps her gold. The problem is Grandma will never leave us alone so we can explore the cellar — that is — until the fateful day.

"I'm going next door to see Mrs. Smith for a few minutes, so please be good little boys, and play nicely until I come back." My eyes widen with excitement. The moment I had planned for has come, and there is no time to waste. I run for the flashlight, and scoop up the papers. The newspapers will keep Billy's clothes from getting soiled. I will hold the flashlight.

"Just a minute!" Billy says, "You can do the crawling; I'll hold the flashlight."

This is indeed a crisis, and I am in no mood to explain to Billy, that I am too scared for that. It is at this time, I discover my powers of persuasion. Billy braves the dangers of the crawl space. I hold the flashlight. Courageously, Billy inches his way to the secret treasure room. Our hearts pound wildly, as we contemplate a world of chocolate ice cream. Then, as suddenly as the vision is given, it vanishes. Alas, Billy reports,

"There is no treasure room on the far side of the crawl space" Incredulously I reply,

"No treasure room?"

"Nope!" says a disconsolate Billy, "There is nothing here. There is only dirt and more dirt."

Our candy vision is dashed beyond repair. As Billy retreats, we retrieve the newspapers. We pile them neatly in the bin, where we found them and put away the flashlight. Minutes later, Grandma returns to see two little boys playing quietly in the kitchen.

The other important memory of the kitchen is the old green cupboard, where Grandma keeps the dishes. We call it the sideboard. Today we'd call it a buffet with hutch. I can still see the well-worn corner where anybody who sits on the rocking chair by the window, can put their feet up on the ledge. All the men do it. There is no need to paint the sideboard, because the corner would soon be worn away by the menfolk. They always use the sideboard to push the rocking chair into action. I dream of the day when I will be big enough to accomplish this feat and feel quite grownup, when at last, at the age of eleven, I too can take part in this rite of passage, one more step to manhood.

One more important memory about the Brunswick Street house is the storm windows. They weigh a ton, and are carefully stored in the garage for the summer. However, every fall they come out of the old garage and, after a good cleaning, make their way one by one to the appropriate window openings. This requires the old wooden extension ladder (also stored in the garage) and the strong arms of Uncle Gordon to put them in place. We always know when to take them down, because the cherry tree in the back yard will bloom to signal in the arrival of spring. Amazing! After all these years, those storm windows are still in use. I would finish this paragraph, if I could, with a few more sentences, but my glasses are so misty I can't see to write.

Grandma was born old and never changed or so I thought. This picture was taken at the beach complete with respectable dress code.

Chapter 2

The Festival City

If someone were to choose the ten most charming cities in North America, Stratford would have to be on the list. It is one of the most beautiful small cities I have ever seen. This observation came home to me long after I left the town of my boyhood. Children are so naïve that conclusions like this only come long after they have matured and seen the larger world. As I look back, well do I remember Ontario Street (our main street). As one approaches from the east side of town, a world of modern progress unfolds. It includes motels, restaurants and big box stores. Gratefully, the city core, as I remember it, is unpolluted by change and vibrantly alive. Stratford had been stunned by the news that the CNR was closing, but hope was on the horizon. Tom Patterson, a repatriate citizen with a vision, in many ways became a sort of town saviour. Thanks to Patterson the city that bore Shakespeare's image discovered Shakespeare. Just as the CNR shops were being phased out to make way for the mighty Diesels that now rule the rails, this visionary romantic in shining armour appeared. Tom Patterson a retired advertising agent bested the skeptics that predicted the town's demise. Cultural David slew the pragmatic Goliath of manufacturing fame and theatre was crowned king.

In deference to the faithful farmers of Perth County, of which Stratford is the county seat, be assured that you are not forgotten. We are (here I claim membership with you) also the bacon capital of the world. I will not attempt to settle piglet wars with Kewanee, Illinois, which claims to be the hog capital of the world. Kewanee produced Edward Robb Ellis, foremost American diarist of the twentieth century. We produced Tom Patterson the visionary that gave us Stratford reborn and thus we became the North American cultural capital of Shakespeare's timeless plays. Our 'Stratford' was

I am indebted to Edward Robb Ellis for his wit and humour which I happily borrow to jazz up my story. He is America's formost diarist and for those who want an eye witness of the halcyon days before World War II and after, he can be read with profit.

Perth County Court House in Stratford: courtesy Perth–Stratford Archives

second to none, save the original to be found on an island somewhere beyond the Atlantic. So whom would you sooner adopt? Ed Ellis a famous newspaper writer of the New York World or Tom Patterson the cultural saviour of our city. And which town would you like to visit next? With all due respect, Kewanee? Get serious!

The Stratford I remember has not changed much. O yes, they ripped up the brick that used to grace Waterloo Street and others (would that we could get those bricks back again) but basically the old town is intact. The facades of over 100 years ago are still there. That handsome City Hall still dominates Wellington Street and Downie, with the old market square paved over for parking. Considering the sack of Rome, this is an anomaly we can accept with one notable exception. The old post office! I reverently remove my cap every time I look at the garden on the north side of Ontario Street where the old post office used to stand. It's gone! Erie Street used to be the Champs Elysee to the former Cenotaph standing guard for the beautiful post office with the clock tower booming out the Westminster chimes. Alas for the bronze soldiers of the Cenotaph. One day when its guard was down, somebody ordered the post office demolished. Others, taking justice into their own hands, ignominiously tore down the Cenotaph for dereliction of duty placing it at the Fort. At first I regarded this, a crime comparable to regicide, but on sober reflection, I suppose it was all for the best. Still, I did shed a tear of lamentation when I first saw the gaping hole where the post office once stood. It reminded me how awful Uncle Frank looked when he smiled, after his eye teeth were removed

How I love Stratford. Its indelible imprint on the landscape of my memory gives me pleasure. I didn't love it when I was young. It seemed like such an ordinary place to me. One must distance oneself to see beauty where no beauty before could be seen.

As a child, I did appreciate the fort. It was originally built to hold back the fill that gave Stratford a level promontory to overlook the river behind the now fallen post office. The cut stone rampart that holds everything together gives the appearance of a fort and just to round out the effect, two ancient cannon were mounted to give the place the illusion of a fortress. The final effect was a wonderfully crafted bulwark that beautifies the park. That fort gives sufficient appearance to inspire a child's imagination of knights in armour, pomp and circumstance, befitting some medieval kingdom. Well do I remember when sitting astride one of those cannons, how I was transported to another world where through smoke and fire, I led my valiant troops on to victory over the vanquished enemies of our glorious Perth county.

At other times we kids, fitting our shoes in the crevices between the large cut stones, would scale the wall, proudly showing off our dexterity as we challenged the fort. Sixty five years later, I see small children doing exactly the same thing. The only addition is the relocated cenotaph. Just for the record, appropriately I suppose, the new location of the cenotaph was suitably placed behind the fortress façade. That's where Remembrance Day services are now held.

Thanks to mother, I did have an appreciation of William Street. She would take me for walks around the river just like today's tourists do. We always included William Street, especially where the lovely homes overlook the Avon River. I still enjoy a drive down William Street. Starting from stately old St. James Anglican Church, I find myself craning my head left and right until we finish the street where the really elegant homes vie with one another for attention.

Stratford's main drag is Ontario Street, a home to many shops and stores some of which are still owned by the families that ran them in my day. The sidewalks are wide and the street is wider still. A recent addition is the shade trees that seem right at home because the city fathers had the foresight to make their main street broad and beautiful. Even in winter, the street was a charmer with plenty of room for the snow banks that lined the avenue. Today they clear them away: in my day the snow just kept piling up.

At the terminus of Ontario Street, where the traffic abruptly turns right to the Huron Bridge, stands the court house. It guards the western end of the street like a secular cathedral that might have been an impressive Methodist church, but it has a square tower instead of a steeple. (That wily Durand wasn't sleeping. As you approach from the east on our main street, the tower lines up perfectly with dead centre Ontario Street, dominating the streetscape. Durand sleeping in his grave knows he will not be forgotten.) It is a building that is both simple in design and imposing in deportment. Architect George Durand gave us a lasting creation in white brick tastefully trimmed in brown stone that speaks softly in appearance but carries that heavy stick that says, 'This is the Law.' Even the county jail, hidden behind the courthouse is a work of masonry art.

On the south side of the courthouse is the library, a place I shamefully admit was not very high on my 'to visit' list. I proudly declare that things have changed. That pastime which I lightly esteemed, in my youth, I now regard as more valuable than gold. On the north side of the courthouse by the Avon River, lay the exquisite Shakespearean Gardens, which appear in the background of every respectable wedding that ever graced a happy couple's photo album. Surely those gardens are the wellspring of much poetry and music in addition to the radiant blooms that even the most indifferent clod could never disavow.

I have not yet referred to the Avon River, that crowning waterway that divides the exquisite parkland, which stretches out for almost two miles. How fortunate are today's visitors. It is almost impossible to conceive that those sweeping lawns almost became the marshalling yards of the Canadian Pacific Railroad. Stratford's city fathers deserve high praise for fending off the pragmatic money-lenders of a bygone era who for the sake of Mammon would have encircled the placid Avon with a necklace of steel. Think of it, with 2000 voters eligible for the referendum, the issue was decided by a slim majority of 127.

In 1830, The Canada Company constructed a dam that created Lake Victoria. This man-made river is home to majestic swans and ducks who think the pond was always theirs just as we imagined, in our youth, that the streets were laid out just so we could roller-skate the length of the town. Patterson Island received its well-deserved name after my time. We simply knew it as the 'island'. Access to the island is by a wooden arched footbridge; this enables boat traffic to make way around that sacred soil.

In my day that meant a canoe or rowboat. Today's boat traffic can also include the dragon boats, which race every September, and the one solitary tour boat, the only motorized craft allowed. Many of the mammoth overarching willows seem to have disappeared. Perhaps they died of old age. They used to enable us as kids to climb their enormous branches with daredevil antics till we were well over the water. Defying gravity and hanging over the water, we could see the fish (mainly Suckers and Carp) with a marvellous view upstream as well as down. The path on the north side of the river was suitably named 'Lover's Lane', where many a romantic kiss was bestowed on ruby lips of blushing maidens who are now octogenarians or better (or worse?). The nameless path on the south side receives most of the foot traffic from walkers and joggers that enjoy its lovely vistas of green against an azure sky of blue.

Paradise? Not quite, but just about as close as it gets to the yet unseen 'New Jerusalem.' Did I understand all this when I spent my carefree youth in the place I took for granted? Hardly! The wisdom of years that makes one wise when finally we get the point, was still to come. What was so wonderfully possessed and taken for granted is now at long last fully appreciated. Thank goodness for the wisdom of the progressive town fathers who now lie sleeping in their graves.

My current residence is in Ancaster: in eighty minutes from my present home through hill and dale and trickling stream, I can enjoy in my old age what I took for granted when I was young. I especially love the back roads that take me through hamlets and villages that modernity has largely ignored. My favourite time is the spring; at this time of year the lacy elegance of verdant leafy lattice is a youthful green. In springtime when the leaves are just emerging from their winter slumber, I love to make my way through Lynden, Troy, St. George, Glen Morris, Ayr, Roseville, New Dundee, Haysville and Shakespeare. These idyllic places, tucked away between rolling countryside dotted with millponds and pasture, could almost pass for England. My pulse always quickens as we approach the 'beauregard' of my youth. Ah Stratford, the city of my memories. The place where I grew up. So having introduced you to the imperial home of my childhood, let me retreat to those golden years when Eden was yet unspoiled by the knowledge of good and evil.

Chapter 3

My Widening World

Janet McLelland and Jackie Griffiths live across the street. They are my pre-school playmates. Jackie lives in the small four-room corner house. Janet lives on the east side of a yellow brick double house with a splendid verandah, tailor made for playing house. I can still remember my disappointment when mother told me Jackie was moving to Detroit. I knew all about Detroit, because Grandma's favourite radio program came from Detroit. WJR was 760 AM on the radio dial, and was the source of Grandma's weekly radio ritual.

Our RCA Victor radio was a small console with a shiny walnut finish that sat on a little four-legged table. Modern technology had given us such marvellous progress that we could control everything with two knobs. One regulated the illuminated green dial where the numbers ran from 55 to 140. The other controlled the volume. I can still see my Grandma who was born old and never changed, relaxed and settled in her rocker, tuning the radio to her station and waiting breathlessly to hear the exciting words; "Lux presents Hollywood, and Cecil B. Demille brings you the best from the world of film. Tonight's drama will be–." I don't remember those wonderful radio scripts anymore; all I can recall is that Monday nights were reserved for big people privileged to listen, and I had to go to bed. I feel so grown up a few years later when at last, I am permitted to stay up and hear the story, just like everybody else. Dutifully and with gratitude in her heart, Grandma always bought Lux soap flakes to do the laundry; everybody agreed that nobody made soap flakes better than Lux.

So Jackie moved to Detroit and, somewhere in that great metropolis, the Griffiths and my friend Jackie disappeared forever. Janet moved away too. Her parents decided to live downtown in a large apartment, above the Dominion store, but that was three blocks away, and too far to carry on a friendship. That's when, with the help of my cousin Shirley, we invented the trampoline. Shirley Gillatly was the cutest three and a half-year old pint one could ever imagine. I loved when she came by to play with me because she loved to laugh. That's my memory of Shirley, always laughing and making me laugh in the bargain. One day Aunt Elsie and Uncle Gordon had dropped by to visit and Shirley and I went up to my room to play. First, however, we perch on the top step of the staircase and do the royal bumps. Our steps curve to the left at the top, so that they were wide on one side and narrow on the other and very steep. Grandma always climbed the stairs on the wide part but I much preferred the narrow; this is especially true when I need a quick start to play the royal bumps. Shirley has a nice soft round bottom and at the tender age of five, I had lots of padding right where it was needed for this drill. Sliding down our staircase was always the first thing any of the kids that came to our house wanted to do. Soon we are polishing Grandma's staircase with the seat of our pants until, Elsie says,

"That's enough or you'll wear out your pants and I can't afford to replace them." She said that to Shirley, but I get the impression she also had me in mind. Next, we decide to play quietly in my playroom with the blocks mother had bought me. Tiring of this, I have an idea.

"Let's jump on the bed." I say to Shirley. Only too happy to cooperate, cousin Shirley joins me and soon we are airborne. Laughing and having the time of our lives, we are oblivious of Grandma who is bent on preserving her furniture. I simply could not understand adults. Why anyone can object to such a joyful experience as jumping on a bed is truly beyond me. For some reason, grown-ups seem to like nothing better than sitting around, trying to figure out ways to spoil a kid's fun. Really, you would think they must have had better things to do.

"Get off that bed!" Grandma hollers. Up the stairs in a bound, Aunt Elsie has followed, and we are unceremoniously demoted to the outside where we are instructed to 'play properly'. Now I am wondering what Grandma means when she says, "You would destroy the place, if I wasn't watching."

Sadly, my cousin Shirley died when I was only six. Once again that old enemy, that took mother's childhood friend, claimed Shirley — appendicitis! Janet was only three and a half, and as sweet as an angel lying in her tiny coffin. I thought she must only be sleeping, but that couldn't be right, because Aunt Elsie was crying. It had only been a little while before, that Grandma had scolded us for jumping on the bed. Somehow I was sure, she would get better, so we could go outside and play. I guess I was right, but I will have to wait until I see her in heaven. Except for the occasional earache and the usual childhood scrapes, I fare quite well in the health department. (With the exception of the croup!) I'll never forget the many times I endured the sore throat I suffered with the croup. Iron manacles grappling at the windpipe hurts — bad. Thank goodness I was not born a giraffe. Then one day a helpful customer at mom's beauty salon

1934, Grandpa Alex and me

1936, me, Jackie, Royce, and Shirley Gillatly

told her to give me a teaspoon of coal oil.

"Coal oil!" mother gasped, "It would kill him for sure." Mother's customer was not to be dissuaded somebody had told her about this old homespun remedy and it had really helped her kids. She recommended it for me. To mom's amazement and my relief, it worked. That wonderful neglected product we used for lamps sure relieved the symptoms provided you stayed away from lighted candles.

To return to my story, just like that, all the women in my life are taken away, so I decide to play with boys. Royce Clark lives at 79 Nile Street, just around the corner, and is one year younger than me. Mrs. Clarke is his grandma but he calls her mother and is she ever strict. I am glad my Grandma is easy to get on with. I can still hear Mrs. Clark calling out, "Roy — ce!" Instantly, Royce is bolt upright.

"I got to go home right now." I never cease to be amazed how quickly Royce would obey that call.

"I think Royce is afraid of his mom." I would tell Grandma.

Royce calls his Grandparents mom and dad. Since Royce had never known his real parents the arrangement seems quite natural. The Clarks are Lutherans, and I don't go to church, so Royce decides to evangelize this pagan.

"My mother thinks you ought to go to Sunday school."

"Is it fun?" I ask.

"Lots of fun!" says Clarkie, "You will like my teacher; he's good." I go the following Sunday with Royce, who proudly introduces me as his best friend. Mr. Lettes tells us many stories. One of them was about the Americans who invented a watch spring so tiny that it could only be seen under a microscope. The Swiss returned it with a hole drilled through it. Naturally I concluded that the Swiss must be very smart. Mr. Lettes also tells us about heaven. That's how I learn that when we die, we don't stay put in the grave, but go to heaven and live forever. I am grateful for this information, as mother used to take me to the cemetery to see grandpa's grave. Somehow, the idea of just lying there in the ground didn't appeal to me.

Me and Royce in our Sunday best.

However, I am not a good Lutheran, because after three Sundays I get bored and never go again. Mrs. Clarke scolds me for that, but the only thing I can think of is that Mrs. Clarke scolds Royce all the time, for just about everything. I have decided I'm not going to be a Lutheran.

In short order Clarkie is now enthusing about an adventure that excludes me.

"My dad took me to the CNR shops today."

"He did? I thought children were not allowed," I enviously intone.

"Yep and I watched the overhead crane pick up a whole train engine and move it to the gate, just as easily as you would pick up a toy." I figure Clarkie must be the luckiest boy in Stratford and wish that it could have been me. Just think about it for one minute and you can see why I am green with envy. Royce gets to see inside those massive walls, where the great steam locomotives are repaired but not me. Life is simply not fair. Royce loves to have a story that is one better than me: and it seems he always has a story. I think the CNR must be the centre of the universe the way Royce describes it.

The CNR dominates the Stratford I know. In its heyday it employed over 1200 men. No one could imagine Stratford without the CNR shops. Its mighty whistle sounded at 8 A.M., 12 Noon, 1 P.M. and at 5 P.M. The old timers still say, 'You could set your watch by it'. For entertainment, my mom would take me to see the products of those mammoth shops and the locomotives they serviced. I can still see the train huffing and puffing as it whistled into town. What a show! For excitement, there was nothing better than a walk to the Stratford station to meet the train. On a Sunday summer evening, we would walk the six blocks to see the 8 o'clock London Special. The station itself looked like a Bavarian Inn, with its overhanging roof. The flower garden was a masterpiece of colour. But the real show was the arrival of the 5800, pulling the passenger cars from Toronto to London. First came the distant wail of the whistle. Next came the panting sound of the steam engine, as she came into view. In those days, we didn't need comic books with mythical monsters from Middle Earth. We had our own real live Colossus, complete with fire and smoke, snorting steam, and right up close. So close you could smell it. Think of it; those wonderful iron wheels, with the long drivers connecting them together working in tandem, powering that train at the unheard of speed of 60 miles an hour! In the background, and to the west, could be seen the formidable walls of the castle that serviced those mighty Behemoths, the CNR shops.

Royce Clark had seen the inside of that fortress. I could only imagine what it was like from the stories he told. Finally (when I was thirteen) I got to see the shops with a grade eight class tour. I got to see the awesome sight of the overhead crane picking up a whole locomotive and moving it over the other engines neatly lined up, row after row, and slowly dropping it into position at the exit gate. Hooray! At last I had caught up to Clarkie.

-o0o-

The other significant friend in my life is Vincent Schooley. Vince has flaming red hair and the bluest eyes. Everybody notices the hair and the freckles and comments. A backyard fence, just behind the Hollyhocks (they are still there 70 years later) separates us. So, we can only say Hi — that is — until one spring day a board goes missing, permitting a small boy to slide over from one side to the other. Royce, Vince and I, a Lutheran, a Catholic and a pagan! Still, we can have deep discussions like the one about what heaven must be like. We must have spent at least five minutes on that ponderous subject, and having quickly resolved those weighty issues moved on to other things like tricycles and toys.

Vince, Royce and I fancy ourselves as the three musketeers, we are inseparable friends, except when we fight. Fortunately, we are so evenly matched that nobody ever gets hurt. We sincerely tried to fight more often but we have this problem, we like each other. To draw a TV illustration, think of the Television Show Happy Days. Royce would be the Fonz, because he was destined to become the guy who had the way with the girls. I would be Richie and Vince would be Ralphie because of his flaming red hair. Now Vince is a Catholic and therefore, goes to a different School. The Immaculate Conception Separate School is three and a half blocks east (now torn down), whereas Romeo School is only a half a block away (where Royce and I attend). When we find out that Vince has to take a bag lunch for noon meals, whereas, we could return home at 12 o'clock, we propose to Mrs. Schooley that all this can be changed. It seems so reasonable to us that we cannot understand why Vince shouldn't change schools, so we can all be together. It would be another five years before I ever heard of a Mick. Innocently I remember asking my Uncle Gordon,

"What's a Mick?" Uncle Gordon who knows just about everything replies,

"A Mick is someone who eats fish on Fridays because they are not allowed to eat meat."

Whereas children are agreeable, parents can be stubborn. Our proposal is flatly turned down. Later on I discover that that big building at the other side of Romeo School was also a Catholic school. Why couldn't Vince go there? Perhaps it's just as well. We used to have snowball fights with the kids at St. Joseph's school. I wouldn't want to throw snowballs at Vince, because he is my friend. Funny thing about Catholics, they just aren't as good as Protestants, or at least that's what we were told, so I guess that's why I felt sorry for Vince. There are always exceptions to every rule; Vince is OK, even if the rest of them are wrong. Don't ask me what they are wrong about, I don't know and I really don't care because Vince and I are friends.

The one advantage I do have, however, is over both Royce and Vincent; I have more toys than both of them put together. Not only do I have more toys, but I also have a playroom. In 1937 Uncle Norman got married and moved out. I graduate to his bedroom, and that leaves my small room vacant. This becomes the most important room in the neighbourhood, because that's where my friends come when it rains. My playroom is smaller than the other upstairs bedrooms, because that very special staircase has to have someplace to fit. My playroom pays the price. This design flaw comes in handy because when we are finished having fun upstairs, we can make a speedy exit down the railing, provided Grandma isn't looking.

You would think friends and a toy room would be enough to satisfy my wildest dreams, but no, with so many worlds to conquer, I need a fresh challenge. So before I was old enough to blow my own nose, I decide to run away which, in retrospect, was quite brave since I had no previous experience. Sensing that it would not be a good idea to tell Grandma, I quietly pack my suitcase and carry it outside, placing it on my wagon. Vince could not be persuaded to join me, but Royce throws his lot in with me and off we go. I have packed sufficient clothes for both of us in a small suitcase and placed it on my wagon. We make it a few houses past Clarkie's house, when a friendly policeman in his black car, pulls up along side of us and rolls down the window.

"Hello boys — and how are you this afternoon."

"We're just fine, thank you."

"Nice suitcase you have there." The officer says, "What do you have in it?"

"Just our clothes."

"Where are you going?"

"We're going to the river," we explain.

"That's nice" says the kindly officer, " — and just why are you going to the river?"

"Oh," we explain. "We just decided to run away from home."

"And do your mothers know about this?"

"No," we politely reply, "we didn't bother to tell them."

"Well, well, well." He smiles, "let me tell you what I think. I think that when your mothers finally discover, that you ran away without telling them, they will be upset. So why don't you tell them first, that you plan to run away, and then, after permission has been granted, — then you can run away."

"We never thought of that," we chorus. "We'll go back and ask them right now. Thank you very much."

"Don't mention it; we're just glad to help." says the officer, and with that, he slowly drives away.

"So who do we ask first?" I say to Royce.

"I think we should ask your mother first," Royce replies. "You know how strict my mother is."

"Sure." So we turn around and go over to my house, where we find my mother, and explain our plans. To say the least, I am nonplused at the response.

"Run away!" Mother exclaims, and unreasonably looks me dead in the eye, "You certainly cannot!"

That's when I learn that women can have that special look that can really be quite frightening. Frankly, I am surprised at the unusual tone of her voice, and can clearly see that it was useless to protest. So I unpack my suitcase, and Royce and I find something else to do. I don't think Royce ever told his mother about our plans. I imagine he reasons quite correctly that if Bruce's mother is against the idea, for sure his mom would never agree. My yen for travel thus thwarted, I put away all such plans for later.

Wanderlust, however, will not be put off. With the advent of more mature years (I am 10 years old now) I receive my first pair of roller skates. They are the latest and most modern kind. My skates have ball bearings; I am lucky to get them before the manufacturers of anything made of metal is subject to wartime requisition. A year later and you could not have purchased a pair of roller skates. The skates made of steel conform to fit any growing foot that a gangling kid can produce. Adjustable, they are strapped to my ankle. A two-sided clamp can be tightened by a butterfly key. When I feel the shoe leather under my foot starting to buckle, I know it's tight enough. This is an important lesson to learn, lest skate and boy are separated and a skinned knee rendered as evidence.

My new liberty allows me to explore Rebecca Street, the next block over where the only smooth asphalt near my house can be found. My explorations of Stratford increased even more when I got my first bicycle. It brought me further south beyond the CNR station and as far North as Ontario Street, which is the limit set by mother until I get a little more experience. Later when I'm old enough to go hiking with Jim Johnston, we will explore the hinterland around our town. We especially loved the 'little hills'. On a Saturday morning we would pack a lunch and take the railroad tracks that parallel Romeo Street crossing over the Avon River on the trestle bridge heading north till we reach the creek winding its way through the 'little hills', a child's version of the Rocky Mountains. Some generous farmer owned that property and never bothered the many kids who played there.

Today the tracks are torn up. There is a condominium on the north side of the creek. South of the creek there is a sterile subdivision of new housing. In my time, we could romp and play by the 'little hills' and snare suckers in the creek. On a summer afternoon, we could lie in the warm grass just watching the lazy clouds roll by, doing good old constructive nothing. That's where I learned that if you rest your chin in your hands, it will keep your mouth shut so you need not disturb yourself.

Growing up with two soft-hearted women as my guardians has a distinct advantage. I am a spoiled child. At least that's what others said. I felt otherwise and eloquently defended my point of view. In hindsight, I confess my detractors were probably right. To start with, I don't want to go to bed early, like I should. Grandma outsmarts me by promising to read me a bedtime story. Eagerly, I climb into my pajamas, while Grandma reaches for ***Hurlbut's Story of the Bible***. In my childhood, we must have gone through that wonderful book several times. The ethics of these stories stick. They will inevitably mould my life. Naturally the meaning of this eludes me at the time. I am more influenced by comic books like my hero Superman, who could leap tall buildings with a single bound, was faster than a speeding bullet, more powerful than a locomotive etc, etc.

One night after my Bible story, I perceive that there are snakes under my bed, which would bite me after the lights went out. I call Grandma to check under my bed to confirm my suspicions.

"Ridiculous," says Grandma, "It's just your foolish imagination."

"Please Grandma, you have to look, I know they are there."

Grandma sighs and rolls her eyes. She accommodates this young manipulator and after kneeling down and looking under my bed she says with a good deal of irritation in her voice,

"No snakes!"

"They disappear when you're here, and come back after you're gone." I complain.

"Nonsense!" says Grandma, "You're just making it up, to put off going to sleep." In vain do I plead with Grandma to stay by my bed, until I go to sleep. Now the lights are out, and the snakes are definitely under my bed. I am too tired to check for myself, and besides, I'm all tucked in by Grandma, and I don't want to mess up the tuck. Suddenly an ingenious idea strikes me, "I will pretend that

I am superman." Imagination is a child's armour against hobgoblins, snakes, and anything else that can do them harm. Now I am smiling at the idea and soon I close my eyes and sleep soundly. The snakes disappear never to return.

Chapter 4

The Andrew Bogie Farm

With the advent of 1939, a new experience comes my way. Mother has decided that it would be a good thing to take me to Lake Huron and enjoy a week's holiday at the beach. Scanning the Stratford Beacon-Herald, she spots an ad that invites inquiries to Bogie's beach, where room and board is provided at the farmhouse of one Andrew Bogie. After suitable arrangements have been negotiated, mother and I take the train to Goderich. What an adventure! After all those wonderful occasions when we go to the train station to see the action, we are now actually a part of the action. Checking our baggage at the station, we watch our valuables carried off in a large four-wheeled wagon. Next, the porter pulls the wagon alongside of the sliding doors of the baggage coach. One by one the suitcases disappear into the bowels of the baggage car.

"Are you sure we will get our suitcases back?" I query mother. Calmly she shows me our tickets, "When we get to Goderich, all we have to do, is show them our ticket stubs, and the luggage will be there, waiting for us." I am assured. Climbing up the stairs into the coach is made easy by a special stool, placed by the coachman, who barks out, "All aboard for Mitchell, Seaforth, Clinton and Goderich."

"That's us," says mother, and we walk right up where I have seen passengers swallowed whole, only to reappear at the windows. Living proof, that they are alive and well. This time, it is us! A surge of excitement pulses through my veins, as we find our way to the wooden benches. Upholstered seats are reserved for the Toronto-London run; progress has not quite caught up to the Stratford-Goderich excursion. That transformation comes the following year. I sometimes wonder what became of those old benches? Perhaps they reappeared in some church mission up north where they could torture the faithful so that sermons, of necessity, would have to be shorter to accommodate newly-latticed-imprinted bottoms.

"Last call for Mitchell, Seaforth, Clinton, and Goderich." sings out the conductor, as he saunters up to us and says,

"Tickets please."

Mother knows the routine, but since all this is quite new for me, to my delight, she has given me the tickets. Proudly, I present them to the conductor, who winks and returns them to me.

"A young man taking his mother for a trip to Goderich?"

"I guess so." I shyly reply while mother smiles.

"That's a long way for a little boy to travel, so you be sure to take good care of your mother."

"I will!" I reply.

Within a minute, we hear the puff and fury of the engine wheels as they spin their forward motion. Our coach shudders and in my mind's eye I can see those massive drivers spinning the wheels, only this time, it is from the privileged position of being inside the train. With each puff of the great drivers, that propel the engine forward, we are in motion. This train is leaving the station behind. Already the traffic barriers are down at Downie Street. A delivery truck, with its driver propped partway out the side window waits. We are 'king of the road.' Next the mighty CNR shops come into view. I think, "Royce Clark, you may have seen them from the inside, but you haven't been this high up, to see them from the train."

The adventure continues mile after mile, as I sit fascinated by the view from the window. I can see everybody's backyard and all their hidden treasures. A rusty lawnmower leans against a battered garbage can. A child's tricycle is overturned a few feet from the back door. Mother says,

"I like travelling on the bus better than the train; that way you can see all the houses from the front, and enjoy the flowers." I prefer the train; this way you can see what a small child is forbidden to explore on Brunswick Street. However, after an hour, I tire of all this, and complain to mother,

"When are we going to get there?" But get there we do, and soon, we are on the platform of the Goderich train station looking for a farmer by the name of Bogie. The stationmaster we speak to gestures,

"I know him, he's been here before, and if you look that way (pointing with his hand) that smiling gentleman is your man."

"Are you Mrs. Woods?' a ruddy-faced man asks.

"Are you Mr. Bogie?" mother replies. Things quickly sort

themselves out, and soon we are on our way north on Highway 21 in Andrew Bogie's 1932 Chevrolet. As we cross the Saltford Bridge, we can see the grain silos. The Goderich Salt sign is also prominently displayed (this accounts for how nearby Saltford got its name). It is later explained to me, the grain silos are not full of salt, although the Goderich mine could fill several thousand, if they were available. The silos are where grain is stored.

"So this is where Goderich salt comes from!" mother exclaims. "We buy that very salt for our table."

"That salt is mined from deep below the earth, right here where it was first discovered." Andrew says.

While mother is focused on salt, I am looking at a freighter making for the port of Goderich.

"People have no idea," said Mr. Bogie, "what an industrious town Goderich is."

"Is Goderich bigger than Stratford?" I ask.

"No," says Andrew, "but Stratford had better watch out or we'll grow so large that they'll never catch up." Relieved that Stratford is still the larger of the two places, I relax and enjoy the spectacular Maitland Valley. I am fascinated with the view of the Maitland River, that broadens to meet Lake Huron; I watch with wide-eyed amazement, as a whole new world opens up to me. Travel broadens the mind, and opens the world, especially to an eight-year old. Leaving Goderich behind, we drive on to Dunlop. As we pass the mill on our right, (now torn down) Mr. Bogie looks at me and says,

"That's where I take my grain to make chop for the pigs, and if you're good, maybe I'll let you help me feed them." I shrink in my seat; I don't know whether to be complimented or terrified. I've never seen a real live pig. Four miles later, we pull into the farmyard, and see the white and aquiline gabled house, where we will be staying. A screened in veranda adorns the front and an open veranda with a view of the lawn looking east gives protection from the rain where one can sit and enjoy a book without getting scorched by the sun or, on rainy days, without getting wet. A few dozen chickens are spread over the lawn, foraging for food. I have never seen a live chicken before, and immediately try to scoop one up, but they are too quick for me.

"Careful young man." says Mrs. Bogie "Don't chase the chickens, or they won't lay any eggs." Mother explains to me how eggs come into the world, and I have the distinct feeling, that this is going to be a holiday to be remembered.

"Andrew will unload your bags," says Mrs. Bogie.

"Come and meet our son Graham, he'll be pleased to greet you and show you around the farm." At age nine, Graham is one year older than me and taller. He is chewing on a Timothy grass head, and I can see that his ears stick out. A friendly kid, he immediately takes mother and me to the drive shed, large enough to accommodate the car, and several farm implements. He invites us to climb the ladder to the loft and see the hay-mow. A new adventure I readily accept but mother declines.

"You can go if you wish; I'll wait here till you come down."

Up the vertical ladder I scamper after Graham, who helps me stretch my way over the menacing opening at the top. Safely arriving at the second floor, I see the hay is about five feet deep and just right for wonderful jumping from the connecting beam that spans the loft. The gentle slope of the hay makes it easy to climb to the beam; Graham deftly walks to the place where the uneven hay spreads out four feet below.

"Watch me while I have some fun," he calls as I hesitate.

"Follow me!" Graham laughs and down he jumps from the central beam that spans the loft. Gingerly, I make my way over the beam so cautiously that I nearly fall backwards. Four feet up seems awfully high, and I am trembling with fright, but honour demands courage.

"Jump!" says Graham, "There's nothing to it."

Taking a deep breath, I jump and squeal like a pig.

"Howdja like it," said Graham.

"Great!" I reply, "But I think that's enough for today." I can hear mother calling from below,

"What are you kids doing up there? Are you OK?" When a small boy crosses the threshold of a new adventure, it is good to sleep on it. In no time, jumping into the hay mow will become a commonplace pleasure. Eventually we will be doing it from eight foot heights in the main barn that houses all the animals; that is, until Mr. Bogie fills it so full of hay that it now becomes a place to play hide and go seek.

Graham scampers down the driving shed ladder, so now it's my turn. Truth is; this city kid is terrified. Getting down is going to be much harder than climbing up. Graham reads my fear and says,

"Just grab the rung; you'll be safe." The problem is the top rung is on the other side of a three-foot opening. I can see the ground 12 feet below. I think, "What if I slip before I grab the top rung." My heart is pounding. I grit my teeth and lunge for the ladder, while Graham laughs at my expense.

"Nuthin to it; when you know

Graham Bogie and his calf

That magnificent barn fell into decay and was eventually demolished

how." I casually reply.

When I finally get back down the ladder, I bravely tell mother all about the hayloft and proudly tell her how I have never had so much fun before.

Next Graham takes us to the barn, where the animals are kept. Pointing to an

Peggy and Lilly, Archives photo courtesy the Milton Antique Steam Association

empty stall, he says,

"That's a manger, where we put the hay for the horses to eat." He explains to me that the baby Jesus probably slept in something like that. It is then that I suddenly learn that Christmas cards are not to be trusted. Meanwhile, Graham tells me,

"The horses are in pasture." (That's why the stalls are empty). Pointing to the rectangular cubicle, Graham says,

"That's where Lily spends the night and Peggy takes the next stall over." Next Graham shows us where the hens that lay those treasured eggs are. It's Graham's job to check them every day to see if the hens are laying or just lying. Finally, Graham takes us to see his newborn calf. He's as cute as can be and comes straight for my hand.

"Let him suck on your hand." says Graham, but I back away,

"No way!"

"Here, I'll show you." and Graham puts his hand into the calf's mouth and says, "He doesn't have any teeth. It feels soft inside his mouth and the calf likes it."

Graham explains to us that a newborn calf craves to suck and that it is perfectly safe to let him suck my hand. Gingerly, I extend my hand to the calf that obliges me by licking and sucking my fingers. I refuse to give him any more of my city-slicker hand. Farm life is a revelation of a world I had never imagined.

After a brief visit to see the pigs (very brief) we make our way upstairs (where we no longer need to hold our noses) to see the granary. Graham laughs at our city sense of smell and pointing, he says,

"That bin is for oats. You can see that we're getting low, but all that will change when we bring in the harvest. We'll fill the bin to the ceiling. If you could stay another week, you could see it." With animated anticipation, Graham explains the adventure of harvest. He has no difficulty convincing me, but mother says,

"That would cost more money. We'll see about that, after I've had time to think about it."

We eat dinner that evening with six other guests. Mrs. Bogie is an excellent cook and with the help of Evelyn, Graham's older sister, she has prepared a roast beef dinner with gravy and most of the things I like except the carrots. Why do adults always have to throw in that vegetable to spoil what could have been a perfect meal?

"No dessert without eating your carrots," Mrs. Bogie chimes. I appeal to mother who apparently wrings a concession out of Mrs. Bogie, earning the gratitude of Rover, who appreciates the carrots far better than I ever could (I care about dogs). I decide, right then and there, that I am going to enjoy this place a lot, as long as Mother is there to protect me from eating the things I don't like.

After supper while the women wash the dishes, Graham and I catch flies. The common housefly abounds. From the dining room ceiling there hangs a long sticky flycatcher which, after a hundred or more flies pockmark their journey's end, will be replaced by another. The sticky flycatcher isn't pretty but its better than having flies in your mashed potatoes. Outside, Graham deftly catches houseflies at the screen door by (as he says) "sneaking up on them from behind." Then he shakes them inside his fist "to make them dizzy." Then, like some baseball fastballer, he hurls them against the cement floor of the porch. Red stains on the cement are the postmortem testifying to Graham's dexterity. I try the same thing with no results whatsoever. Graham is a skilled fly-catcher. This amateur has some catching up to do to match his skill. After the dishes are done, Evelyn proposes a game of Hide and Go Seek. To my amazement, she invites the adult guests to join, and gamely they accept the invitation. I can hardly believe my mother as she chases her way to home base. It's so out of character as I perceive things. Mother just says,

"Remember, I was young once." I conclude, when on holiday, young and old seem to feel free as birds, thoroughly enjoying a fresh lease on life.

We awake the following morning to a glorious summer day with plenty of sunshine. After breakfast mother says,

"We'll go to the beach in the afternoon." and sends me out to play with Graham.

"C'mon to the sandbox," Graham says,

"We will play (what else?) farm." The sandbox is located about 50 feet past the outhouse, which brings up a topic that must be explained. At home, when I want to go to the bathroom, I simply go upstairs, and when I am 'done', I flush the toilet. The farmhouse has no such luxuries. When the call of nature comes, you go outside to the backhouse (outhouse). Inside the 4 by 4 room is a bench with two holes side by side (I do wonder about that extra hole). For privacy there is a hook on the inside, and when you are 'done', you are ready to do the paper work. In the farmhouse there are porcelain commodes under each bed with a lid, if you need to 'go' in the night. Fortunately for me that proves unnecessary. If for any reason you need a light, there are matches for the coal oil lamp, as they have no electricity. That backhouse is an education all by itself. Mother explains to me that at one time in Stratford, years ago, every house had such a contraption. Just then I remembered that there was one in Uncle Gordon's back yard, which had fallen into disuse, but was great for kids who wanted somewhere to hide.

Summertime, wonderful summertime! Next we graduate to sandbox, but as Graham's pupil I have a lesson to learn. I am looking at the windmill. I see Graham is filling a pail with water from the pump located at ground level. Fortunately that night, there has been a breeze, and Mr. Bogie had hooked the pump to the windmill. All night long, the water reservoir in the barn is filling up, without a human hand to help. Ah, the wonders of modern technology! Graham tells me that sometimes when the wind fails, his dad will pump for 20 minutes just to get enough water to the reservoir for the animals to drink. For Graham to master the pump, he grabs the handle with both hands, and jumps up high enough with his feet curled up while the weight of his 70 pounds brings the handle down. Eureka! Out comes the precious water. We need this water for the sandbox. As soon as Graham has filled a pail with the necessary water, he soaks the sand, so that we can shape it. A few cedar shingles beside the sandbox, is the source for all our implements. Graham splits off a slice of shingle, about the size of a dinner knife, and says,

"This is your plow." Dividing the sandbox between us, he starts to make walls for his barn, chicken house, and driving shed (somewhat reminiscent of yesterday's tour). Following his lead, I do much the same on my side. First we have to divide the farm up with four fields: one for wheat, one for oats, one for hay and one for pasture.

"Next," Graham says, "we have to plough the soil." Breaking his knife sized cedar in half; he starts to plough his fields. I learn quickly, following Graham's every move.

"Now we have to disc the fields; the real disc is in the driving shed and looks like a long row of iron wheels held together by a steel frame. Graham breaks off another slice of shingle that doesn't look too different from the make-believe plough.

"Now you have to store the plough in the driving shed before we disc the fields." Graham's driving shed is a miniature version of a leaf house we make every fall. Next, he proceeds to turn his shingle on its side to smooth out the ploughed field. A similar piece of cedar becomes the cultivator (a steel flat grill with long spikes in several rows). Of course each farm implement has to be hooked up to horses that have to be bought, and named, and bedded down for the night. A child's imagination, a few cedar shingles, and the next thing we know, its time for lunch.

Graham's grandfather raised a family of seven, five of whom were born in a log cabin just a little east of the present farmhouse. However it fell to Andrew to carry on the family farm. After serving in the Canadian army in World War I, Andrew married Ethel Graham, and took possession of the farm that eventually became Bogie's Beach. Assuming ownership of the farm, no one at that time could have imagined that the real value was in the sandy beach, on the Lake Huron shore. It took the combination of paved roads and the automobile to bring this to light. One day a Stratford spinster by the name of Margaret Casson approached Andrew Bogie with a specific request, to purchase a parcel of land on the bluffs,beside the canyon overlooking the lake. Andrew Bogie knew a good thing when he saw it, and sold her the lot for the princely sum of fifty dollars. Others soon followed, so Andrew had the beach surveyed, and divided into lots. Cottages bearing family names, such as MacDonald, Wade, Saunders, Davis, and Dunlop sprang up along the lakeshore. Bogie's Beach was born. The road on the bluff was Evelyn Street (named after Graham's sister). The street that made its way to the beach was called Graham Street.

In 1936, a Stratford doctor by the name of Nichols was looking for a spot on Lake Huron to build a cottage. Since the drive to Goderich was only 45 miles, he checked out Bogie's farm, another 6 miles north, and found the pristine beach. Nichols knew a lot of people. In time the word got out, and by 1939, there were only a few lots left. Stratford had discovered Bogie's Beach. Dr. Nichols became a legend, not only because he was a well-liked doctor, but also for his driving record. He collected more speeding tickets, and spread more dust than any man alive, racing back to Stratford to care for emergencies.

The beach was like a thousand others that have attracted sun worshippers all over Canada. The thing about Bogie's was its proximity to Stratford. While people from other places did discover Bogie's Beach, Stratford was the principal source for visitors. One such was Margaret Dennett, a girl from London; meeting Margaret would prove to be a fork in the road for me, that would alter my life, but I'm getting ahead of my story.

Returning to Bogie's Beach, that pristine sand stretched for almost a mile from Point Farm on the south, to Hunter's Beach on the north, where once again the beach gets stony. Bogie's Beach on the other hand, had beautiful soft sand. Great for making castles, and broad enough for tourists like me and others to bake in the sun and swim in the surf.

Bogie's farm has a canyon. The locals call it a gully, but to me, it is a canyon. In that part of the world, the small creeks that make their way to the lake erode the soil and create gullies. Along the bluff that

The Canyon with Lake Huron in the background

overlooks the lake, many gullies are formed; they take on a life of their own. When Andrew Bogie buys the farm, the gully compels the need for a small bridge, just behind the driving shed to reach the 30 acres that make up the northern side of the farm. However, the relentless erosion by the annual rain makes its indelible advance, and the bridge will have to be moved further east, for the horses and wagons to cross. Incredibly to me, Mr. Bogie predicts,

"One day that gully will cut its way back so wide and so deep, that I won't be able to get to my land on the northern side." As a child I can't imagine such a disaster, so I put it out of my mind. However, time and erosion works it way, and now as an old man, I have to tell you, that's exactly what happened. Mr. Bogie was forced to sell the north side to the Hunter farm.

The gully fascinates me from the start and Graham knows the hidden trails. We romp and play in the gully. At times, we encounter Spanish conquistadors, and shoot them all dead. At other times, we are ambushed by Indians and, to boot, kill wild beasts of every kind. Of course we never lose a battle or get hurt by a lion. Then, at other times like some famous explorer, we will make our way from stem to stern, through the tangled trees and scrub, until we emerge at the mystical ocean, colloquially referred to as Lake Huron.

To me, a farm that no longer is a farm is a lonely place. Today the lively animals that contributed to the life of Bogie's fame are only a memory. The present owners are bereft of barn and driving shed and the fields are rented out. What pasture that remains have no cow pies because the cows are gone. The chicken coop is still there, and has been transformed into outside sleeping quarters for visitors, "complete with picture windows." says the present owner,

"I sometimes like to go out in that shed, and just sit for hours and look at that amazing canyon." he says. I still love that canyon too; but

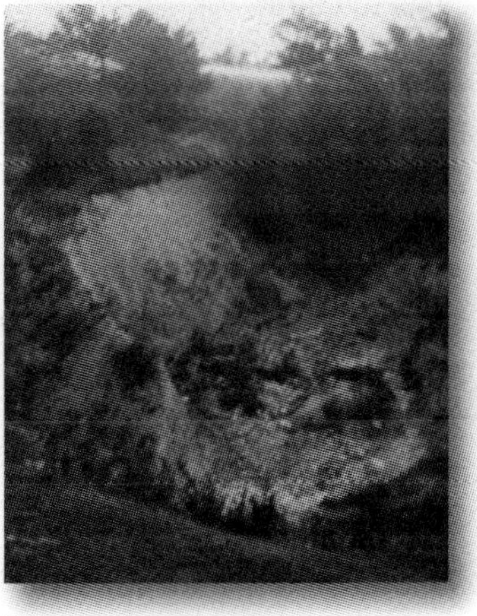

The view from the chicken coop.

there is a sadness about a farm that was once bristling with life that is now only a memory. Mixed farming that teemed with activity and chores has become a mirage leaving Graham Bogie and me with only our memories.

I recall once the most incredible sight (I cannot tell you exactly, because as I returned summer by summer the memory dims); Graham and I had decided to scale the steepest part of the gully. Suddenly two deer appeared on the south side. They paused for a moment, looking totally elegant as they scanned the horizon; then, as though aided with invisible wings they darted down one side of the gully, and flew up the north side never missing a step. Graham and I mastered the same feat, but it took us a half an hour. Perhaps 3000 years ago in faraway Greece two adventurous boys saw a similar sight and (provided that deer can translate into horses) the myth of Pegasus was born. Respect and awe for the spectacle of creation is universal.

The best week of my life goes fast. I have had several best weeks since but, for the time, it was the best. This time I didn't get to see a harvest. I have to wait another two years, before I see that. I did get to see the Milky Way and the marvellous show of brilliant stars by night. It happened after the campfire we had at the beach to which all the guests were invited. To see what I saw in those days would require a trip 100 miles north of Sudbury or, for second best, a visit to the Toronto Planetarium. Progress has exacted a price. Atmospheric pollution from our brilliantly lit streets obscures the beauty of the night skies from our eyes. The silent music of other galaxies in view is hidden unless one has travelled beyond the reaches of modern civilization.

Our vacation at Bogie's Beach was a great experience. Four weeks later, I am back in school, in grade three

Chapter 5

War comes to us

As a veteran of two years at public school I am now a pro. The year 1939 is my coming of age. I have returned from Bogie's farm and am looking forward to the first day of school. Mind you, only the first day, after that I prefer the calendar to read July. Alas, no such luck. Like everybody else, I have to go to school. For me, that means Romeo Public where the bell rings at 9 A.M., 11:50, 1:30 P.M. and 3:40. Counting a morning and afternoon recess that means eight significant bell rings to regulate our school life with an hour and forty minutes for dinner. We never called it lunch as we do these days. Noon was dinner and supper was always at 5:30 P.M.

All the schools in Stratford are named for Shakespearean characters. I suppose someone must have explained all that, but for kids who knew nothing of Shakespeare the significance was lost until we became adolescents. Well do I remember the time when I first discovered that Romeo was a Boy and Juliet was his girlfriend. With this newly acquired information, I figured it out like this. For many years Romeo pined for company, so as the city grew, the town fathers had mercy and built Juliet School a half a mile away. The heyday of this love affair was during my time. I assumed these two romantically inclined schools were always there, before I was born, and would always stand where I knew them after I had died and gone to heaven. Today both buildings have been torn down, a destruction which to me is as tragic as the original story.

My Romeo School was an old two-story white brick building (well do I remember that first day of school and the tears). With fondness, I recall its formidable walls and cinder playground. How could they tear it down!? The old school was eventually replaced by a modern building. The travesty of it! Who will relate the story of how my Uncle Gordon and some of the other big boys attempted to hang Mr. Slaughter (their Principal) out the second story window, just to scare him. Mr. Slaughter was a small man and the big boys could well have done it. I suspect the story grew in proportion to the number of times it was told. It's one thing to make a threat. It's another to carry it out. I remember how shocked I was when

I heard about the fracas that ensued. The trick didn't work. After suitable punishment, the hoped for expulsion was not granted, and Mr. Slaughter still continued to use the strap on undisciplined boys who were compelled to accept the routine miseries of childhood. I know that Romeo School still exists and that the building is new and modern. But, when I close my eyes, I see the old two story white brick building and the memories come flooding in of kids whose faces I recollect knowing that if, today, I passed them on the street, recognition would elude me.

Romeo School was the place where we traded pink eye and impetigo and learned that life is larger than Brunswick Street. Like all children, I tremble at the discipline of my teachers. Mother has assured me the teacher really likes me even when she gets cross. This year, I am pleasantly surprised, because I like our teacher, Miss Hazel Nash, right away. She doesn't look like a teacher (I'm not sure if I know what a teacher ought to look like) but Hazel Nash had a kind face, and didn't scold us like the others (or so I thought). I can still see her flaming red hair neatly curled on the head of this diminutive woman that you couldn't help but like.

She introduced us to Finland. She and her sister Eva, who taught grade four, had taken a tour of Finland, and had fallen in love with the country and its people. She had wonderful pictures, and soon we were all ready to take out citizenship to Lapland if the Finns wouldn't have us. Then one month later, terrible things happen; bad old Russia turns its army on Finland. Mars has awakened from a nineteen-year slumber and turned his evil gaze on Europe.

Miss Nash is outraged at the Russians, and it isn't too long before 27 third grade pupils share her wrath. To reinforce my venom against the Russians, there is the newly subscribed Life magazine, which comes every month, complete with graphic photos of the war. Next, occur the stunning reversals the Russians receive at the hands of the skillful army of Finland. We are certain that David will slay Goliath. Sadly, the advent of spring brings reality. The badly outnumbered Finns cannot withstand the Russian bear. Our hearts, as much as it is possible, for eight year-olds to comprehend, are as sad as the heart of our teacher.

Then there is that little matter of Germany and France, with England thrown in as well. We don't talk much about that at school, but we sure do at home.

"We beat them before," mom says, "We will beat them again."

"Churchill was right;" Grandma said, "they should have listened to him." Month by month, the graphic pictures of the war come in and are devoured by my fascinated eyes. Then the unthinkable happens; the Germans defeat the Allies in battle so badly that France surrenders. There isn't much talk around the table about that, until suddenly the stilled table conversations between Grandma and mother reveal to me the mood. Finland, fresh in my memory, makes me uneasy about the war in Europe. I can still remember the fateful news on June 16, 1940. We are listening to the evening broadcast on the radio, when the announcer says,

"France is fallen!" I can read the fear in mother's eyes, and feel the same emotions. We are a family that discusses the news. I understand the gravity of the situation, even though I am only eight years old, and I start to cry.

"They will take England next, and then, they'll come to Canada and kill us all."

"Don't worry Brucie," mother reassures me;

"Before that could happen, the Americans would step in and stop them." With this reassurance, the pessimist climbs into bed and falls asleep. The following morning the optimist wakes up ready to fight the Germans.

The fall of France created a diplomatic dilemma for Canada because it cut France into two countries: occupied and unoccupied France, with a new capital at Vichy in the south. Vichy France kept the semblance of a free country complete with the French Empire and the third most powerful fleet in the world. This truncated France was a diplomatic coup for Hitler, because wherever Frenchmen lived, the problem of a divided loyalty arose. On this side of the ocean Canada was one third French. To further complicate the story there is St. Pierre and Micquelon, both of which were part of territorial unoccupied France.

The story quickly became a drama played out by two newcomer warriors, Charles DeGaulle and Emile Muselier, who as of yet were unknown. Meanwhile, General Marechal Petain, a famous World War I hero, became the Prime Minister of France. Admiral Jean Darlan was already the commander of the French Navy. These men made the tragic mistake of collaborating with Hitler and caused no end of confusion in Quebec. In opposition to these two men, General DeGaulle and Admiral Muselier, fled to England and set up the Free French movement. Both sets of French leadership appealed to the French in Canada for support. For a year and a half, Prime Minister MacKenzie King had a delicate tightrope to walk just to keep Quebec's loyalty focused on the war effort because many Quebecois venerated General Petain. To compound the problem, the twin islands of St. Pierre and Micquelon in the Gulf of St. Lawrence was ruled by Governor de Bournat who was loyal to Vichy France.

When France surrendered to the Nazis, Admiral Muselier had managed to pirate a submarine and three corvettes from the French Navy and deliver them to the Free French cause. A little over a year later, on Christmas day in 1941 with his little Navy he 'liberated' St. Pierre and Micquelon. It wasn't much of feat as it was done without firing a shot; however in a year when there was no good news and Hitler seemed invincible, we all cheered this minuscule victory as an omen of better days ahead. Even the Quebecois agreed.

Now the pictures in Life magazine take on special meaning. I am thoroughly engrossed with the war. I want war toys. Mother, who always obliges me, furnishes me with a wonderful array of dinky toys, which I loyally give to the cause. With my Hawker Hurricane, I shoot down every imaginable German bomber that dares to threaten England. My fleet of battleships engages the enemy, sinking all German submarines in sight, and come through unscathed. Of course I generously enlist Royce and Vince in my army, and together, we are invincible. At night while drifting off to sleep, Winston Churchill and King George VI gratefully award me the appropriate medals. Eventually our contribution turns the tide, and the British win the war. Of course the Americans help, but that is another story. The reality is between the British, Canadians and Americans the Canadians always make the best soldiers. That's what Clarkie says, and I agree with him.

One day at school it was announced that Mr. McDougal, who taught grade 7, was leaving because he had joined the army and was now in the Perth Regiment. At 900 strong the Perth trains just outside of town, and is soon ready to go on parade. I shall never forget the day they march along Downie Street, looking proud and strong, three abreast. I think all of Stratford showed up to line the street cheering as the band led the way. Naturally, my friends and I cheered too, and couldn't imagine, why some of the women were crying. Later with the hindsight that comes from experience, Stan Scislowski would write, "How naïve we were! How blind to what battle would really be like! If we had known that, once we had our taste of it, we wouldn't be so hungry for a second helping." The honour roll at Stratford High has eighty-four names of young men who paid the supreme sacrifice. They were barely out of school when they found themselves in the armed forces.

Chapter 6

Mother

My grandfather had cut a dashing figure in his youth and was recognizably a handsome man right up to his sixties. In 1902 he married the beautiful Rachael Langstroth. In eight years they were blessed with three children. Ethel (my mother) was the precocious middle child. In 1911, when my mother was six years old, grandpa takes the family west to live in Camrose, Alberta. Grandpa said it was to seize the opportunity. Grandma said it was to avoid the embarrassment. Grandpa had invested his savings in the stock market against the advice of his family and lost everything. Alberta reaps the benefit of a good carpenter with empty pockets. The Gillatlys are now the new family from the East. So mother went to school in the Prairie town of Camrose and loved it. Grandma, separated from everything that was familiar, hated it. The young always have the advantage of making the best of the only world they know.

Mother soon finds a kindred spirit in Alice Ballard. They do everything together, and love to play in the tall grasses that grow wild around the house. Mother is smart in school, and excels in music. She doesn't have the opportunity to take lessons, but learns to play the piano anyway, all by herself. Then comes tragedy; Alice is stricken with appendicitis, and dies three days later. The funeral is the saddest day in my mother's young life. The resultant grief has its ways of coming to the surface, at the most unexpected times. From that event on, mother can burst into tears at the least provocation. Still, the advantage of youth works its magic, and mother learns to live again. Her love of the only world she knows is a healing balm that enables her to adjust. When she turns 16 — at last, Alexander Gillatly has caved under the pressure. Grandpa announces that the family will move back to Ontario, to Stratford, so that his

Mom in the middle, when she was 14.
Alice Ballard to her left.

1919 Mother was fourteen years old when this picture was taken in Camrose, Alberta

wife, Rachael can return to family and familiar territory. Grandma's sister is Julia Wade. Rachael and Julia had been inseparable until Grandpa imposed his Western exile. The sisters will be reunited, and Grandpa, as a carpenter, will find work in Stratford. For my mother, the move is full of anxiety; she must leave the world she loves for the unknown.

1921 Mother at sweet sixteen

George Wade is a hard working man, who loves flowers. Julia, his second wife, had given him six children in addition to the two she inherited. May and Rena were raised by the Grandparents in St. Catherines, Alice, Edith, Beatrice, Jack, Lorne and Frank grew up in Stratford. Frank, the youngest, will eventually become a household name in Stratford. The old Northways building, across from the cenotaph, is purchased by Frank and becomes Wade's Florists. For over 46 years Frank and Margaret run the business. Margaret will eventually become a city councillor, and even deputy mayor. Margaret loved to tell patrons that Frank's parents brought in the first Clematis that was ever planted in Stratford. Frank inherited George's love of flowers, and the locals know the rest.

In 1921, Dad and Mother Wade live at 136 Water Street, and their backyard is a virtual paradise, producing colour for the windows, and vegetables for the table. After being apart for 10 years, the sisters are eagerly looking forward to their reunion. As the Grand Trunk lumbers into Stratford, Rachel tells her children how to get to Auntie and Uncle Wade's house, and announces,

"You walk slowly, while your father and I go ahead to prepare the way. I don't want Auntie Julia to think she's been invaded by a bunch of wild Indians." Now the Indians consist of Frank 17, Ethel 16, Gordon 11, and Camrose-born Norman who is eight. After a joyous reunion of the sisters, the tribe shows up a half an hour later. With excitement and pleasure they meet their cousins. The Wades put them up for two weeks, while Alexander scours the town for a house that he can afford, which means a fixer-upper. Brunswick Street is the prize, and for the grateful Wades, the tribe moves into their new home, and the population of 136 Water Street shrinks from 14 back to 8.

I never thought of Grandma as beautiful. Like so many others without proper dental care, she had her teeth extracted. This alteration changed the shape of her mouth, and made her look dour. As a young woman she was a beauty.

Back, Mother and Frank, front, Grandpa, Norman, Grandma, Gordon

While mother and father Gillatly and the boys adjust quickly to Stratford, Ethel does not. In 1921, Stratford is an untidy industrial town, whereas Camrose is a rural village, where western hospitality makes room for everybody. Ethel pines for the west. She finishes high school doing well, getting a job right away, and quits in two weeks' time. Ethel is now a shapely beautiful girl, suffering all the unwanted attention that accrues to that select breed of women who catch the wandering eyes of men.

When the boss's son makes advances, mother gets scared and that's why she quit. People would stop her and say,

"You look just like Janet Gaynor, the movie star."
This compliment follows her around to the point where it will do her harm. Meantime, Ethel becomes a telephone operator at the Bell. 'Number please?' is the usual question that most people have never heard in today's automated phone system. It was standard fare when I was a kid. In those days everybody had a party line. If you try to use the phone when your shared line is in use and heard voices you politely hang up and wait a few minutes. If however, an emergency crops up, you would say so, and polite people would immediately defer, hang up, and let you make your call. After a minute or so, surreptitiously, your second party lifts the receiver to find out what's up.

Beautiful and charming, Ethel does not lack for admirers. Her problem is which one to choose. No ordinary man will do. They have to be something special. Or to be specific, the kind of ambition that means moving away from Stratford. There is a world of adventure out there somewhere where success and possibly even fame awaits the challenger. Freddie O'Conner (not his real name) was madly in love with Ethel, but Freddie worked in a factory. His secure and happy life in Stratford made him content. Freddie's idea of living was to buy a house in Stratford, settle down and have a family. His friends all lived in town and he had no desire to meet new people. Sure Freddie was kind, helpful, and respectful of his parents. He even went to church, but Freddie was boring. There were others too. Ethel had no lack of admirers, but Ethel was picky. She was waiting for Mr. Adventure. The man of her dreams who would take her away to the palace of Prince Charming where she would live happily ever after. She would not have to wait long. Her vision of romance was about to be realized. It was just around the corner.

A year later, a smooth talking Casanova salesman by the name of Bruce Woods, representing Maclean's Magazine, is in town. Boy meets girl at a dance, and Cupid snares two hearts with one arrow. But Grandma didn't like him from the start.

"He's a smoothie and I don't trust him, and you're not the first

1926, Mom and Dad and their convertible, their courting days

1926, Mom and Dad just married

girl, he's ever dated," she says.

"And just what do you mean by that?" Ethel protests.

"You know what I mean!" Grandma declares.

1926, Style in the roaring twenties.

Grandma never put into words what she had in mind and to her everlasting regret, she wished that she had. She rightly assumed that her daughter understood. Ethel knows all too well what she means, but she is totally infatuated with Bruce and refuses to hear. In today's parlance, we would call it denial. It is a combination for a certain inevitability that forebodes an ill wind right from the start. This is to become a cautionary tale for Ethel, who for five years has been plotting her exodus to a 'promised land' somewhere else, where all one's dreams come true. Alas, she discovers too late, that bad things can happen to beautiful girls, if they don't watch out. Lacking mother's approval, Bruce Woods Sr. and Ethel elope. Damage control consists of a sad announcement card to family and friends that reads, "Alexander and Rachel Gillatly wish to announce the marriage of their daughter, Ethel Irene to Bruce Woods of Toronto, October 3, 1926."

Having no specific plans for married life, Bruce brings his new bride to St. Thomas, to live with his father Bertram Arthur Woods, and Arthur's second wife, Mary Ann. One week later, Bruce heads out on a western tour for Maclean's, and informs Ethel that he will be back in two months. Enter the gods Pan and Puck to work their mischief. What would have been a ruinous start for any marriage is resolved by an infatuation with Wray, Bruce's younger brother. Ethel never misses a dance, or a movie, always accompanied by Wray. No one quite knows what Bruce is doing, away from home, but like his womanizer father, Bertram Arthur, one can guess.

Ethel does a lot of learning and growing up in St. Thomas. One of her surprise lessons is her father-in-law Arthur makes extra cash by doing illegal abortions. In fact, Arthur makes extra cash by any means, fair or otherwise, but always passes himself off as the gentleman. In due time, Bruce returns home, none the wiser about Ethel's manner of entertainment. The newlyweds begin their city life in Toronto, where all the excitement can be found.

Ethel now receives a crash course on how to avoid bill collectors, as Bruce has an easy way of smooth talking just about everyone to give him credit, on his solemn word that they will be paid as soon as his commissions come in. Ethel and Bruce are constantly on the move, as exasperated landlords evict them. Bruce could always afford the things he wanted as the photos of the Terraplane Hudson coupe he drove reveals. Ethel looks chic as she poses for a photo Bruce took of that very impressive looking car.

Their big break comes when Bruce announces that he has met an important American businessman named Sammy. Sammy is an Italian entrepreneur, who drives a black Cadillac. Sammy has contacts and needs a partner who is a good salesman. Bruce fits the bill and is hired at the unheard of salary of $50 per week (in 1926 a new car could be purchased for $600). In no time, the happy couple move to an upscale apartment, with brand new furniture, purchased on credit. However, the joy of affluence is short lived; the police pick up Sammy and put him in jail. Ethel had suspected something fishy from the start but, blinded by the lure of easy money, had put her suspicions aside. A month later, the department store picks up the

1924, people told Mother she looked just like Hollywood movie actress, Janet Gaynor (public domain photo)

new furniture for non-payment, and once again, Bruce and Ethel are apartment hunting. Meanwhile Bruce flits from one sales job to another. It is always a feast or a famine. At other times, Bruce will head out west, once again working for Maclean's. Weeks go by and Ethel begins to wonder if she will ever see him again. In order to eat, Ethel will work where she can; it is 1929, and the great depression has set in; furthermore she is pregnant and desperate.

Eventually Bruce returns, and solves the problem. He has seen it all before in his own St. Thomas home. He knows exactly what to do. He finds a religious, hard-pressed doctor, who amongst other things, thinks it's a reasonable thing to be paid for sending unborn babies to the happiness of heaven ahead of time (preferably for cash but in the case of my father, on credit). He must have done one too many, because not only did he lose his license, but he also went to jail. After his release, he looked up Bruce for payment. Ethel said,

"I felt so sorry for him, he looked so sad." Unfortunately he fares no better than the rest, who try to collect debts that are owed by the super salesman. Such tensions as these do not work in favour of the marriage. There are frequent arguments.

The crisis in the marriage comes when Bruce meets the other woman. Phyllis Christian. Phyllis, who was originally from Hamilton, had married an American and did newspaper work in New York. Phyllis, who was good with the pen, did a society column pursuing scandal ridden Long Islanders ad nauseum. Finally the subject matter of her column overcame her own tortured marriage. Phyllis and Gilbert Christian decide to split up. After a stormy divorce with a baby girl in tow, she moves to Toronto. Phyllis is a seasoned newspaperwoman, who knows what she wants and knows how to get it. As Ethel would later ruefully say,

"Her name was Christian, but she was no Christian." It all starts as a family friendship, but shortly Bruce always has these sales meetings to attend after supper. Suspicious, Ethel phones Phyllis, who will cheerfully lie,

"Oh Bruce just stopped in for a coffee after his meeting."

To compound the problem, Ethel is pregnant again, and can't be bothered with sex. Once again my parents get the evangelistic fervour to populate heaven and make an appointment with the friendly abortionist, and being of an agreeable nature and somewhat naive, I went along. To my everlasting gratitude, this time, the abortionist is confronted by my guardian angel or some such act of Providence, because try as one might, they didn't get me. Now Ethel worries that she might have injured the baby. On October 31, 1931, I came into the world and mother, in deference to dad, called me Bruce which showed real foresight because that's what all the kids call me at school. Ethel now goes to work in order to save her marriage. Her solution is to get the baby on formula immediately and after her newborn is weaned, war for her marriage. She will pretty herself up and take on the 'femme fatale.'

Oddly enough, these two women have something in common. They both have a parent that warns them not to marry Bruce Woods. Furthermore, both these women have loved a man that who bring them grief. Since Ethel is still the first wife, she decides to fight for her marriage with fire. Unfortunately, fighting fire with fire doesn't work, because I refuse to cooperate. To preserve her stylish figure, mother weans me right away and I go on formula. After a few weeks, as a connoisseur of mother's milk, I decide to accept no substitutes. I react to cow's milk; so begins my lifelong affinity for proudly making a noise. I am a compulsive talker from birth. While Ethel tries one formula after another, Bruce Jr. (that's me again) is losing weight, and looking very sick. (Some people are sure I never got over it, because that's when I began my lifelong battle to put on weight, despite my propensity for cheese and extravagant desserts). Desperate to save her baby, Ethel travels to St. Thomas, and appeals to her father-in-law for help. Bertram, who seems to know just about everything, tries a formula that is so wretched, that mother is sure her baby will die.

The last hope is Stratford. Braving Grandma's "I told you so," we wind up on Grandma's doorstep. I had voluntarily accompanied my mother looking like I can't last a week. Dr. Harold Kenner is Grandma's physician who (when he sees my winsome ways) says,

"All this baby needs is Carnation milk." The formula works. For the first time in six weeks, mother and baby sleep the sleep of exhaustion. Bruce Jr. thrives (Look at my baby pictures and judge for yourself!) Bruce Sr. moves into a flat with Phyllis Christian. The marriage is over; however Ethel does not comprehend this, at least, not yet. She tries a few letters, and dutifully Bruce Sr., eight months later, comes by to see the baby.

The other woman, Phyllis Christian

Mother putting on a bold face after Bruce asks for a divorce

There are photos of the happy couple holding the kid. Mother, who looks gorgeous and is dressed fit to kill, is still trying desperately to restore her marriage. However, the damage is done; finally but firmly, Bruce Sr. explains to Ethel the marriage is finished, and that he will be seeking a divorce. Mother is devastated. There is however one significant hurdle to overcome. This is 1932 and the only cause for divorce that the law will recognize is adultery. To obtain the divorce, Bruce Sr. asks mother to charge him with due cause, and he will pay the lawyer. This is one time, when Bruce Sr. seems to have the money to pay bills, (except for child support). Ethel capitulates and meekly complies. Janet Gaynor's, double stars in her own melodrama written by others who are beyond her control. However, there is no reward for her career; the girl with so much potential finds herself abandoned and sad. This Cinderella story has no glass slipper and the fickle prince Charming will build his Castle for someone else.

Coming home after five years away, for Ethel is not the homecoming a 26-year old, attractive brunette has envisaged. She is oftentimes despondent and lonely. For Bruce Jr. it was fun. He had three men to dote on him: Grandpa Alex, Uncle Gordon who is 21, and Uncle Norman who is 18. He is sharing all the same relatives and communicable diseases. It is not until Bruce turns 15, that he begins to understand the tragedy that beset his beautiful mother, and the gradual subversion of her life.

OK, so I've let the cat out of the bag; I was born in Toronto, I shamefully repent. But have no fears, because fortunately I was snatched away before I could be corrupted. I lived my first sixteen years in Stratford, minus a few weeks, that I don't remember. (You see, I was very young at the time.) That minor detail explained, I will have you to understand, I am a Stratfordite through and through. As proof, I submit my blood line pedigree, (all dead or comatose), who would witness to my claims, if they could.

Chapter 7

The Pre-War Years

In 1931, when mother moved back to Stratford, her brother Frank had already married Margaret Wilkinson. Margaret was a colourful character who loved to talk even when she had nothing to say. Margaret had plenty of advice for just about everybody and as the Bible says, 'It is more blessed to give than to receive.' Getting a word in edgewise with Margaret was like threading a sewing machine with the motor running, and how she did love to drop by and chat. We were always glad to see her because for entertainment, she was better than any modern sitcom you can imagine. When Margaret dropped by to talk, we listened. Did we have a choice? Meanwhile, we did our best to muffle a smile. When she left, Grandma would patronizingly commiserate with Frank.

"There's no way that Frank could have proposed marriage to Margaret." Grandma said, "It was all her doing, and Frank was too quiet to object." We had plenty to laugh about at Margaret's expense, when she wasn't around. The absent are always in the wrong.

One day Aunt Marg decided she could drive a car without troubling herself with bothersome lessons. Choosing a road less travelled by; she headed for Snake Hill, and backed a Model A Ford right into the Avon River. After that, Margaret never thought about driving again until 25 years later, when she gave it some serious consideration. Although she still couldn't drive, she took a notion to buy a Jeep. When her sons Bill and Gordon came home from work, they looked at each other in astonishment,

"Where did this Jeep come from?" Meantime the uneasy salesman who sold this unusual female the vehicle wondered if he had done the right thing. He soon found out when the sons showed up with the Jeep and quickly made their point. With explanations made, the dealer took back the vehicle and life returned to normal. Today, we would say Margret was bi-polar.

Frank's recreation was work. After an eight-hour day, he would take odd jobs washing windows or painting houses. We joked about that,

"In his situation, who wouldn't work day and night; it was easier than getting a word in edgewise with Aunt Marg." However I have to take my hat off to Margaret's boldness. One day she discovered that 30 McLagan Drive was for sale. The city had taken possession of the house for non-payment of taxes. The house was unpretentious, but its location by the river was priceless. Margaret saw value; that showed a rare insight for the occasion. She borrowed $1700 from her mother and closed the deal. She bought a property that on today's market would certainly bring a hefty price, so who's laughing now.

1957, my cousin Marylou and Bill Allman

There is no joy to a parent like seeing your children succeed. The joy is compounded when early failures give way to later triumph. Margaret and Frank Gillatly had three children. Billy, after he did a stint in the armed forces, became roads superintendent for the town of St. Mary's. Next came Marylou and then Gordon, the youngest. Gordon too, did his overseas tour with the forces before he retired to Victoria. The charmer however is Marylou. Everybody in Stratford knows Bill Allman, the manager of the Stratford Arena. Well, Bill was sweet on Marylou and the attraction was mutual. However, in the course of events, Marylou got swept off her feet with the arrival of a German soldier by the name of Ralph Willie. How does Bill Allman who clears the ice between hockey games compete with this? He is sad when Marylou marries Ralph, but Bill Allman licks his wounds by learning how to ride horses becoming a respectable trainer in the process. Alas, Marylou realizes her mistake all too soon and after bringing two children into the world, she leaves her abusive husband and comes home to mommy. Seems like this kind of story runs in the family. Marylou also had twin girls, but they were put up for adoption.

By now Bill Allman, who everybody likes, is climbing the ranks at the arena. He will eventually become the manager. Bill, who has largeness of heart, pardons Marylou and the romance blossoms once again. Together they have a life. Bill's health is none to good at the last, and in his need, a generous heart is rewarded by Marylou's care and devotion. What a lesson on the joy of forgiveness! When Bill Allman dies, Margaret Wade is deputy mayor of Stratford and determined that the city will not forget Bill Allman for his lifelong service to all who ever used the arena. There are other contenders, but Margaret Wade has her mind made up. She is not without her critics,

"Imagine," said one, "naming an Arena after a janitor when there are so many good men to honour." What is that line from the Magnificat? 'He hath put down the mighty from their seats, and exhaulted them of low degree.' It is settled. The refurbished arena is called the William Allman Arena in honour of a good man. Nobody is more pleased than Margaret Gillatly and her family.

Back to the beginning of my story. Frank marries Margaret Wilkenson and moves out of the house. Two years after Frank had married Margaret and moved away from home, mother comes home from Toronto with a brand new baby as Frank's replacement; the population at 156 Brunswick still stands at six. It didn't shrink to five until September 5, 1933 when Gordon suddenly decides to marry Elsie Deacon. Since I was only two at the time my memory of the event comes afterward. Seven months later a full explanation is revealed. On March 31, the following year, Shirley Gillatly is born.

Gordon was a born athlete, and excelled at every sport he played, including billiards. Good looking and popular with the guys and the ladies, Gordon was a man to be reckoned with, and despite his stuttering problem, was regarded as a 'catch'. Elsie was the winner, and we often wondered if, afterward, she didn't wish that she had lost. Certainly Elsie's sisters thought so, and didn't mind saying it. With three sisters-in-law, Gordon never lacked for advice, but alas, it just went in one ear and out the other, so maybe that explains why Gordon wasn't smart at school. Gordon liked to party. As is so often the case with athletes, Gordon liked to drink, which exacerbated his stuttering. Bacchus may have a smiling face, but he can be a monkey on your back. There were times when Elsie had to contend with a husband who partied with one pint too many. Mother succeeded in keeping that side of my Uncle Gordon a secret. Meanwhile, Providence sided with Elsie. Every time Gordon got to his fourth beer, he would get as sick as a dog. Frustrated, Bacchus had to look elsewhere for patronage.

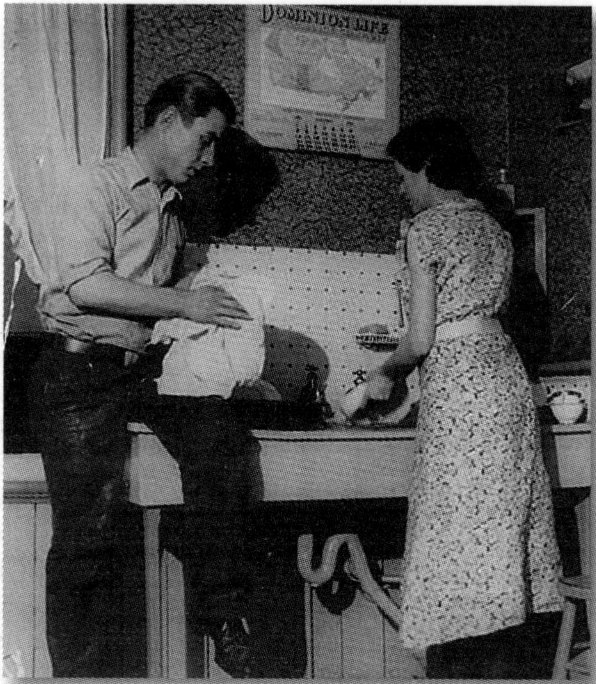

1934, If mother resembled Janet Gaynor, her brother Gordon [in my opinion] resembled Humphrey Bogart

I hero-worshipped Uncle Gordon because he was good at sports and what kid wouldn't like to have an uncle who excelled in athletics. Uncle Gord would tell me stories of Howie Morenz and that other Howie from New Hamburg, Howie Meeker, both of NHL hockey fame. I often wondered if Gordon might have made it in professional hockey if he hadn't had to hunker down early in his career with a wife and baby. Now I'll have you to understand that even though Uncle Gordon was not smart at school, he excelled with his hands. Not only did this include a puck and a hockey stick, but it also included furniture. His home-built furniture rivalled anything to be purchased in stores.

One thing more about my Uncle Gord. He introduced me to my lifelong love of maps. Mother noticed my affinity for maps and bought me a grade five geography textbook a year before I would need it. I was fascinated with the maps in that textbook. In no time I could draw freehand the map of Europe and write in the capital cities. I even dreamed of being a cartographer so mother took me to Toronto to see the Ontario government map making offices. When I saw the painstaking effort of mapmaking, I must confess a little of the glamour wore off. How did Uncle Gordon figure in all this? He acquired the first roadmap I ever saw when he bought a 1926 Essex and parked it in our garage. Pouring over this roadmap of Ontario, he pointed out where Montreal was located. Uncle Gordon was planning a vacation trip to Montreal. I was bewitched with that roadmap and examined it for hours. I located Goderich and Bogie's Beach. I marvelled that such a map could be drawn and that you could find exactly each town and village in Ontario. Later in the war years, I clipped every war map the Stratford Beacon-Herald printed and filed them all in a cardboard box. Three years after the war's end I still had four hundred of them until one day I just decided to throw them away.

Oh yes — about Uncle Gordon's Montreal trip. He never took it. There was always something wrong with the car, and even after hours of work, it barely made the rounds in Stratford, although once it was driven to Tillsonburg. Another reason was that Gordon simply didn't have the money. His kids, Cheryl and Bobby, remember one time when they were treated to a car ride and an ice cream cone. The money for the ice cream came from a quarter Gordon found on the street. I was so inspired by this story that I decided I would give all my earthly treasures to Gordon for his birthday. I had come into possession of a quarter, so I wrapped it up and put it at his place for the weekly Friday supper visit that Gordon always made at our house. You cannot imagine the relief I felt when after opening his present, Uncle Gordon gave it back to me. (I loved chocolate milkshakes and that quarter would buy five of them). The car was finally sold to another automotive devotee who would dream of going places even if they could only find out where those places were by locating them on the map. Those were the days when everybody was poor.

Having disposed of two uncles, I turn to Uncle Norm. Uncle Norman was twenty, when Gordon got married, and was still delivering groceries on his bicycle for Lloyd's store on the corner of Brunswick and Nile. Not much of a job for a twenty-year old man, but this was the Great Depression, and any job is better than none.

Norman, like mom, is artistic and learned to play the French horn in the Stratford Boy's Band. Clever with his hands, he made his own violin out of a wooden cigar box, and was sometimes asked to play his unique instrument at church suppers. At other times he would make three dimensional flower pictures out of shells. His creative bent expressed itself in practical ways as well.

One day an exasperated Mr. Lloyd complained,

"I've got a pear tree loaded with pears, but the tree is so big, I can only harvest bruised fruit after it falls to the ground." This was the kind of challenge that Uncle Norman loved to hear, and it resulted in an unusual invention, which he called his giraffe. Collecting a batch of throwaway silk stockings, (nylon had not yet been invented), Norman had a plan to harvest pears. For such a worthy cause the neighbourhood ladies rallied. Silk stockings didn't last long. After he had collected a dozen pair spoiled by unsightly runs, Uncle Norm cut off the feet, and sewed them all together. Mounted on a pole, he could snag a pear and it would Adam's apple its way, down the stocking safely into Norman's hands. Even the neighbours came out to watch the show, and laugh at Norman's giraffe.

The sudden and unexpected death of Grandpa Alex in 1934 created a financial crisis, which brought mother to the fore. Mother could not find employment in Stratford in 1931, but had acquired a big city talent from her Toronto years. She had learned how to do a Marcel, a popular 1930's hairstyle. For 50 cents mother would cover a lady's head with pin curls and bobby pins. After the hair had set, and the pins were removed, the customer was ready for her date or special occasion. A Marcel only lasted for one night, but shucks, what do you expect for 50 cents. A Marcel was fine employment for weekends, but provided no work from Monday to Thursday. Mother had pleaded with Grandma to let her set up a hairdressing salon in the front room, but Grandma wouldn't hear of such an outlandish idea. Suddenly with the passing of Grandpa Alex and no income, Grandma gave her consent.

Mother would go into the hairdressing business. However this was the Depression, and the friendly banker wouldn't lend mother the $75 to set up shop, which in those days would have been a king's ransom. At this juncture mother turned to her pastor, Rev. J. F. Reycroft of the United Church where she attended. The minister took the money from the benevolent fund. The $75 was enough to make the down payment for equipment from the suppliers, with the balance to be paid off in monthly instalments. The beauty parlour, as it was called in those days, was an instant success. Later mother would say,

"From that time on, there was no Depression for us." This was wonderful vindication for mother. In no time she paid off the $75 and for Rev. Reycroft's pains promptly stopped going to church. From now on, she had money to spare and a son to spoil.
I accommodate mother with reckless abandon. Needless to say Grandma was relieved. When grandpa died, he left nothing but the house. Grandma's security came through mother's success in the hairdressing business. While no one would wish the troubles that mother had endured, her trials have a redeeming effect for Grandma and me. Grandma is cared for in her old age and Bruce Jr. is provided for, growing up apart from the dysfunctional Woods clan with its plethora of affluence and multiple divorces.

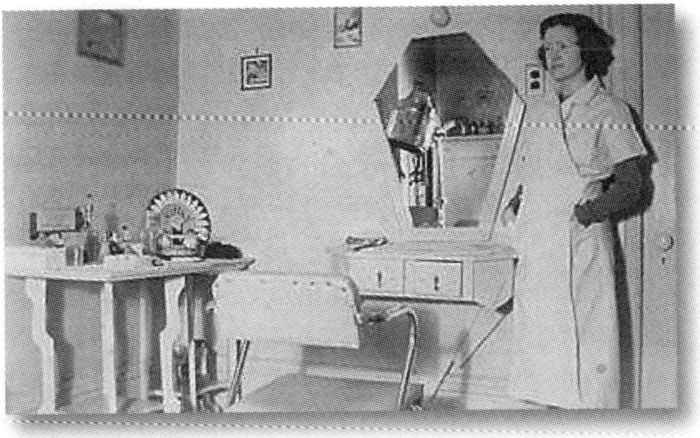

1937, once Mother got the beauty parlour up and running, there was no depression for us

Soon Uncle Norman gets interested, and quickly learns the trade. In 1937 he marries the girl of his dreams, Jean Timms, and moves to Tillsonburg, where he sets up shop on the main street above Richardson's 5 & 10. A fun loving couple, they quickly became an institution. When I would visit Tillsonburg, it seemed that everyone knew Norm and Jean. Once again mother becomes the redeemer-sister who makes happiness for her brother while her own happiness goes wanting. After Norm and Jean got married, I graduated to Norman's bedroom with that wonderful view of the street.

In those early years the two most exciting things that I remember I now will relate. The first was bad and the second was good. In 1937, when I was five, Stratford had an exciting visitation of fire and water. The fire was in the building on Ontario Street where the Stratford Beacon-Herald is printed.
The flames were so high you could see them all over the city.
The water part was the rain. That winter the rains were so bad that they took out the dam and the John Street Bridge. People on the north side of the city, who had no car for the round about trip, couldn't get to the hospital. It was a calamity that took months to correct. On the other hand, those were the idyllic days when life was slow. On occasion when the lazy drone of an airplane could be heard coming over town, we would drop everything to run outside and witness the miracle of modern flight and talk about it for a week thereafter. A more frequent adventure was the fire bell from the old Fire Station at Albert and Waterloo Streets. Most of Stratford could hear the clarion call and watch in fascination, provided proximity gave you a view, as the shiny red fire trucks rolled by. A better conversation piece than this was hard to imagine, unless you had been made famous by having visited Callander and seen the Dionne quintuplets.

In 1937 due to the heavy rains the dam washed out

I guess the really good news story that happened in those pre-war years was the discovery that the King and Queen of England were coming to pay us a visit and all the kids at school were invited to the party, or was that invitation for the grown-ups as well? There we were, as kids in Grade 2, starry-eyed and full of anticipation.

"Imagine," I said to mom. "The King and Queen of England coming to Stratford!" We thought the King and Queen were coming all the way from England just to see us. We were unaware of the politics. Foreseeing the coming of Word War II, with an eye on a reluctant French Canada, Prime Minister MacKenzie King and his cabinet felt that a royal visit would help unify the country if another war was declared. The ruse worked. Canada's unity never was in doubt despite the reluctant French. Oblivious of the real reason for the royal visit, all of Stratford was buzzing with preparations.

J. T. Priest was the music director for most of the public schools in Stratford, and loved his job better than we loved to practice. Practice we must, because there was to be a school choir of all the kids singing patriotic songs in celebration of the monarchy. Appropriately, the big occasion fell on a beautiful day, Wednesday, June 7, 1939. With the sun shining brightly in a cloudless sky, the anticipated occasion had arrived. Obviously Providence had smiled upon a most favoured city to bring together some very important people. As we assembled on the Romeo School grounds, Miss Dunbar had her hands full to contain our excitement. Brimming with patriotism, we made our way to the Station Park, expecting to have a front row place.

"What are you going to say to the King when you meet him?" I say to Clarkie.

"We won't get to talk to the King." Clarkie sternly replies.

"Sure we will." I confidently reply. "After all, this is why they are coming." Clarkie turns up his nose and says,

"That's what you think."

Meanwhile I imagine myself at the very front, talking to the King. I can picture the whole thing and can see myself catching the King's eye just as the train pulls into town. I have it all planned out in my head, "We are small people, we deserve a front row; it's only fair. Short people to the front, tall people to the rear." The problem was, that when we got to the station, there were already five thousand people who had arrived there first, with thousands more making their way to the park. To say the least, I am intimidated. Royal fever had spawned a contagion, and everybody had caught the virus. A thousand people from Listowel, who had boarded their train at 4 o'clock in the morning, had the best standing room, and they weren't even from Stratford. I don't know how many came from St. Mary's. More from Mitchell! On and on it went.

“Romeo School children to the right;” Mr. Priest boomed out through the loudspeaker system. “There it is,” I think to myself, “we will be right at the front as I imagined.” My difficulty came with the people who simply would not stand aside and let us through. I had a wonderful view of a broad shouldered man and his wife. Standing tightly beside them, a hundred other backs of total strangers, all craning their necks to see the platform. Suddenly, Mr. Priest announced,

“The train is coming, school children of Stratford, get ready to sing; here comes the royal train. Vainly I look for Miss Dunbar to lead the way. The kids from Romeo school are scattered and in disarray. Suddenly the crowd roars, “Here comes the train.”

I suppose the train pulled up to the Stratford platform, so specially prepared for the Royal couple. You could tell by the cheering of the people who could see, even if we couldn’t. Next, Mr. Priest invited a thousand or more children to sing. As school kids, we could hear the train, but that’s about all. Meanwhile, Mr. Priest sang as credible a solo as he was capable of. As children, who had spent weeks learning six or seven patriotic songs, we were too smitten with awe to sing a single note. The silence of the children was deafening; meanwhile, Mr. Priest sang as though the cherished privacy of his bathroom had travelled with him before an audience of thousands. To this day I can still sing a ‘Tow-row tow-row to the British Grenediers’ so I guess all those school choir lessons were not in vain.

Since the train was an hour late, Stratford was deemed worthy of only 15 minutes of time. The thousand or so people who were spread along the tracks to Romeo Street (in those days the city limits) got a quick view of the coach, but that’s about all. To make up time, the train, which was supposed to be going five miles per hour, whizzed by at twenty. The organizers of the tour must have been napping because they realized too late, that the train was already well inside the city limits. By the time they rushed the King and Queen to the railing of the viewing porch, the train was stopped at the platform overlooking the Shakespeare Street Park. At this juncture it was all downhill in magnificent disarray. Speeches were scrapped and dignitaries ignored. The Royal couple did make their appearance. It was long enough for a photo op, and then the organizers rushed them back into the special coach that eventually travelled all the way to Vancouver. Meantime I caught Clarkie by the sleeve and said,

"C'mon let's see, if we can get closer to the front." Snaking our way around the legs of hundreds of adults, who were in the way, we finally made it to the tracks. We were just in time to see the Royal Coach disappear, around the bend.

I know the King and Queen came to Stratford, because we saw their picture in the Stratford-Beacon Herald the following day. Mayor Tom Henry vented his rage in a letter of protest that claimed 17,000 people had been shamefully ignored. The Beacon-Herald agreed, and just about everybody was sure Stratford had been given the royal snub. However, in the end, everybody forgave just about everybody else, or how could you keep flying the Union Jack at City Hall.
In my memory the Royal ballyhoo became the Royal busteroo, but it was still a success because we got the day off from school. As for what I might have said to the King — well, it just never got said. Probably for the best!

Chapter 8

Canada at War

Tom Brokaw, news anchor of NBC called the young men of World War II, 'the greatest generation'. They were certainly deserving of the title. That greatest generation came from men a little older than me, some right from Brunswick Street. They were a special class forged in the hardships of the depression years and challenged by the perils of those anxious times. For the men who survived, it was the adventure of a lifetime. For us kids with war toys hitherto unseen, it set a standard of play unequalled by any previous generation. The volunteers, and later on the draftees, were men like my Uncle Norman and his friends. Frank Wade is another example of that generation. He volunteered for the Air Force but was rejected because of a hernia suffered from a simple bicycle accident. In 'guy' language, boys call this 'cracking your nuts' and any kid, who ever rode a bicycle, knows what I'm talking about. While most of us usually recover quickly, nobody forgets the pain. In Frank's case his accident became a barrier to the Air Force. To overcome this rejection, he joined the army where medical attention was free. After the surgery for his hernia, he transferred to the Air Force and became a gunner, which happens to be the most dangerous job a man could take. Such is the stuff of that generation.

As a child, I was too immature to understand this kind of dedication. I was among those who were too young to go to war, but not too young to be moulded by the small sacrifices that were required. January 8, 1940, the ration books that were issued in the previous year came into effect. Meat, sugar, and butter had to be shared with mother England. Those invaluable coupons are our passage to the essentials. Red coupons for sugar, green for tea and coffee, yellow for butter and brown for meat. At times some people unpatriotically swap coupons for staples that are in demand. We never used up our quota for meat coupons and were surprised at those who would swap meat coupons for sugar. We never seemed to have enough sugar, but patriotically we refused to swap with those of a carnivore appetite who longed for our meat coupons and would offer us sugar in return. I do remember Grandma giving away meat coupons to someone who was having a special occasion, but such transactions were rare. These minor privations taught us that the war we heard about on the six o'clock news had finally come home to us. The more ominous experience came when the air raid siren sounded its alarm. We have read our instructions from the paper and are pre-warned. Obediently, we turn out all the lights and sit in the dark for fifteen minutes waiting for the all clear. When the siren sounds for the second time, life returns to normal. The longest blackout occurred in January 1943, when without warning the sirens sounded, and we were blacked out for half an hour. In retrospect, the danger of being bombed by the Germans was sheer hyperbole, but the psychological and propaganda effect was real. For those brief moments, the news-reels we saw at the movie house, was lived in our imagination. The closest thing to a bomb we ever saw was in 1944, when a German V-l flying 'dootlebug' was reconstructed in England and shipped to Canada for public viewing. It made the rounds through Canada for loyal Canadians to see. I remember viewing it, parked beside City Hall, and thinking how big the thing looked and how expensive it would be to produce. "War is such a waste of money!"

It is spring 1940; we are sitting on our porch. The Spirea blossoms white. The veranda is our platform. A place to meet and say a friendly hello. Our entertainment is to greet family and friends. George Wade, a widower since Julia died in '34, comes less frequently now, but there are many that appear regularly. It is the common recreation that disappeared with the arrival of television. I am convinced that for good times, we had the better end of the stick. Young as I was, while I don't remember the conversations, I do remember sitting on the veranda and feeling very much a part of the fun. Tonight it is a beautiful evening. It is hard to appreciate that there is a war going on in Europe. The daily news is a ritual at our

The Germans launced almost 2000 V-1rockets against London. They were a scientific marvel or so we thought. They could fly at 350 miles per hour but were programmed to slow down over England and crash into populated areas. Only one of every ten V-1 pilotless rocket bombs got to their target as the British shot them down when they slowed to detonate.

house at 6 P.M, and the news is bad. Mother doesn't burden me with these things, but as I have already informed you, I find out by bits and pieces.

A few days later, it is Sunday and Uncle Norm and Aunt Jean are coming for dinner. A pork roast is kept in the cellar-way. We have no fridge or icebox.

"It's cool enough to keep meat in the cellar-way." Grandma always says. The visit from Norm and Jean is a treat, because gas rationing means we don't see them as often as we'd like. This afternoon, we will go for a car ride. This is indeed high adventure. In minutes we can visit Uncle Gord and Aunt Elsie. At other times, it takes a brisk 20 minute walk to get to 475 Albert Street. Norman is 27 and so far has eluded the draft, but we all know the inevitable: very soon he will be called up to the join the army. We enjoy our dinner that day. Pork roast, thinly sliced, and gravy on my potatoes never tasted so good, and to boot, Uncle Norman with his wit and humour makes us laugh. We savour more than the meal: Uncle Norman could receive his conscription notice. If that were the case, it would be some time before we would have a Sunday dinner with Uncle Norman present, even though Aunt Jean would continue to make her regular pilgrimage to see Grandma. We just don't know. This apprehension will be with us for another 18 months, when finally the fateful conscription call came in 1943. After supper mother lies down on the couch.

This picture tells a story.

"Come over here Brucie and lie beside me," says mother. I dutifully obey. Norman decides this is a photo op, and snaps a picture. It turns out to be a good one and makes its way into mother's photo album. Years later and a little bit wiser, I observe how sad mother looks in that picture.

In the summer of 1940, mother and her newfound friend, Yulanda Latter, have planned a vacation. It turns out to be a cruise on Georgian Bay, stopping off at picturesque islands and finishing off at Manitoulin. I go to Bogie's Beach for two weeks. Once again I encounter the war. Radar training is at Clinton. Young Englishmen learn to fly from Goderich's Sky Harbour on outmoded Tiger Moths, a biplane from World War I. In 1941 the single engine Harvard Trainer eventually replaced these aircraft. We got so used to seeing them overhead that the novelty finally wore off and we didn't even bother to look as they flew over. In 1942, the Anson Trainer arrived at Port Albert. They were designed to teach the air warriors how to fly the long-range bomber. Names like the Lockheed Hudson, the Douglas DC 3, the Halifax, and the Lancaster, identify the flying machines that will ultimately reveal the truth that to be an airman is the most dangerous of all possible careers. Many of these young men will die in action.

George Luxton is one such pilot in training. He is one of many to come. The Commonwealth Air Training program will eventually graduate 50,000 pilots for combat. The winds of war will ultimately turn against Germany. These men in training are destined to become a hurricane spreading destruction over Europe. They are far from home and restless. The confinement of the cockpit demands a change of pace. George Luxton is looking for a little relaxation. He discovers Bogie's Beach. I can still see his handsome face, and wonder if he survived to live a normal life. The adult guests are just getting acquainted. George is the centre of their curiosity. They are full of questions about England and George is only too happy to accommodate them, describing his beloved homeland. Mrs. Bogie invites us to the table. She has a special treat. The menu at the table includes corn on the cob. Mr. Bogie has noticed something unusual about the corn leaf, which he picks out and shows the guests. The leaf has the letter "B" imprinted clearly.

"It just grew that way," says Mr. Bogie. We all discuss the leaf and decide that God must have put it there as a prophecy that Britain will win the war. Evelyn brings in a platter of the steaming freshly boiled corn. We are salivating the feast. The guests have pooled their yellow rationing coupons to buy a pound of butter, purchased in Goderich, for the special treat. Mrs. Bogie makes butter, but, it is requisitioned by the food inspector for Britain that in turn ships us woolen goods of every kind. To use this butter for oneself would be tantamount to treason. Besides, what would we do without those woolen sweaters packed in mothballs to wear on winter days; I can still smell them, and remember with disgust when despite our best efforts, the moths ate them full of holes. There will be no special treatment for anybody we know. Mrs. Bogie's butter is for Britain.

Evelyn and Graham had been picking fresh corn for the last hour. The community pound of butter is the table centrepiece. The guests around the table are rubbing their hands with anticipation. First, Mr. Bogie says grace. Now we take turns, rolling our corn in the precious butter, remembering we have to make it last. Ramrod stiff, George is aloof and non-conversant. We are feasting, but George isn't eating.

"Have some corn, George," Mr. Bogie implores.

"Corn is for pigs," George replies. The guests burst out laughing. The implications are obvious. No amount of persuasion can tempt George. His prejudice against corn is fixed. I shake my head in amazement; Englishmen are a stubborn lot. Two weeks at the farm go quickly and while I am reluctant to leave, a new adventure awaits me in Stratford.

Mom loves me alot even when I object.

-oOo-

Mother loves me a lot. She showers her affection on me in every way she can. If I see a toy that catches my fancy, I will probably receive it on my birthday, or at Christmas. She wants me to succeed in life. She always tells me how important it is for me to go to college. She talks to me like a confidante. Mother is a good mom. Copious love received has to be expressed outwardly somehow, but I discover there are exceptions. I beg mother for a dog; that's when I discover the limit to human affection. Grandma lays down the law. There will be no dog in our house, at least not until the miracle happens. One day, shortly after I had returned to school in September, God the giver of good gifts provides a dog for me right out of the blue. A boy I have never seen before comes riding by our house on his bicycle. He has a dog in his carrier. He says to me,

"Wouldja like a puppy, it's free." I cannot believe my ears,

"You mean you are actually giving away this valuable puppy for no money at all."

"Yep." says the stranger, "My mom says I have to give it away." With authority like that; who can dispute my good fortune, I agree to the terms and the stranger-boy, who seems to be as pleased as I am, rides away without Ricky. That's my dog's name. I knew it the instant I laid eyes on him. Ricky gets as much love and affection from me, as I get from my mom. I take my new friend gently in my hands and carry my blessing to the kitchen. That's when I learn, when I make my blessing Grandma's requirement, my blessing becomes Grandma's burden. Grandma is not blessed.

"Look Grandma, the most wonderful thing in the world has happened to me, I have a puppy. A boy gave it to me just now, and it's free." Grandma does not share my enthusiasm.

"You take that puppy, and give it right back to him this very minute."

"I can't give him back," I wail, "he's mine and it's free." Grandma takes me by the hand and marches me right out to the front yard, to find the generous boy who gave me the pup. He is nowhere to be seen. Next we have a family pow–wow.

"I'm not taking care of any dog," says Grandma. Now there are times of crisis when one must step up to the plate, and accept responsibility. This is one of those times.

"Grandma, you won't have to do anything, I will take care of him, I promise."

I am amazed at how quickly the issue is resolved. All I have to do is make assurances to take care of him through the night when he cries. I don't know puppies can cry, so unaware of what's waiting for me, I agree to the terms. As things turn out, this peace treaty will prove to be an example of those rare occasions when parents actually do know more than their children. Meantime, Ricky gets my undivided attention, until it's time to go to bed. I fix the pup with a cardboard box for a bed; add a few rags for company, and we retire for the evening. The action starts when we turn out the lights. Ricky whimpers most pathetically. He is obviously one of a litter, and he misses his siblings. I get up and comfort him. He settles down and I return to my bed. No dice! Ricky is not comforted! I pull the box beside my bed and dangle my hand where he can feel it. It is not enough. The lifeless hand of his loving, but sleepy master does not suffice. Ricky is inconsolable. A half-hour later, Grandma says,

"I'm not losing any more sleep over that dog. Put him in the kitchen and close the door. He can howl all night, and no one needs to listen." This is indeed cruel and unusual punishment to a tender-hearted boy who loves his dog, but exhaustion wins the day. I have to go to school the next morning. I reluctantly put Ricky in the kitchen, apologize profusely to Ricky, and close the kitchen door.

The next morning, I awake early and race down the stairs to a grateful Ricky who wags his tail and showers me with kisses. There is something sticky on my hands, and my nose tells me it is Ricky's pooh. No sacrifice is too great for a generous lover. I do what has to be done, and after 'ugh' putting Ricky's nose into the used vitamins, (the received wisdom of the day for dog training). I really didn't, I just put him close and told Grandma I actually did. Next, I put him outside and return to the kitchen to clean up the mess. I hadn't bargained on all this but I'm learning fast. Ricky is now howling at the back door.

"Patience Ricky, I'm too busy to let you in." Water and paper applied, I sigh,

"Alright Ricky, I'm coming. You will make me late for school," I tenderly say as I pick up my dog and let him kiss me on the cheek.

I'm beginning to learn that caring for a dog has its downside. After breakfast, I kiss Ricky goodbye and go to school. It's hard to concentrate on schoolwork when you are tired. I slouch in my seat. I am glad when noon hour comes. I race home to see Ricky. I am rewarded by his affection. Grandma hasn't given him any love all morning.

I barely have time to eat my dinner. Ricky is taking all my attention. I don't even take time to play. Proudly I show Ricky to Royce. After a while Clarkie tires of the fun, and leaves me to take care of my dog. I refuse to admit it, but I'm beginning to have my doubts. The evening ordeal is a rerun of the night before. The following morning, when it's time to go to school, I am so tired, I am crying. By noon hour I have reached a decision. Ricky is too much for me. I cave in to mother and Grandma's advice. Give him to the dog pound. They will pick him up, and I can get on with life. Years later when I have kids of my own that imagine our dog is their exclusive possession, I think of Ricky. Dog owning kids are blissfully unaware that it's the parents that do the hard work. Forty-eight hours of dog ownership and its attendant responsibilities have done me in. I give him to the dogcatcher, and he takes him away. I am relieved. My first lesson regarding the brevity of infatuation has been learned.

Posters courtesy Hamilton Public Library, special collections

Meanwhile, my personal pilgrimage has caught the attention of another world. Unbeknown to me, the gods of puppy love exchange a knowing wink; they know when they have found an easy mark.

-oOo-

The Stratford of 1941 includes many horses. The Silverwoods Milkman delivers milk in glass bottles from a horse drawn wagon. In wintertime the cream freezes and lifts the round cardboard cap as much as an inch. The bread man also has a horse and wagon. The ash man comes by every Thursday with his horse drawn wagon. It is my job to carry out the ashes and place them curbside. The garbage man also has a horse and wagon. The evidence is frequently found on the street. As kids, we never tire of shouting, "horsebuns" every time we see the evidence. Meantime, there is always the war. I sometimes wonder if there might be a way to combine horsebuns with bombs. A secret weapon to win the war.

"Buy War Bonds" posters are everywhere. Mother buys a $50 war bond; she can afford it. As kids we are encouraged to buy war savings stamps. For 25 cents, I start my own book; it doesn't occur to me that others are not patriotic just because they don't. The truth is their parents can't afford it. At war's end when I cash in my coupons, I collect 3 dollars plus 26 cents interest at the local Bank of Montreal on Downie Street. I have now entered the world of high finance.

Eleven months have gone by since the war started. By now we have learned that Quebec is not interested in fighting Britain's war. Prime Minister Mackenzie King has announced that all eligible young men in Canada must be registered. On August 3, Montreal's mayor, Camillien Houde defied the government and denied all use of public buildings for registration. Houde, like many Quebecers, had no intentions of allowing French Canadian young men to fight Britain's war. For his pains, Mackenzie King arrested Houde, who as Pierre Burton writes, "became a guest of His Majesty's government, behind barbed wire in an interment camp for the next four years." Released in 1944, the following year he was re-elected as Mayor of Montreal.

Now we are deluged with patriotic slogans, "Don't you know there's a war going on." is one we will hear again and again. Consumer goods start disappearing; "Use it up. Wear it out. Make it do!" These are the slogans we live by. Girls now wear 'Patriot' red lipstick. Meantime, Mackenzie King is leading a nation with one-third of its people who are marching — away from the war. I must pay tribute to the brave French minority who did volunteer and who supported the war effort. These were delicate days when prewar pacifist Mackenzie King, now converted to waging war, walked a tightrope-balancing act and to his credit kept Canada united until at long last, our country was fully committed to the challenge.

When October arrives, so does Eaton's catalogue, delivered to us by somebody who also has a horse and wagon. The war effort has not yet started to bite into consumer goods, but that doesn't concern me; it's the toy section in the catalogue that gets my attention. I tell Aunt Margaret that I want an electric train, she says,

"Your mother is spoiling you rotten; you don't deserve an electric train." Mother reads my letter to Santa Claus. I want her to read the letter because I know there is no such thing as a real Santa Claus?

However just in case I'm wrong, I've got my bases covered. My appeal to mother will ultimately prevail. Christmas 1940, I get my electric train. Christmas Eve excitement has me awake long after I was supposed to be asleep. I distinctly recognize the sound of a train going around a track. Bolt upright in bed, I leap to the hole in the hallway (where the heat comes up) and listen to the voices coming from below. I also hear the sound of the train and Uncle Gordon saying,

"It works, look at the way it travels around the track! Now you can wrap it up." I can scarcely contain myself.

"Has Santa come yet?" I call down the hole.

"Cripes!" moans Uncle Gordon, "I thought that kid was asleep." Mom says,

"Santa has not come yet; go to sleep."

"How come I can hear the sound of an electric train?"

"You're hearing things," says mother, "that noise is something else."

"Sounds like a train to me," I mutter.

“Go to bed or Santa won’t leave you any presents.”

With a threat like that hanging over my head, I return to bed.

“I know an electric train when I hear it.” I reason it all out in my brain; there is no Santa. Your parents are your Santa! I roll over and go to sleep, and I have ceased to be a believer. Christmas morning, I keep up the charade and pretend, but Grandma knows I know. There is no Santa Claus. I can just feel it. Later that day Aunt Margaret calls on us for a visit. Margaret is nonplused, shakes her head and says,

“They’ll spoil that kid rotten.”

Chapter 9

Winter, Kids and Cars

For kids, the arrival of snow is always cause for celebration but especially so at Christmas. This Christmas was no exception; it had been snowing all December. Up till now, when we played road hockey, we had to use a tennis ball. It is only a matter of time when we can retire the tennis ball for a puck. We were playing hockey with a puck on Front Street three weeks before Christmas. This is the era before salt trucks and perennially bare asphalt. Snowfalls bring out the horse drawn plows for sidewalks only. Mountains of snow line the sidewalk dividing it from the street. The snow on the street is never cleared; instead, it is packed smooth by car traffic. Plows don't bother with streets unless there is a record snowfall. Early December is also the time when my sleigh replaces the wagon that I pull to help Grandma do her Saturday shopping at the Farmer's Market. The shopping day I like best is when we buy the Christmas tree two weeks ahead of time. Everyone is in a festive mood and without exception they greet one another with the familiar "Merry Christmas." They wouldn't have known how to respond to "Season's Greetings" but then, those were the days before political correctness.

Christmas 1941 - Mom spoiled me with gifts.

The exhilaration I experience pulling that sleigh with the Christmas tree and the groceries are still a happy memory. I plead with Grandma to put the tree up immediately.

"No Brucie, the tree will keep nicely in the garage until a week before the 25th of December or it will dry out and the needles will fall off." Every day I check the garage and admire the tree. Meanwhile I help Grandma decorate the house with the now faded green and red paper spun rope we droop around the perimeter of the walls. Next we hang the tinfoil icicles on the rope. At last the great day comes when we can bring in the tree. By modern standards, that tree with its decorations would look pretty drab, but to this child's eyes, our tree was always the best.

The slippery surfaces of the snow-packed street slow traffic to a crawl, but the white asphalt is perfect for road hockey. Wartime traffic is so intermittent that we can play on the roads with very little interference from cars. Now we use a real puck, and not a tennis ball like in November. A little sand is spread by the city trucks at intersections for limited traction. This is the age before stop signs, so cars approach the corner with care. Cars need to have something abrasive (sand) to slow down and check for oncoming traffic. It is perfect for hitching a ride on the bumper. Motorists complain in vain. We hitch a ride for half a block, and then after receiving a good cussing from the driver, we relent and run away. One cold January evening after a night of road hockey, I hitch a ride on Front Street at Albert. When we get to Ontario Street, we let go, except when I release my grip, my gloves stick to the bumper. Terror strikes my heart.

"Mother paid good money for those gloves; what will she say if I return home, gloveless." I race after the car. "I'll never catch him." I despair. Mercifully the car stops two blocks up. Panting, I retrieve my gloves, grateful that I will not have to face Grandma's rebuke.

January is cold and the temperature plunges. Mother thinks it's too cold for me to play hockey after supper. The temperature is twenty below zero (-29 Celsius). I protest because the outdoor rink at Immaculate Conception School is in prime condition. We can play hockey with real skates, just like my hero Bill Mosienko of the Chicago Black Hawks. By nine o'clock the kids are thinning out because they're too cold to play hockey anymore. My feet were cold too but they have warmed up and I'm good till ten o'clock. When I finally get home I tell mother I could have played hockey till midnight. When I remove my skates, I find out why. My feet are frostbitten. I can feel nothing. I even try jabbing my big toe with a sharp pair of scissors. I feel nothing. Mother screams,

"Put those scissors down, you don't realize what you are doing." I put in a miserable night trying to sleep. My feet are still frostbitten the next morning. Later on in the afternoon, I can walk, but stiffly. At five o'clock, my big toe is throbbing with pain where I stuck in the point of the scissors. Four days later my feet finally feel normal. I have learned a hard lesson. When cold feet get warm on a frigid night, it's time to go home.

The creeping traffic over the snow pack not only provides entertainment to kids who can't resist a free ride, it also makes for high drama. One such incident occurs at Brunswick and Front. Our hockey game is interrupted as two cars collide. The collision makes such a bang, that three customers from Thistle's grocery store are instantly on the street. I watch in fascination, and marvel at the dust cloud that envelopes the two vehicles. Two very unhappy drivers figure out what to do. Do I ever have something to talk about as I relate to Grandma the very first car accident that I ever saw. Years later, I recall how few cars there were in Stratford in 1940. None of my friends that I played with had family cars. For kids, wartime was that idyllic period when the streets became our Domain. Road hockey in the winter, a game of catch in the summer! The streets were 'our' playgrounds. The roads belong to the kids. Those epochal days caused an unemployment problem for underworked overpaid guardian angels, who had to find other things to do to while away the time. They were in marked contrast to today's traffic situation, when one wonders if there are enough overworked guardian angels to go round. What a great time to be a thirteen-year old, and to boot, we had the Commons. When the Optimist Club put in a wading pool for tots, it never occurred to us that sinister plans were afoot. As young teens we thought we owned the Commons and made sure the little kids stuck to the sandbox, the swings, or the octagon wading pool, so we could play softball or a game of tin can cricket. Our eviction notice came subtly when I turned sixteen.
The Commons was to be made over for younger kids.

After the war was over the cars showed up en masse and pushed us off the streets. Billy Murphy's dad bought a brand new '47 Studebaker, which surprised all the neighbours because the Murphys were poor. The car disappeared as suddenly as it arrived, when Billy's dad had to go to jail for doing illegal abortions. We all feel badly for Billy, because our parents won't tell us what Mr. Murphy did wrong. The likeable Mr. Murphy would pack his car with kids and take us for a ride out to the picnic grounds at Embro.

We missed the jovial Mr. Murphy, and especially his car. When it comes to the good life, there's more to it than meets the eye. Years later those rides in Mr. Murphy's car, while they lasted, had something to it that I didn't know. In fact, as I was to learn much later, it was his daughter Audrey who was behind all this generosity. More of this in a later chapter. There is one thing I shall never forget that I learned from riding in Mr. Murphy's car.

"Close the door Bruce."

"Sure." say I, not noticing that my thumb is resting on the door jam. Slam–OUCH! Suddenly I am howling while I reopen the door to remove my flattened thumb. Grandma to the rescue.

"Hot salty water to remove the infection," she says. I now know that what I needed was icewater, but I acquiesce to Grandma's time honoured wisdom. That thumb hurt so much I can still feel the pain when I think of it. O the innocence of tender years. There seems to be no end of the things one needs to learn. No wonder it scares me to grow up.

Poor Billy Murphy. I liked him a lot, but Billy had to pay for his father's misdeeds. In 1948 when I had decided to quit my paper route, I gave the job to Billy without bothering to inform Miss Lougheed at the office. After Billy had learned the route, I figured my duty was done. I can still see Billy's tears that day when Mabel Lougheed self righteously said,

"The Murphys have a bad name. I have to protect the reputation of the Beacon-Herald, and remember Billy has to collect the paper money every week. Sorry, but Billy can't have the paper route."

It took me a few years to figure that one out. It is amazing how some people, who think they are helping society, can get it so wrong.

Chapter 10

Music Lessons 1942

Mother has decided that her son needs to develop his singing voice. We have heard some wonderful soloists at church who, I have to admit, even inspire me. I remember one visiting soloist from Buffalo who sings 'The Holy City.' Mother buys the music. I learn the song and sing it with enthusiasm. The decision is made; I will become a singer. Miss Hall, a music teacher who lives on West Gore, accepts me as her pupil. I remember thinking, "She would be a pretty woman if she didn't have buck teeth" She must have been a thumb sucker kid; too bad pacifiers weren't invented sooner. I practice a half an hour a day (for a while) and soon am entered into a singing festival held at St. John's United Church on Waterloo Street. I don't win any prizes, but I am challenged to do better. Winners get 10 cents; second prize is a nickel. That's enough to buy a chocolate milkshake. I am motivated. I am ready to do battle at the next music festival; meanwhile, Miss Hall arranges to enter me in a London competition. We get there in Miss Hall's car. Mother comes along. I give it my best but this dog meows like a cat.
The results are disappointing. I win no prizes.

Stratford City Hall is the location of the next music festival. I warily scan the competition. They do badly. I can taste the sweet smell of success. At last my name is called. Brimming with confidence, I take my place on the stage, and cup my hands just the way Miss Hall has instructed me. My masterpiece is a song entitled, 'Robin in the Rain.' Miss Hall plays the introduction on the piano and I sing.

"Robin in the rain, such a saucy fellow
Robin in the rain, mind your socks of yellow
Running in the garden on your nimble feet.
Digging for your dinner with your long strong beak.
Robin in the rain —

Suddenly, I forget the words. My lips are moving, but there is no sound. What is the second verse? Miss Hall sees my stage fright, and replays the introduction. Nothing happens. My mind is a total blank. The audience feels my utter humiliation and is stony silent.

"Would Bruce like to start over from the beginning?"

The adjudicator says. It is too late for recovery. Mortified, I burst into tears and run for cover beside my mom. I bury my head in her lap and sob,

"I want to go home."

Mother replies,

"After this session is over." I'm looking for a hole to climb into, but mother's arm is my only recourse. I don't want to look at anybody. After an eternity, the session ends. The adjudicator comes by and says,

"Better luck next time, don't give up."

For the benefit of my readers, the part I forgot is as follows.

"Robin in the rain, you don't mind the weather
Bet the worms are wishing you would stay at home
Robin on a rainy day, you don't get your feet wet.
Robin on a rainy day."

I'm quite sure the world was watching, and from now on, I cannot go outside. To confirm my worst fears, the next day on the way to school, a kid I barely know says,

"I hear you forgot your words at the music festival." My reputation has reached the street. I am ruined. I vow never take another music lesson, as long as I live, but mother persuades me to try. I have a future; I just have to get on with it.

That was when it happened. I call it my great temptation. Mother has given me the 75 cents for my lesson, but as things turn out, I forget to pay Miss Hall. She also neglects to ask. Just as I am passing Bert Comley's Downie Street Booth, I feel the money in my pocket. "I forgot to pay Miss Hall for my music lesson!" I know I have to walk back to Miss Hall, and give her the money. As I retrace my steps, I look at the confectionery booth and think, "Seventy-five cents would buy a lot of candy." Perhaps Miss Hall will forget that I have not paid. Who will know the difference? Needless to say right about now my guardian angel is very upset. Just at that point, the devil whispers in my ear,

"Buy yourself some candy; enjoy yourself, no one will ever know." If one is going to sin, it is convenient to blame the devil. This way it is not my fault. Now I know from Sunday school, never to listen to the devil, but with such an opportunity as this, maybe this devil guy has a point. I will spend five cents for a candy bar at the ‘music box’ as Comley’s was affectionately called. So named, because of the Jute Box that played 78 rpm records for a nickel. The Proverb says,

“Bread of deceit is sweet to the taste, but afterwards his mouth shall be filled with gravel.” With fear and trembling, I wonder how candy could ever taste like gravel, but I decide to take the chance. I finally return home with 38 cents, a stomach ache, and a guilty conscience. I hide the 38 cents in a jar. Two days later, Miss Hall phones to say that she has not been paid. The jig is up; my ill-gotten gains are exposed.

“Where is the money?” mother angrily asks. Quickly I empty the jar and surrender the 38 cents. I’m beginning to taste the gravel.

“Where is the rest of the money?” Grandma sternly demands. Ashen, I confess my crimes and vow never to do it again. I take a few more lessons from Miss Hall, but finally we agree, this fish don’t sing. My career as a singer and a thief is in shambles. The report to Gabriel that day by my guardian angel reads as follows:

“I have good news and bad news. The bad news is the little thief squandered thirty-seven cents that could have been given to the orphanage. The good news is this; he was caught and suitable restitution has been imposed. Furthermore, we don’t have to worry about that kid singing flat in the choir.”

Chapter 11

Old Tyme Religion

The early months of 1941 was full of bad news as far as the war was concerned. However not all the news was bad; Britain had not been invaded by Germany. Hitler had made the foolish mistake of making Russia his enemy by invading that unfortunate country, but the ultimate good news was that United States came in at last to join the Allies. December 8, one day after Pearl Harbour, there is a joke going around that I hear at school.

Yula Latter

Why is Uncle Sam's face red? Answer: 'because the Japs caught him with his pants down!' I fail to see the humour. At last what had been table conversation has come to pass. With the United States in the war, the Nazi peril is not so threatening. Closer to home, I guess the really bad news for us is that mother is depressed. Not that I really noticed at the time, but looking back I figure it out. Mother had already experienced too many sorrows. She was about to experience another. After eight years of loneliness, mother had met a kindred spirit, Yulanda Latter or Yula for short. They did things together. Here was a single woman with similar interests to share a friendship. At last mother had a life. Then, the unspeakable happens. Yula is diagnosed with an incurable disease; it is cancer. Mother wants to pay Yula a visit. She takes me along. First we drop in on the only Grandpa figure I can remember, George Wade. He apologizes for his garden, which we figure is still a masterpiece.

"It's not what it was before Frank went into the army." He sighs. After seeing the garden, we walk along the river to the Waterloo Bridge. Our destination is Yula's house. She greets us warmly, and her mother serves us a cup of tea. Yula looks pale and doesn't have the strength to rise from her couch. We talk awhile and leave; I am not really aware of mother's pain. She grieves alone and tells me nothing. She always keeps me well protected.

-oOo-

Keith Spackman works at Gregory's drug store as a pharmacist. This is an anomaly, because Keith is a tee-totalling Christian and Greg is a drinker. This is partnership glue that will not stick. Bacchus and Belial have an uneasy deal. Washed out of medical school for drinking too much, Greg became a pharmacist, no easy course to master. Greg's solution to stubborn ailments was, 'Mix it with whiskey.' Many a grateful patron was glad to be sick, just to get one of Greg's concoctions. The truth is, responsibility for running the store is falling on Keith more and more, until finally, Keith had had enough. Keith talks it over with his wife, Florence; they are together on this. Keith will start his own business. Bacchus never seems to know when to quit. The hapless Greg will have to fend for himself.

Keith Spackman now has a drug store that is called Spackman and Ross, located on Ontario Street. It is a partnership. Meantime mother's friend Yulanda has died. I have no recollection of the funeral. I only know that mother is sad and, sometimes, she cries. Florence Spackman is a customer of mother's beauty parlour. One day she talks to mom about her church, and invites mother to come to the Congregational Church located at Brunswick and Waterloo.

1941, Rev John McLeod (left) his wife Rita is on the right

The Congregational Church dwindled, today it has become the Church restaurant.

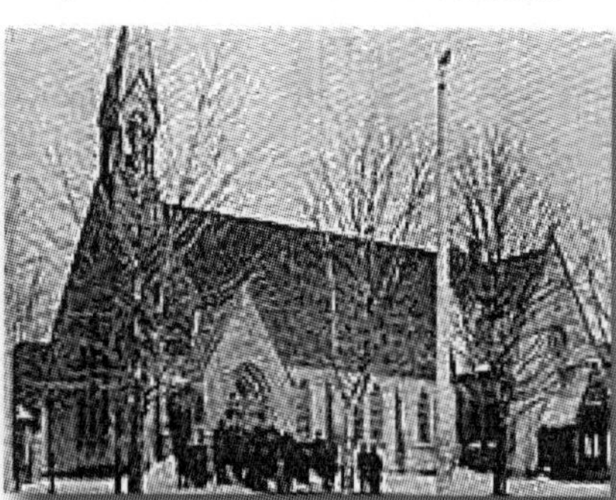

Times change, the once robust congregation dwindled, and the building was put up for sale. The building is still there, but today it is called the Church Restaurant. Keith Spackman would roll over in his grave.

Back in 1941, a commanding speaker by the name of Rev. John MacLeod preached to a packed house every Sunday at the Congregational Church. His smallness of stature belies his power in the pulpit. Mother is spellbound and returns the following Sunday.

The church has social functions, which provide sorely needed friends. Up till now, mother's only recreation is to go to a movie – alone. She draws great comfort from reading a new book she has purchased. It is called the Bible. Those were the days when faithful Christians went to two services to keep the soul in repair. Suddenly her life becomes the church. She hasn't gone to church since she paid off the loan to Rev. Reycroft and abruptly left the United Church. Now she attends church both Sunday morning and evening. She goes to every meeting the church announces and revels in her new Christian life. This has a profound affect on me. I now go to church with her every Sunday. On Sunday afternoon I go to Sunday school, which starts promptly at 3 P.M. The Spackmans take a special interest in mother. Looking back, I can now perceive their genuine compassion for an attractive, but lonely, divorcee. One day we are picked up by the Spackmans to attend the annual Sunday school picnic held at Matheson Park in Embro. I have an old picture of the congregation that was taken that day (with me sitting on the grass in the front row) by an unknown photographer. Where did 65 years go? It seems like it was just yesterday.

Memorial Baptist Church is a square three story red brick structure that was meant to be both a Church and a Sunday school mission started by the Ontario Street Baptist Church in 1916. All the Sunday school rooms on the main floor and the balcony opened up to the auditorium. Every chair in the auditorium was made of molded plywood with seats that would fold up and down. It was a wonderful invitation for children to bang their chairs just to make a disturbance. My memory of the place was 300 noisy kids on a Sunday afternoon creating a racket so loud that no demon in hell would dare come near the place. My mother's memory is how many silk stockings she lost on the ragged edges of the plywood chairs. Our reward for reaching 300 in Sunday School is a picnic at Embro, which we enthusiastically anticipate. Happy with the record attendance the new minister quips,

"Next year, make it 400 and we'll go to New York." Everybody laughs, but for me the idea sticks. In five years, I actually get to experience the Big Apple for myself.

Parsonage and Memorial Baptist Church, the church relocated on Bruce Street. The site is now a service station (photos courtesy of Memorial Baptist Church)

Rev. Howard Chipchase is the new minister at Memorial Baptist Church at 555 Downie Street (now torn down and replaced by a gas station). He is a firey preacher! He has red hair to match his Irish temperment. Word spreads around church people quickly. Abruptly, we transfer from the Congregational church to Memorial Baptist. This works an extra hardship on me, because now I have to trudge a full mile to go to Sunday school, instead of just the one block, that separates our house from the Congregational church. Mother says when I ask why,

"Because Memorial Baptist is better." I accept her wisdom without question.

It is now January 1941 and I am in grade four. Old enough to make mature decisions, at least, I thought so at the time. After the evening sermon, the preacher invites people to the altar to be saved. I decide I ought to go. With mother's permission, I walk down the balcony stairs to the lower floor, and stand beside several others while the congregation sings,

"Just as I am without one plea, but that Thy blood was shed for me." I go to a room where a kindly man explains to me the way of salvation. Since I have now made my decision, I am scheduled for baptism. A few weeks later on a Sunday evening after the service, I am baptized in warm water by total immersion, wearing a black baptismal gown. I remember thinking, "This water feels so nice and warm, I'd like to — just stay here for a while, and enjoy." However, I am ushered up to a room to dry off, and put my clothes back on. As I rejoin mother, who had proudly watched her son, I hear the water draining from the baptismal tank. I think, "The least they could do, is keep the water in for a while, for children, who would like to swim around in that wonderfully warm water on a cold February night." It was a hot tub before hot tubs were invented. I tell this to mother afterwards, and am surprised that she doesn't agree with me. Meanwhile my inexperienced guardian angel excitedly reports the good news to Gabriel who seems unimpressed. Deflated, my angel, feeling the need for a lift, heads off to choir practice and decides to drown his disappointment in the singing of hymns.

Mother meets Mrs. Campbell. She is her newest customer. Next thing I know, we are going to the Ontario Street Pentecostal Church. Mrs. Campbell invites us to a Sunday dinner. I meet her daughter, Gayla. She is the first person I have ever met who has more toys than I do. Naturally I like to play with Gayla. She is rich. She has her own playhouse complete with front door, lock, and key. Her father built it just for her. Mr. Campbell doesn't go to church, but I forgive him because he can do magic. He pulls a dime out of my ear, but doesn't give it to me. Now I know he's not a Christian, but I think, "If the dime was in my ear, it really should be mine." Even though he didn't give me the dime, I like him a lot.

Mr. Campbell is an insurance salesman and drives a shiny new Hudson coupe. He stays home while the rest of us go to hear an evangelist at the Pentecostal church. It is located in a basement on Ontario Street. They will build the rest of the church, when they get the money. The service is lively, and the preacher goes on far too long. I fidget. Suddenly, several people go forward to the altar. The evangelist prays for them and they fall over. They call it being 'slain in the spirit'. One of the deacons has a blanket to cover the ladies, so that no one will look at their legs. Years later when passing the church with friends, Vincent falls to the ground and does a mock holy roller, to the amusement of us all. Such is the reputation of the Pentecostal church. I think to myself, "I was there a few times, that's not quite the way it happens." While I am aware of the facts, I make no defense for Pentecostals; I just laugh with the others while my conscience bothers me.

One day, mother announces to me, that she is not going to church today. I decide, "If mother is not going to church anymore, I'm not going either." From that time on we become Presbyterians. They don't have to go to church if they don't want to. However, Grandma is different; she goes to church every Sunday at St. Andrew's. I go with her, but only on Easter and Christmas Sunday. Rev. B.L. Waldon is the minister. He has a sing-song voice and I daydream through the sermon. Grandma tells Rev. Waldon that she enjoyed the sermon. It's a good thing nobody asked me what I thought, but then who is interested in an eleven-year-old opinion. For the present, my Church-going days have gone into hibernation.

We still see Mrs. Campbell occasionally. I remember Christmas 1942. It is Sunday, December 20. Mother and Mrs. Campbell have decided to take in as many Christmas Sunday evening concerts as they can in two hours flat. Gayla and I go along. We go to Knox Presbyterian for a while, and then skip out to St. John's United. After a fifteen minute sampling, we slip out and join St. Paul's across the street. We finish our evening at Zion Lutheran. I guess as much as anything, the object was to see how nicely the churches were decorated for Christmas. All the churches were packed with people. To the ushers, we must have seemed like a nuisance. I conclude there are a lot of people who like to go to church at Christmas time. Stratford has a lot of beautiful churches.

Chapter 12

The Great Snowstorm of 1942

The year 1942 closes out with a snowstorm to remember. It is Saturday, December 27 and mother puts me on the bus heading for Goderich. I will spend the Christmas holidays with Graham Bogie. The bus is a prewar design. It is drafty and rattles every time we hit rough pavement. It was snowing so hard we were lucky to get to Goderich. I am looking forward to seeing Mr. Bogie, but instead, I am met by a total stranger, Mrs. Gorrie, whom I have never seen before.

"Is your name Bruce Woods?" she asks.

"Yes, that's my name," I sniffed.

"My friend, Ethel Bogie called me twenty minutes ago; Mr. Bogie can't make it to Goderich for the snow. He tried but couldn't get out of his own driveway, let alone the sideroad. The drifts are six feet high and climbing by the minute. Naturally, she was concerned about you so she called me and asked me to take you home with me until they can come out to pick you up."

"How soon will that be?" I nervously enquire.

"Probably not until tomorrow; the plow cannot go out until the wind dies down."

"Where will I sleep tonight?" I ask.

"I'm afraid you will have to stay with me, but don't worry I have a nice hot supper waiting for you and tomorrow Mr. Bogie will pick you up as soon as the roads are ploughed." I am clearly disappointed. This eleven-year old kid fights to hold back the tears but has no choice, so I pick up my suitcase and put it on Mrs. Gorrie's sleigh. She is a widow and doesn't own a car. She makes a noble effort to comfort me as I trudge along pulling the sleigh while I talk with this total stranger.

"Does my mother know where I am?" I ask

"Ethel Bogie has already phoned her; she knows all about it."

"Okay." I meekly submit.

We are at Mrs. Gorrie's house and I eat my supper with a lump in my throat. The table talk is definitely one sided with Mrs. Gorrie trying to make conversation by asking me questions. She is trying hard to make me feel at home, but I feel very much alone and isolated. Shortly after supper the phone rings and Mrs. Gorrie calls me,

"Your mother is on the phone and wants to talk to you."
Just knowing that mother is on that phone helps. We haven't even spoken a word but already I'm feeling better.

"Hello Brucie, I've talked with Ethel Bogie and she has explained everything, you don't have a thing to worry about. Mrs. Gorrie is Ethel Bogie's friend and she will take good care of you. Tomorrow Mr. Bogie will come by and pick you up and then you and Graham will have lots of fun. So be a good boy and don't get upset, because everything will turn out just fine."

The phone call helps to calm my fears and I go to sleep that night looking forward to Sunday. I am not to be relieved of my apprehension so easily. The following morning, Mrs. Gorrie awakes me trying to be cheerful,

"Time to get up, Bruce, I have a hot breakfast for you."

"Will Mr. Bogie be coming for me today?" I ask.

"Well Bruce, I'm afraid I have some news that you may not like. It snowed all night and the snowdrifts are ten feet high in some places, so you will have to stay here till Monday before Mr. Bogie can come and get you." Deflated and disappointed, I eat my breakfast slowly and once again, I am fighting back the tears.

Sunday is the longest day I have ever put in. Mrs. Gorrie, as a widow, has no toys and lives in a neighbourhood where there are no children. I am bored and homesick and can do nothing about it. I wish I had never come, but I know I am stuck, so I have to make the best of it. Monday brings no relief. It has stopped snowing, but the wind just keeps piling up the drifts. Goderich has come to a standstill. Tuesday morning is not much better, but Ethel Bogie has come to the rescue. She calls with a plan.

"The snowplow is going to come up the Highway followed by the mail truck. It doesn't help the motorist, but it will get the mail delivered. The winds will make it impossible for Andrew to come with the car because the snowdrifts will fill in the highway as soon as the plow goes through. John Steward, who runs the plow, is a friend of ours and he has agreed to take Bruce with him and drop him off at our sideroad. Andrew will be there to meet him and they can walk to the farmhouse together."

Saved by the mailman! Now I am getting excited. Even if cars can't use the highway the mail must get through. I await the adventure of riding with John Steward. At last I am released from my hospitable prison. Mrs. Gorrie bundles me up and walks me to the municipal office. The happy John Steward welcomes me aboard,

"So this is my passenger to keep me company on the plow." I give a timid smile and Mrs. Gorrie thanks the man for taking me off her hands. I am oblivious to her undisguised relief. There is more than one person who is pleased that I am finally on my way. The snowplow turns out to be a grader used for road building. I ride in the cab with Mr. Steward who tells me this is the worst snowstorm he has ever seen. Meantime the six-mile run stops at every mailbox. Following close behind us is the mailman in his car. He hugs the plow; if he lags too far behind, the drifting snow might trap him on the spot. The usual fifteen-minute trip takes an hour and a half. Finally when we get to the Hunter farm mailbox, Mr. Bogie, who has been waiting in the Hunter farmhouse, has been watching through their front window. He emerges grinning with a cheerful hello, and has a toboggan for my luggage. Excited, I am happy to see him; my joy is shortlived. Mrs. Gorrie who had long forgotten how to dress kids had loaned me her rubber boots instead of the snow boots mother included in my luggage. She will retrieve her rubber boots the next time the Bogies come to town. She meant well, but the decision was a bad one for me.

I am grateful to see Mr. Bogie and after a brief interchange between Andrew Bogie and John Steward, we begin the walk to the farmhouse, three quarters of a mile away (one and a quarter kilometers). We are akin to good King Wenceslas and his faithful page heading out into the 'bitter weather'. The deep snow is falling into the rubber boots and we are stopping every few minutes to clear out the snow. I have one pair of socks on. My feet are getting colder by the minute and soon I am crying for the cold,

"Oh Mr. Bogie, my feet are so cold."

"Is it time to empty your boots again?" he replies.

"It's no use," I complain, "they fill up as soon as they are empty."

"Well, all we can do is keep walking." Mr. Bogie tries to comfort me but unlike Wenceslas, there is no heat in his footprints. To ride on the toboggan would only slow us down and is no help to me. I have to keep walking to stay as warm as possible.

"Think of how good, you'll feel when we get there," says Andrew

Bogie.

"I'll try," I weep, "but Oh Mr. Bogie my feet are so cold."

For the next twenty minutes, we slog our way through swirling snowdrifts, while I moan and complain about my cold feet. Falling snow and wind adds to my misery until we arrive at the farmhouse where a wonderful reception is waiting for me.

"Welcome, child," says Mrs. Bogie who hugs me, "but what on earth are you wearing on your feet."

"Mrs. Gorrie gave me her rubber boots to wear." I wail.

"For goodness sake," exclaims Mrs. Bogie, "doesn't that woman have enough sense to dress a child in proper winter boots?" She is plainly disgusted about the rubber boots. She takes off my coat and plops me in front of the stove. Soon the oven door is open and my feet are propped up in the oven while I slowly thaw out. Relief finally comes as my feet return to normal. It is time for lunch and a hot bowl of soup. I have successfully overcome the first hurdle of my arrival. I now must overcome the second.

"What kind of soup are we having?" I ask.

"Why do you ask?" says Evelyn, Graham's older sister.

"Because, I don't like soup very much," I complain.

"Especially mushroom soup, so I need to know what kind of soup it is before I have any."

"Well, I'll bet you will like our soup!" says Evelyn.

"Perhaps I will, what kind of soup is it?" I ask again.

"It's just soup;" says Evelyn, "When you taste it you will like it."

"But what kind of soup is it?" I ask for the third time

"It's just soup; I can't tell you anything more than that."

After my frigid walk the hot soup feels good to the touch, but I am suspicious about what I'm about to eat. I gingerly take a very small sip.

"How does it taste?" says Evelyn. I completely miss Andrew Bogie's wink to his wife. Hungry and still feeling cold I eventually confess.

"I guess it tastes alright." After I finish a bowl of the mystery soup, Evelyn offers me seconds. I accept and finish the second bowl of soup. Then Evelyn leans forward on her hands and says,

"Now would you like to know what you just ate?"

"I guess so." I cautiously reply.

"You just finished two bowls of mushroom soup, and

furthermore you told us that you liked it."

"I only liked it a little bit," I protest. Suddenly the whole family, who was in on the secret from the beginning, breaks out in laughter. Sheepishly I grin,

"I guess I like mushroom soup better than I thought, but I don't think I want any more for a long time." I don't remember any more mealtime stories, so I guess things went fine and Mrs. Bogie didn't try to make me eat any boiled carrots. My holiday adventure with Graham was a great success. I have a picture of Graham and me dressed in our snowsuits and tobogganing down the hill behind the farmhouse. When it came time for me to return to Stratford, the roads were plowed with drifts so high it seemed like we were driving between two mountain ranges; nonetheless, getting home went smoothly.

1942, Evelyn, Graham and me, snow sledding behind the barn

That winter mother bought me a comic book. It was a history of Adoph Hitler made into comics for children. A serious treatment of the man, it outlined his rise to power up to the present war being fought in Russia. I shall never forget the last double frame. It was a face-off between Hitler and Napoleon Bonaparte. Hitler looks shocked and perplexed. The ghostly figure of Napoleon is unmistakable. He is standing in swirling snow with his arm outstretched and pointing at Hitler, he says, "Beware Adolph, I too attempted to invade Russia and failed." That comic book, which was undoubtedly intended as propaganda to patronize kids like me, found its mark. I am encouraged to hope that despite the string of war disasters that seemed to come along unabated, ultimately, all would be well.

Chapter 13

Father 1942

Robert Woods was a foot soldier in the British Dragoons stationed in Belfast, Ireland.

He and his fellow comrades shipped out to Canada in 1814 to teach the Americans a lesson. There were 20,000 British soldiers ordered to the new world that year. Sensing that it was time to settle matters quickly, the Americans sued for peace and by the time Robert Woods got to Lake Champlain, there was no battle to fight. Given the opportunity to return to Ireland or settle in Ontario for free land, Robert became a farmer near Lindsay. In 1820, he became a father when Thomas Woods came into the world. Thomas married pretty Eliza Shaw and she gave birth to Bertram Arthur Woods who definitely did not want to be a farmer. Bertram was my paternal grandfather and settled for the big city of St. Thomas. He became a failed city slicker running a corner store and hatching developement plans that never materialized. So that's where I pick up the story to bring fame and fortune to the family name.

When a mother and father split up, somebody is bound to get hurt. I am better off, because I grow up in a household that was relatively normal. I get the advantage of the family village, where aunts and uncles get a crack at raising the kid. In this case, I suppose father is better off, because he hitches his wagon to a comet that makes him toe the line. (Years later reading the signals, I have a feeling that he was not without his regrets.) Mother was too kind hearted to get tough with Bruce Sr. 'Spoiled him rotten!' applies to both father and son. With Phyllis Christian, Bruce Sr. had better get up and go to work or, he faces the wrath of a newspaperwoman, who can fire off a volley of words that would melt a mountain. It is Ethel who gets the short end of the stick. It is a soul-destroying thing to know that one is talented, hardworking, caring, and beautiful, yet be rejected and very much alone.

My 'other' grandma Clarissa Woods - in her wedding dress
Died giving birth to her 7th child at age 34

My other grandpa - Bertram Arthur Woods from St Thomas

Getting back to father, when Bruce Sr. was born, he led the way for five more in rapid succession, because Bertram was as vigorous at procreataion as he was at bootlegging. Clarisa produced six babies in 14 years, not counting the ones Arthur took away; and finally died in childbirth in 1920. Bertram Arthur's grief is short lived. He is now a widower on the prowl to find a replacement. The eligible ladies of St. Thomas pass around a joke, "Down Arthur, down." As luck would have it, he meets Mary Martin on the train. After a whirlwind three days' romance, he marries her without benefit of the information that there are six kids waiting for her in St.Thomas. Those are the days; when as the saying goes, 'Marriage is a knot that you tie with your tongue that you cannot undo with your teeth.'

The kids have a surprise waiting for them, when Daddy comes home; so does Mary. After she recovers from the shock, Mary's preoccupation becomes, "How do I get rid of my surprise responsibilities." Solution! Children are out of the house as soon as they turn sixteen. Bruce is the first to discover she means business, so, for employment, he lies about his age and joins the army. After 3 months, he falls off a horse and breaks his arm. He has had enough, so Bertram Arthur Woods buys him his freedom, but he can't come home. In 1922 what does a 16-year old do to stay alive? Answer! Sell magazines. Bruce makes a discovery. A smooth talker can make real money selling magazines. Bruce is a born salesman. His handsome brother Jim, who is one year younger, soon joins him. Together they quickly become a Casanova pair of city slickers with an eye for the ladies. Once Bruce Sr. discovers his true talent, he never lacks for cash in his pocket, especially when he has sufficient motivation. Phyllis Christian has plenty of that. Unlike Ethel, who would plead for Bruce Sr. to get up and go to work, Phyllis brooks no nonsense. From now on Bruce Sr. will do very well in the world of sales even though this is the hungry thirties.

Anna took this picture of mom.

Anna Woods is Bruce's sister, a worldly-wise woman who, unlike Ethel, knows her way around. Ethel and Anna are friends. The marriage break-up alters some things for Ethel, but not Anna's friendship. When mother lived in Toronto, these two women did things together. They have a lot in common. They have both loved a man with their souls and their bodies. They have both suffered the pain of betrayal. In Anna's case, it was a fiancé who kept on delaying the wedding date. After seven years of postponements, Anna agonizes a heart-wrenching verdict. She gives

Mom at the rail. Anna is seated.

an ultimatum, and finds herself alone and abandoned. These two beautiful women are intelligent, artistic, and persons of character. They both have taken up the painting of pictures with oils. Mother's paintings are revealing. They are either landscapes or seascapes, without benefit of people. In Anna's case, her paintings have people, including some significant portraits. I think the contrast illustrates mother's sense of aloneness. There is one exception. I remember the faceless girl looking out to sea. Now that I am an old man and wiser, does the girl in the painting, with her wide brimmed hat and flowing dress, depict mother's nostalgia, for a life she was denied? The questions that a wiser son would now love to ask go unanswered. Silent graves do not talk. How I wish Anna and Ethel could have enjoyed the friendship that could have been, if they had not been separated by distance. It might have averted the storm to come.

Anna has planned a shopping spree in Montreal, with an excursion through the Thousand Islands. She invites Ethel to join her and in the offer makes a suggestion. Bruce Jr. is eleven and Anna thinks he ought to meet his father. Anna and mother could take a vacation together, while Bruce and his father get to know each other. Ethel is hesitant, but in the end, acquiesces. In contrast to Ethel, the proposed meeting is warmly received by Bruce Sr., who has often wondered what his son is like. The occasion is late August. It coincides with the Canadian National Exhibition, a spectacle Bruce Jr. has never experienced. Anna has figured out everything. Ethel will come with Bruce Jr. and stay overnight. The two Bruces will meet one another at last. The meeting will take place at Anna's. I am to sit outside on the front porch at the appointed time, under the watchful eye of mother. There is no meeting between Ethel and Bruce. The time is 11 A.M. I wait for a dark blue Cadillac, whatever that looks like. The car pulls up, and a strange man opens the door.

"Are you Bruce?" I ask.

"Are you Bruce?" the stranger replies. Anna comes out of the house, and assures me that this man is indeed my father. After pleasantries are exchanged, I climb into the car and we drive away. Later that day, Anna and Ethel board the train for Kingston.

I sit in the front seat, and we drive off. I have the strangest feeling that leaves me uncertain and afraid. Bruce Sr. senses my unease and talks nicely to me. After a while I decide that the adventure will be okay. I just have to get used to it. Our destination is 15 Bedford Park Avenue, just west of Yonge Street. The house looks like the kind mother and I walk by on William Street, when we want to see Stratford elegance. I meet the notorious Phyllis. She greets me warmly, and introduces me to her daughter Pat who is one year older than I, and excited to meet her very own brother (Of course, we are not related at all, but Pat introduces me to all her friends as 'brother.') Phyllis tells me she is knitting a sweater that will keep me warm at the Ex, because it is often cold by the lake. We have lunch, and there is no food served that I don't like. She tells me, I will be sleeping with Pat, and hopes that I don't mind. I'm too innocent to figure out that this is unusual. We unpack my suitcase. Pat and I go outside to play in her sandbox. Whenever I address my father, I call him Bruce. I am confronted with my first lesson, in having a father.

"From now on, I don't want you to call me Bruce; I want you to call me DAD." I've never called anyone Dad in my entire life. The adjustment comes hard, and I frequently slip up, and call him Bruce. I am always corrected.

Dad owns a lot of things I have never seen before. I admire his array of tools. The furniture seems posh compared to what I am used to. I am taken with his electric record player. He shows me how to use it, and stacks the records, so I can play six records in a row without touching it. I discover classical music and play Grieg's piano Concerto in A minor as often as I wish. The first contribution of my father to his son is a love of classical music. The concerto is recorded on six 78-rpm records. I watch in fascination, as one record after another falls into place, played with a stylus that contains a diamond needle. The playing arm swings back and forth. The records drop on the turntable without the aid of a human hand. I marvel at modern technology.

Bedtime is for talking. Phyllis reprimands Pat, but by implication, I figure I'm included. We whisper, but soon the laughing gives us away. Phyllis gets stern. We comply and go to sleep. There are no problems until the third night when Pat pinches me on my bottom. I sternly protest.

"I didn't do it." Pat denies.

"Then who did?" I demand.

"The ghost did it," she pretends. "It's the pinching ghost; you never know when she comes around." I am naïve, and my confidence waivers, but I challenge my tormentor.

"There's no such thing as a pinching ghost, you did it." Pat denies the whole thing, but the next thing I know, I get pinched again.

"Stop it or I'll tell your mother." Pat denies it again with the same lie.

Frustration gives way to relief, when Phyllis appears to reprimand our talking. I take my case to the highest authority in the household.

"All I can say," says Phyllis, "is that this pinching ghost had better go away, or she's in big trouble." Magically, the ghost goes away never to return.

"It was you!" I accusingly declare, but Pat denies it. No matter, I have no more trouble with the pinching ghost.

The week goes by quickly, and I am starting to warm up to Phyllis, who makes no special demands. She teaches me a game. All four of us play. She starts a story that she makes up out of her head, then, abruptly stops. Pat who has played the game before knows what to do, and continues the story, taking it wherever her imagination desires. Dad takes his turn and then it's mine. It becomes a Who-done-it mystery, and carries on for two days until Phyllis winds it up. I like the game. We do three of them in the week. Phyllis is also a mine of information on things I'd never heard of before like the venomous Hoop snake. For the uninformed, there is no escape from the Hoop snake. He just takes his tail in his mouth and projects himself forward faster and faster until he can outrun a horse and bite his victim dead. After scaring me half to death with the Hoop snake story, Phyllis comforted me with the knowledge that this only happens in the desert. Since I had no plans to visit deserts, I am safe for the moment. How I relished scaring as many as would hear of the dangers of the Hoop snake. Years later I discovered that the fable of the Hoop snake was urban myth, just like a lot of nonsense that passes for truth when we hear it from the lips of an authority figure.

We go to the Canadian National Exhibition on Saturday, which turns out to be a hot day. Again, while the exhibits are wonderful,

I'm only interested in the midway. I don't wear the green sweater that Phyllis knit, but carry it around my waist by tying the arms in a knot. The exciting sounds of the Merry-Go-Round is now the focus of my attention. Pat and I ride the plastic horses that go up and down. Dad buys me anything I want like candy floss and hotdogs. The next day, I return to Aunt Anna's and say goodbye to my father. My green sweater unused is in my suitcase. Mother and I take the Stratford train home. She asks me how it went. I freely tell her it was okay, but I firmly declare, I sure wouldn't want to live in Toronto.

"He made me call him Dad," I complain. "It wasn't easy; I felt he was more like an uncle." I am oblivious of her response. I have no recollection of how she felt, entrusting her only son to the man who deserted her, and to the woman who took him from her. From time to time, Aunt Elsie would remind me that Ethel never stopped loving Bruce Sr. At the time these thoughts are beyond me. I have had plenty of time to think about it since. I have become a father and a grandfather. I have known and experienced the splendor of love and feel compassion for those who have loved, only to have that special delight stolen away. Write a book. I recommend it. It restores things forgotten which in the light of experience yield information that never occurred to you when you were young. One such memory for me was my mother's jewellery box. In that box was two locks of baby hair. One was mine; the other was my father's. Somehow, mother had come into possession of my father's baby hair which was cut and preserved by Clarissa, Bertram's first wife. Mary must have overlooked it. These two locks of hair tell their own story. The fact that they were preserved speaks of love. Mother could not have had mine without Dad's. They both symbolize a love story. The first, a love lost, the second, well — if you meet my mother in heaven someday, you can ask her about mine.

How did mother enjoy her holiday, knowing that for the first time, her personal treasure was, for a week, out of her hands? As I tell her about father's possessions, what did she think? She is a divorcee at a time when divorce was rare. None of my friends had a single parent. I never thought of Royce Clark as a kid from a broken family. His grandparents were his father and mother. He always called them that. I have now lived long enough, to see one of my grandchildren divorced in an age when it is common. I think of the personal turmoil it caused for me. How did mother feel, living in a time when divorce was a disgrace! A subject of whispered conversations! Her sensitive nature was already badly damaged by the death of her two dearest friends, one in childhood, the other, after losing a husband when she was still young. Without a kindred spirit, how do you cope? Mother is struggling, and I am too immature to understand why she is always hugging me. I vigorously wipe her kisses from my face, and wish she wouldn't treat me like her little boy.

Something strange happened shortly after I returned from Toronto. One of the travelling beauty supply salesmen who provided mother's permanent wave solution (I've long forgotten his name) asked mother if she would go to the movies with him. They went out for dinner somewhere and then took in a movie at the Avon theatre. Grandma and I ate supper by ourselves.

When mother came home later that night, I am curious and with a naïve question I ask her,

"Mother, would you ever consider marrying that man?"

"No Brucie, he is just a friend, so don't worry about that."

"Are you sure?" I query.

"Yes!" That was the end of the conversation and although I worried about it at the time, relieved, I put the whole thing out of my mind.

School starts on Tuesday, September 2nd. Mother has a surprise for me. I return home from Romeo Public School. There is a shiny red bicycle parked by the kitchen door that I've never seen before, and wonder why it is there. It is my best surprise to date. None of my friends have a bicycle. Mother proudly tells me,

"This is for the best boy ever." Aunt Margaret complains,

"She'll spoil that kid rotten." I don't mind. I like the way mother spoils me. After a few spills, I learn to ride the bike. The thrill of freedom is intoxicating. I explore the streets I know, and learn of more. I conquer Nile Street, and all the streets south, right to the CNR station. My only boundary is Ontario Street. As Stratford's main street, it is busy with traffic, and mother doesn't want me to take any chances.

Chapter 14

The Crisis Breaks

I never saw the kid before. He says to me, "Dja want to know how babies are made?" Up until now, I never thought about that, so I figure it wouldn't hurt to know. Wide eyed in disbelief, I make a life altering decision.

"If that's how babies are made, I shall never marry." I am embarrassed every time I look at Barbara Schooley, Vince's younger sister. I have no doubts about my future. I shall be a bachelor as long as I live. Anyway, who needs girls when comic books like Superman, Captain Marvel and Flash Gordon are available.

Life magazine arrives and I eagerly follow the war. Things in Russia are going badly. The African war is also bad. The British are defeated by a guy named Rommel. I worry that Russia may collapse before American help arrives. In Egypt, the German army is only 52 miles from Alexandria. The plight of European Jewry is table conversation. On the other hand, I rejoice at the news that the British are bombing German cities. What a difference time makes. Fourteen years later, I was living in Dallas, Texas. At that time I met Georgi. He was a Ukrainian and was the object of perverted Nazi medical research during the war. Transferred from hot water tubs to cold water tubs and back again, his vital organs were tested. Supposedly the object was to see how much the human body could stand. It's been eleven years since the war is over, long enough to learn that the Germans suffered too. I cannot shake my prejudice; I think, "Just like the Germans."

One year later while still in Dallas I meet Seline, who married an American GI Originally from Cairo, Egypt, she tells me how, in 1942, when it looked like Rommel's army was about to capture Egypt, out of sheer terror, everybody intended to desert the British and acclaim the Germans. I relive the anxiety of those days all over again. It is a reminder to me, how shaped I was by that war. The things that I feared in my childhood never happened. A British general by the name of Montgomery changed the course of the war, with his victory over the German army at El Alamein. By now my Christianity has informed me, we must forgive our enemies. Yet I am amazed at how easy it is to revive my prejudice against Germans. Years later, I am a tourist visiting countries in Europe. In 1995, I am in Germany with my wife and friends. We are staying at a Bavarian Inn, just outside of Munich, the birthplace of Hitler's Nazi party. Our host is Basi Erhardt. After a wonderful dinner of spatzel, sauerkraut, and schnitzel, Basi invites his guests to a concert that he personally will provide. I think, "We are where the Nazi party was born, but music has replaced the guns." I am about to be wonderfully moved by this talented musician.

Basi tells us it is a Friday tradition to entertain guests with song. Basi takes out his Zither, and thrills us with his incredible voice and his ability to yodel. My mind goes back 53 years, to those war pictures in Life magazine. I am in the heart of what I once despised. Travel broadens. I have walked the streets of Jerusalem, and hiked in the Bolivian Andes. I always knew that people are the same the world over, it's just that my heart has to catch up with my head. My world of 1941 was very small, but it was the only world I knew. My prejudices of yesteryears are shattered, but it takes a lifetime to see the light.

1941, my eleventh birthday, I'm the one with the big grin. Within 25 years, two of these kids will have committed suicide. There are other kinds of wars to be fought. In the battle of life, two out of eleven is a high casualty rate.

Halloween 1941, my mother gives me a birthday party for my 11th year. The kids I play with are invited. I have a picture of that party. There are eleven of us. We have noisemakers, party hats, and I am wearing a clown suit. I am grinning from ear to ear. It is my record of the joyful innocence that makes children who they are. Looking back, I am struck by the inequities of life. In Europe, a war, in Canada, a party, but why should childhood be spoiled by such conflicting knowledge? Someday, I will find these things out. What a blessing that it comes in bits and parts so that I can accommodate the trials slowly as I am able to cope. Life affords this luxury to some and denies it to others. I only knew the war from pictures in magazines and newspapers. However with first hand experience, I am to learn very soon that there are other kinds of wars. Invisible wars that defy photographers and historians. I am about to enter a war zone that will shake me to the core. My place in this mortal conflict is the no man's land between the two most important people in my life. There is no preparation adequate for this kind of war. This is an unwanted lesson in warfare I have never experienced before. The theatre of operations will be within my own house. This war will touch me personally, and dramatically alter my life.

School is out and I run home with the picture I drew. As I approach the kitchen door, I hear mother scolding Grandma. She is sobbing, and crying, and shouting all at once. Alarmed, I run into the kitchen.

"You never taught me anything," mother cries. "How was I to know what the world is like? You could have warned me. You could have told me what men are like. You threw me to the winds —." Just at that moment, mother sees that she has a startled audience of one. I have arrived and witnessed a bewildering volley of anger directed at Grandma that baffles my understanding. Shock at the sight of me has silenced mother. Grandma is ashen and shaking. Mother runs upstairs and throws herself on the bed weeping. Grandma says,

"This has been coming for some time. Your mother blames me for everything that has gone wrong in her life. Now you know what I have endured. I'm sorry you have to know all this; I've tried to keep it a secret, because I didn't want you to worry. But now you know." I hear her words but I cannot process the meaning. I imagine this to be some kind of quarrel that mother will forget. Like some kind of disease one catches and then after ten days in bed, you recover. I shrug my shoulders and wait for mother to get over it. Meanwhile Mars rubs his hands with glee and can hardly wait to tell the good news to Apollyon. Pan and Puck feel awkward and don't know what to think. Mischief is one thing but this sort of behaviour is over the top.

We eat our supper in silence. Mother seems to have recovered, and asks me what I did at school. The conversation is awkward. My eyes dart back and forth between Grandma and mother. They avoid eye contact. The evening goes as usual. The experience is surreal. Relieved, I go to bed and assume, "it will never happen again". It does happen again, with long intervals in between. In time, the intervals are shorter. I'm in a battle zone between the two women I love. I try to protect both as best I can. Children explain nothing; they accept what is, and make the best of it. I have no understanding of why mother blames Grandma for things that were completely beyond her control. Baffled, I find myself taking Grandma's side, yet trying to accept the mother who continues to shower me with love and affection.

Royce is now a sixer in Cub Scouts, note the body language

In 1941 the Boy Scout movement was 34 years old and in its prime. Founded by an Englishman, Sir Robert Baden-Powell; this organization had spread all over the world and in Stratford was a power to be reckoned with. Clarkie goes to Wolf Cubs, the division for boys under twelve. In 1941 over a thousand boys belonged to the junior division, not counting the Boy Scouts who number over 400. Royce tells me all about it. He has become a Sixer. That means Royce is the leader of his own Cub pack of six boys. He recruits me, and mother buys the uniform. Clarkie has two yellow stripes on his sleeve and eight badges. He displays them with pride. If I hurry up and join the Cubs, I can be in the Scout parade for November 11th, and march to the cenotaph. I plead with mother who always gives me what I want. I get my sweater and cap just in time. We assemble at the armouries building, where two wonderful World War I artillery guns used to mark the entrance. In a flurry of patriotism, they disappeared for scrap metal a year before. I am excited to march down Ontario Street, just like the soldiers do, with people lining the streets to cheer.

Remembrance Day is cold and raw. I have to wear my coat and gloves. Like some snapping turtle, the only thing to declare that I am a bona fide Wolf Cub, is the little green cap on my head. I am disappointed at the non-existent crowd that I imagined would be watching. A few bundled up stragglers are making their way to the cenotaph, but some of them look and wave at us. A surge of pride warms my heart, but it soon passes as my feet get colder by the minute. It is worse at the cenotaph, where we stand, while sleet and wind make us shiver. Important people make speeches, and somebody plays taps on a bugle. I am so miserable, I am glad when it's over and we can go home. I vow, if ever I go on parade again, it will have to be in the summer, but I am still keen on Cubs.

I have a long way to go to catch up to Clarkie, and I am a year older. Twelve-year olds are automatically promoted to Boy Scouts which means in the badge department, I have to start all over again. If I am to catch Royce, I've got to earn two badges and a stripe, to even start on my quest to become a Sixer. In no time I make the first level and gain a yellow stripe. Gaining that two-stripe status is however another matter. The zeal of the newly converted motivates me. I am a Seconder; I have 10 months to catch Clarkie. I give it everything I have. I never make it.

Church parade is my second opportunity to march. It is springtime and the weather is warm. We assemble at the cenotaph and parade to St. James Anglican Church, where the weekly Wolf Cubs meet. I decide that Pentecostal services are more interesting. However, since mother has decided that I don't have to go to church, I opt for the life of a pagan. I now sow the wild oats of my misspent youth; later I will pray for a crop failure.

Chapter 15

Christmas l942.

"I don't like to complain mom, but you bought me the wrong bicycle."

"So what's wrong with your bicycle?" says mother.

"It's a juvenile size," I complain.

"What's wrong with that?" says Grandma.

"It's smaller than what the other kids ride," I explain.

"Is it slower than the regular size?" mother asks.

"No. It's just that, it's not the kind that all the other kids ride; I want a man's size!"

"I could have bought you a man's size for the same price," says mother. "I just thought you would like this one better."

"Well, I don't like it; it's one size smaller than what the other kids ride."

"The other kids don't have a shiny new bike like you do," Grandma chimes in.

"I don't care. I just wish you had bought me a full size bike."

"Well, it's too late now to do anything about it. With the war effort, there simply are not any bikes for sale. You will just have to make the best of it."

The conclusion is beyond dispute. I know this, but I just wish mother had thought about the fact that everybody else rides man-sized bikes, even if they are hand-me-downs.

Mother has decided to take me to see the Santa Claus parade in Toronto. It is sponsored by Eaton's Department store, which supplies that wonderful catalogue with all the toys pictured that I love to covet. We take the early train to Toronto. The crowds on Yonge Street are lined up on either side five rows deep. The parade is late. We wait and we wait.

"Mom," I whisper, "I have to go to the bathroom."

"You will just have to hold it," mother firmly replies.

"Mom, I can't hold it any longer."

"Look Brucie, here comes the parade." I grimace and watch; I cross my legs in misery and try to enjoy the parade.

"I don't care if I see Santa Claus, I gotta go bad," I whine.

"Just hold it, you can do it if you try harder," says mom.

We repeat this conversation several times until Santa arrives. I was never so glad to see the end of Santa. I am in total misery as we rush to Eaton's Department store. Mother is laughing while I fight off the leaky plumbing. At last I make it to the washroom. I tear down my pants and sit on the toilet.

"Aaaaah, sweet relief, how wonderful it is." At last I reappear to mother who waits at the door. Energized, I exclaim, "Now let's go to Toyland!"

On the way to Toyland, we see an incredible sight. A CCM bicycle is for sale. The price is $42.50. Furthermore, it is a man's size. It has gray painted handlebars instead of chrome (nickel is requisitioned for the war effort) but it is a full sized bike, painted a wartime black. I am oblivious of how unappealing a black bike with gray handlebars would be compared to the bright red bike I ride.

"I have to have that bike; we can sell my bike through the want ads in the paper." I plead with mother.

"I can't buy that bike, it will take all my spending money," mother explains. I will not take no for an answer. I trot out all the arguments and chutzpah known to spoiled brats until at last I wear her down. Mother counts her money and says,

"I can do it, but I have certain things that I must buy. The only way we can arrange it is to skip supper." In today's world we would not have had a problem. Credit cards make debt so easy these days, we never heard of such things when I was a child.

This spoiled kid will endure anything. I agree to the terms. Mother buys the bike. She then completes her Christmas shopping, measuring her money because of the unexpected drain on her finances. Mother's plans include a night in a tourist home because Anna, dad's sister, has moved away. If Anna still lived in Toronto, we would have had supper and free lodgings. With these arrangements, the bicycle has cost us dearly. We go without our evening meal. We hunker down that night, and my stomach begins to grumble. The lady at the tourist home has pity on us, and gives us four slices of unbuttered bread. It is a miserable way to spend an evening, but the bicycle redeems everything. When I complain how hungry I am, mother tells me to go to sleep. Once asleep, I won't feel the hunger.

The following day we take the train home checking the bicycle into the freight car. I am embarrassed at how the loud grumbling in my stomach alerts the adjacent passengers. Noon hour on Sunday, we detrain with my prized bicycle. We will soon have a decent meal at Grandma's. I ride beside mother on my new bike and grimace at how hard it is to peddle.

"There is something wrong with this bike," I say to mother. "It's too hard to peddle!" I wail. By the time we get home, I decide we've made a terrible mistake. In retrospect, I marvel at mother's patience. The next day mother calls Whetlaufer's bicycle shop and solves the mystery.

"Sorry Brucie but the man explained to me that the bicycle doesn't have any ball bearings to make the wheels run smoothly. It is definitely a wartime bicycle." The war effort has requisitioned ball bearings; there are none available to fix the problem. At long last guilt has caught up with me. I wonder, "How do we get rid of this white elephant, and retrieve the money?" Mother tries an ad in the Beacon Herald. To our amazement the phone rings off the hook. Because mother doesn't want to deceive anybody, she explains the problem to the would-be buyer. The buyer doesn't care. Any bike is better than no bike. This is wartime. Consumer goods are getting scarce. Even pots and pans are hard to come by, if at all. The depression is over, with wartime prosperity, people have money just at the time when there's nothing to buy. With relief, the wartime bicycle exchanges hands for exactly the same price as we paid. Conscience eased, I gratefully ride my bike for five more years with no complaints. Deprivation teaches lessons that affluence never knew.

Christmas 1942 is the best ever. About a week before Noel, a warm wind from the south melted all the snow and Old Man Winter fell asleep. The only reminder of winter was the icicles outside our kitchen window four feet long. Jack Frost seized the opportunity and sent the temperature to eleven below zero (minus 25 Celsius). Free to roam as he wished, Jack Frost painted every picture window in town with a prodigious array of cold weather Art, and turned the Avon River into a frozen but navigable strip of ice for unimpeded skating — even Santa was laughing. After school and also at night, we have the thrill of a lifetime skating wherever we wish under the stars until

Old Man Winter awoke with a snort. Begrudging what Jack Frost* had accomplished while he was sleeping (O.M.W. was always the jealous sort); he promptly dumped six inches of the white stuff before the smiling New Year's baby could do a thing to help, and — snow it goes. But do we care? The kids of Stratford enjoyed a week of exquisite skating fun to match anything that Ottawa could boast with their famed Rideau Canal.

Santa brings me lots of presents, although I can't remember any of them except one; it is the life of Christ in a cartoon format. It comes in three thick comic books. Apparently, if I no longer attend Sunday school, mother feels it would be good for me not to forget my Bible lessons. Uncle Norm and Aunt Jean are home from Tillsonburg. The family sings Christmas carols around the piano. Mother plays the accompaniment. She is a good pianist. 'Joy to the World' is my favourite carol. Norman has received his conscription call, but there is hope on the horizon; the German army is defeated in the Russian north. Life magazine publishes a photo that astounds me. Fifty thousand German prisoners of war are marched through the streets of Moscow. How quickly a year can turn things around. To quote Peter Ustinov,

"It is only a little time before many minds have been eased in their wartime tasks by the pleasant prospect of hanging Adolf Hitler." My fascination with the war knows no bounds. I decide to draw a map of Germany and carefully print every city that has been bombed by the Allies. In this way I memorize the names of over seventy cities. Fifty years later, when I am a tourist in Germany, I recognize many names and am ashamed of how I depersonalized those I once regarded as enemies.

*In today's world of insulated windows, we rarely see frost art. In my day when houses were drafty and windows leaked air, a cold morning presented us with artistry in frost that now is only a memory. For youngsters today, the closest example is dad cleaning off the frost on the windshield of a car. Alas, there is no picture frost to see here; one requires a house not insulated and a tug of war between hot and cold separated by a pane of glass.

Clara Berglind, the only girl in a family of nine siblings is my friend. I met Clara in Vancouver. She was, as I, a child of the war, except she was born in Germany. All of her eight brothers were drafted into Hitler's army. She lost three brothers on the Russian Front, two more died in Italy. Clara endured her own personal hell, narrowly escaping death in the bombing of Dortmund. Crammed into a bomb shelter with 400 civilians, her world disappeared in a firestorm caused by the Allied bombing of her city. When the all clear was sounded, a frantic effort to open the iron doors of the shelter revealed that they were welded shut by the heat of the firebombing. With oxygen running low, and the ventilation damaged by the heat, they faced a slow death by suffocation. Her pastor, a Baptist minister, (not all Germans are Lutherans) calmed the terrified civilians. He said,

"We must pray for a miracle." When the pastor had completed his prayer a powerful blast shook the shelter and suddenly the doors flew open. The explanation came later. A stray allied bomber with a few unused bombs was practicing what was called 'dumping.' When returning aircraft had been unable to find their target, they looked for an alternative city and 'dumped' their bombs at random. Invisible hands guided one of those bombs to a place where it would actually do some good. The explosion blew open the iron doors of that shelter with its imprisoned occupants thus setting them free.

War makes us into intolerable beasts, and not even children are exempt. I made my own scrapbook of coloured war prints, which is now in the possession of Nathan, my grandson who has a love of art. I have no desire to see it again, I decided a long time ago,

"There is no man anywhere on earth that is not my brother."
It took me a lifetime to learn that lesson, although I must confess, I still have this inexplicable fascination to follow world events when the news is all about war. Europe is now a far better place since we laid our weapons down. Alas, this world still has a long way to go.

There were eleven children in the Amy family from Waterloo. Three sons went to war.

The war affected many families like this photo illustrates. Reginald Amy age 25 (insert) is already overseas. Ross age 21 (back left) enlisted one month after this photo was taken. Bruce, age 22 an Army Sargent is in summer uniform. Three days after the Normandy invasion in 1944, Bruce survived a mortar attack thanks to someone who pushed him to the ground seconds before the explosion. When he looked around to see who his benefactor was there was no one to be seen. Reginald, wounded in an enemy air raid was shipped home in 1945. Years later in 1995, Bruce Amy (now my brother-in-law) some friends and myself attended Holland's Golden Celebration of the liberation of Holland. Eventually, our travels took us to a small hotel in Heidleburg near an American Army base. At breakfast, we engaged four American GIs in conversation. I casually mentioned that Bruce had been with the Canadian Army at Juno Beach in the Normandy invasion. As though on cue, the four GIs stood to attention walked over to Bruce and said, "We want to shake your hand."

Chapter 16

The Turning of the Tide

When Britain and France declared war on Germany in 1939, they faced the enemy convinced they could win the fight. There was a good deal of bravado that gave false hopes. The eight months' standoff was called the 'phony' war. Then Hitler invaded the Low Countries and we quickly learned the enemy was stronger than we thought. There had also been a 'phony' war going on in our house for quite some time, but I was unaware of it. November 1941 came as an unexpected shock. As the verbal battles between mother and Grandma heated up, I only needed to walk into the room, and the angry words ceased. How does an eleven-year old kid cope? In one way I felt a sense of empowerment; my presence acted as a peace intermediary. In another way, I felt as though I was walking on eggs. In vain, did my counsel work. The very idea of it is ludicrous. I live in two worlds; one is real the other is fictitious, or so it seemed to me. Unfortunately, both worlds are real. As things turned out, I have six more years of class work to do, in psychotherapy. From this kid's perspective, there is no textbook; my teacher is what I perceive to be the truth and my perception is, "Mother's world is slightly out of focus. She always seems to be looking at life through the wrong end of the telescope."

The complexity of mental illness is rarely understood by the unfortunate families that are compelled to face it. Our family was no exception. It is tragic to witness the inevitable alienation between siblings who once loved each other because they misunderstand the deterioration of the mind. Such was the case between Uncle Norman and my mother.

Uncle Norman has been watching our increasingly unstable household for some time. Uncle Gordon has mentioned a few things and so has Uncle Frank. He has talked it over with Aunt Jean and they have decided that a brotherly talk to an unruly sister must be held. A disturbing letter from Grandma reads, "I don't know how much more I can stand." The time for action has come. Norm and Jean are to have supper with us on Sunday. Norm sends me out to play. Jean is helping Grandma in the kitchen. The confrontation takes place in the privacy of the living room.

"Ethel, what on earth are you up to?" Norman is blunt. "Are you trying to destroy our mother? I hear it from Gordon. I hear it from Frank. Every time we visit here, I can see it in Grandma's eyes." He doesn't mention Grandma's letter. He is afraid that after he is gone, Ethel will use that information against her."

"I don't know what you are talking about," protests mother.

"O yes you do! Don't deny it. Look at our mother; her palsy is getting worse and you are partly to blame. You accuse her of ruining your life. You have had a tragic marriage go wrong. But you cannot blame mother for that. I lived in the same house as you did. I heard our mother warning you not to marry Bruce. So what did you do? You disregarded her advice and eloped and you have the gall to blame mother for that!" Mother is now in tears. She is hurt and angry.

"I do blame mother. We were happy living in Camrose, and what does mother do, she nagged Father till at last he gave in and dumped us into this dirty railroad town. I hated Stratford from the start. She only thought of herself. She never talked to me about life. She never warned me about men. How was I to know?"

"Ethel, you are trying to excuse the inexcusable. People move from place to place all the time. Don't avoid the issue. Mother raised four children and buried a fifth. She had her troubles too, but she didn't blame others for that and neither should you."

"It's so easy for you to talk; you have a wife and friends, I have nothing." Ethel is sobbing now.

"I'm sorry Ethel, but just because you married the wrong man doesn't make Mother responsible for your mistakes and irrespective of what you say, I know that mother warned you because I heard her myself."

"It was too late by then," wailed Ethel, "I wanted to get out of Stratford and by then I was in love. By that time, it was too late. Mother never talked to me like a mother should. She should have told me these things before it was too late. It's all her fault that my life turned out like this." Ethel is now weeping uncontrollably.

"Ethel, you were always a dreamer. Mother raised you no differently than anybody else would have. I admit that you've had it tough. But you cannot blame our mother for that. Now you hear me and pay attention to what I say. You have got to stop blaming mother for things that were beyond her control. I'm telling you the truth. This foolishness must stop or you will be worse off than you are right now." There is a long silence; Ethel has stopped crying and is saying nothing.

"Ethel, listen to me, I want to hear you say with your own lips that you will stop blaming mother for all your troubles." Another long silence. Mother whispers,

"I promise." Later that evening, after suitable farewells, Norm and Jean are driving home in the car. Aunt Jean turns to Norman and says,

"Well? How did she take it."

"She cried and tried to justify herself."

"— and?"

"I wrung from her a promise that she will stop all this nonsense."

"Do you think she will?"

"Well, let's call it the turning of the tide." Norman's confidence is short lived. Mother cannot help herself. She willingly forgets the promise she made to her brother. The accusations increase in frequency and intensity. Sadly, mother lives in a world with invisible walls that cannot be breached by words of correction. The gates of her mind are locked and barred and the only other person allowed in is the son that she loves. As much as it is possible, for an eleven year old to love and understand, I try, with mixed results.

-oOo-

Cub Scouts is a good diversion for me. Akela leads the Cubs and is a role model. I am greatly attracted to Akayla; he seems to be such a kind man. I have only seven months till my twelfth birthday. I have courses to do and badges to earn, if I am to make it to the rank of Sixer. My motive is not very altruistic. I'm trying to catch up to Clarkie. Akela encourages me to work at it. He will help me. I am now learning how to flag the alphabet. Akela tells us stories of how messages in battle are signalled from Captain to soldiers. Life and death depend on reading the flagman. I imagine myself on a ship in the Atlantic, signalling to other ships, warning of dangerous shoals to be avoided. I cannot be a Sixer unless I master the flag alphabet. Grandma shakes her head and says;

"I can't see any value in knowing how to send messages by flags." I try to explain to her how important this is, even to the saving of life. She is not convinced. Diligently I attempt to memorize the flag alphabet and practice on a longsuffering Grandmother. I have no flags; my hands are my flags. So, I spell out messages by my hand movements. Uncle Gordon teases me as he peeks through the window on one of his weekly visits.

"Why is Brucie trying to catch flies in the middle of winter?"

Akela tells us there will be a paper drive in early March. All of Stratford is mobilized to collect and tie their newspapers in bundles. It's all part of the war effort. As a patriotic Canadian, I rise at the unheard of hour of six. We are to be picked up in cars. Yes, there were some of the better-off kids with parents who owned cars. At 6 A.M. like the light of dawn in the book of Genesis, Grandma wakes me, but I decide I don't want to be patriotic today. Grandma will not relent. That's when I learn that if you don't feel like getting out of bed, just jump out and get dressed and the feeling will go away.

At 7 A.M., I am picked up for battle. We are to collect the bundles of paper, placed curbside, by other patriotic Canadians who have put them out the night before. Slowly the cars fill up until there is just enough room for us boys to squeeze in between the papers. We pull up to the line of cars ahead of us, and inch our way forward, until it is our turn to unload our paper into a waiting freight car, sitting at a railway siding. Ray Hopwood is helping to load the freight car along with his older brother. Ray is my classmate at Romeo school. We are all in this together. At noon hour, we have hot dogs and pop, provided by Whyte's Meat Market and Schneider's Wholesalers. I down three of them quickly, confirming the axiom: 'the appetite expands with the availability of food, especially when it's free'. Ken Hopwood, Ray's older brother, finishes six. He continues to work, but he's looking a little green around the gills. We have an arduous afternoon ahead of us. By 4 P.M. a very tired Wolf Cub staggers home after a hard day's work. We have done our duty. We have contributed to the war effort. Ten months later, Life magazine has all the pictures of the surrender of the German Army in North Africa. Two months later, the Allies invade Sicily. It must have been the paper drive that turned the tide.

-oOo-

With the arrival of spring comes the slush, and the breaking up of the white asphalt. Racing matchsticks replaces road hockey as the city pastime for kids. Rivulets run curbside everywhere. They are kid-sized, and perfect for running match races. You don't even need a match, a broken twig will do. The incline on Nile Street between Brunswick and Rebecca, is perfect for match racing. The water is at least an inch deep and 6 to 12 inches wide with partly frozen snowbanks. We compete, two matchsticks at a time. We imagine our matchsticks as boats that disappear under the ice ledges only to reappear as they make their way with the current. In matchstick racing, you have a 50% chance of winning the race. You only need a pair of rubber boots (indispensable for the sport) unless you like soaking wet feet. I particularly like this sport better than the annual ritual of playing marbles. The part that is marvellous is that the odds are even. Even at marbles, the athletic have the advantage. I am not a good athlete. A bag of marbles only lasts me for two days. I was actually breaking even until I challenged Ralph Fryer. By the time Ralph is through with me, I am marbleless. Alas, match racing has a short season. Mr. Sun has a prejudice against match racing, or at least, so it seems. Like me in marbles, hard frozen snow pack doesn't stand much of a chance against the sun.

War movies are frequent fare at the Ontario Street Classic theatre. Royce, Vince and I go to see a movie about an American submarine that sinks a Japanese warship. It is a thriller for us, and we are still talking about it the following Sunday afternoon. We are at Vince Schooley's house, 177 Albert Street. They have a veranda both front and back of the house. The back veranda is plain with no railing; it has three slender posts that hold up a sloping roof. Mrs. Schooley and Vince's grandma are also present. They are sitting on chairs, knitting. It is a warm spring day and it is gently raining. We decide to play submarine. The game resembles the movie we have just seen. All the control panels are on the brick wall and in our imagination. The periscope comes down at our command, and even though Mrs. Schooley can't see it, we can. That white brick wall has every gadget that a child's mind can manufacture: the instrument panel, the torpedo controls, the levers and the steering mechanism, are all on the white brick wall. We improve on the movie that was only an hour long. Our game is made up on the spot, and goes for two hours. Not only are three kids thoroughly entertained, but also, so is our audience.

In 1943 we loved to watch the war movies. In hindsight, I suspect that truth mixed with propaganda fueled those Hollywood flicks. Oblivious to all that, we devoured them with the quiet assurance that given a little time, we would surely win the war. Two films especially stand out in my memory. The first was **Mrs. Miniver**, an MGM movie starring Greer Garson and Walter Pigeon. The second was **So Proudly We Hail** starring Claudette Colbert, Paulette Goddard, Veronica Lake, and the strong and shy, Sonny Tuffs. These movies of the era celebrated our crushing defeats, first at Dunkirk and later at Corrigedor, but held out the hope of a better day to come. The first movie depicted Dunkirk, in France; the second was America's defeat in the Philippines. Miniver won best picture of the year in 1942. Churchill said of the making of Miniver that it was worth a flotilla of destroyers. **Proudly** might have won the following year had it not been for the immortal **Casablanca** starring Ingrid Bergman and Humphrey Bogart. All of these films, cast in the dark days of World War II, gave us hope that at the cost of even life itself, we would eventually win the war. They can still be watched with appreciation today by a later generation.

Even the music of those days reflected this hope. I could whistle the song 'There'll be Blue Birds over the White Cliffs of Dover' in those days with impunity. Today I cannot sing through those words without misty eyes. Here's the lyrics, written by Nat Burton:

There'll be bluebirds over the white cliffs of Dover
Tomorrow just you wait and see.
There'll be joy and laughter and peace ever after,
When the world is free.
The shepherd will count his sheep the valleys will bloom again
And Jimmy will go to sleep in his own little bed again.
There'll be bluebirds over the white cliffs of Dover
Tomorrow just you wait and see.

We blamed the war for the starlings. These imports from Europe invaded our skies by the millions in 1943. Their formations in flight are actually quite beautiful to watch and are a dance of delight to rival the Northern lights. We hated them. They came at dusk and left at dawn. Their squawking and screeching I can hear to this very day. Noisemakers would drive one squadron away only to be replaced by another. They bombed us every night. Their droppings made the sidewalks white and no one walked the sidewalks after dark.

1943, my Victory garden

Pedestrians took to the middle of the road, and dared only to brave the sidewalk, to let a car go by. Everybody had a story of being hit by bird dirt. They left in the fall only to return in the spring. I remember reading an article in the Beacon-Herald saying that eventually their natural enemies would pare them down to manageable size. Despite my love of natural creatures, we prayed for that day. Then, mysteriously as they had come, they left; by 1946, we reclaimed the sidewalks, just in time, to save us from the deluge of new cars that eventually drove us kids from the streets back to the sidewalks and playgrounds where adults thought we belonged.

The Women's Institute is a force to be reckoned with. W.I. is knitting socks, canning jam, and sending vegetable seeds to Britain by the ton. At school we are encouraged to plant a Victory garden. 'Sow the Seeds of Victory, Plant a Victory Garden.' I am inspired and over the kitchen table I declare our need for a Victory Garden. I find out that means me, since Grandma can hardly dig a garden. We have had a garden of sorts over the years, but it has gone to weeds with inattention. I decide to revive the dead. After I get the garden dug, it is time to plant.

Dutch Sets! I learn that Dutch Sets are really seeds for green onions, about the size of a marble. I plant Dutch sets. Potatoes, corn, carrots, lettuce and beans round out the garden. I soon learn that I have competition. Weeds! At first, I vigourously weed the garden. With the coming of warm weather, play competes with weeds, and play wins out in the end. In vain does Grandma plead for the garden. Now hard work never killed anyone, but why take a chance. The beans and onions seem to fend for themselves, and we harvest a few. Everything else is having a rough time, as this gardener has more important things to do. My morning glories are the big surprise. They wow all my visitors; I'm giving Grandpa Wade some competition. My contribution to the war effort lags. Alas, there seems to be little that I can accomplish for the war that comes under the category of pleasure. Loyally, we play cops and robbers by day and hide and go seek at night, but I'll have you to know that I can sing at the top of my voice, 'There'll always be an England.' Furthermore, I knit two six-inch squares with my very own fingers for an Afgan that was sent to Britain.

Chapter 17

Back to Bogie's Beach

Mr. Bogie has traded his 1932 Chevrolet for a 1937 Plymouth. Back in 1939, he could have bought a brand new Ford for 900 dollars. With the scarcity of new cars, the price of used cars has gone up. He settles for the Plymouth. I admire its clean lines, and the dashboard, which is modern and shiny. He made the deal in 1942, just in time to take advantage of the market. The shrinking used car population is driving up the prices. Detroit stopped making cars in early 1942, and has switched over to making Sherman tanks. In the next two years they will make 50,000 of them. Had Mr. Bogie waited much longer, he would still be driving his old Chevrolet. Used cars are scarce and new cars nonexistent. Rubber is also scarce; new tires are not available. Used tires wear till they are bald. Anybody who owns a car has a flat tire story and you can't buy replacements. It's a wonderful time for kids. We virtually own the streets. No wonder street hockey proliferates; the competition is down for the count.

It's great to be back at the farm again. Graham has news for me. There is going to be a threshing. This time I will be around for the action. I love work; I could watch it for hours. But that's not all; there is a new business on the farm. With gas rationing, cottagers are having a hard time getting milk and cream from the stores in Goderich. At any time of day, vacationers who want to buy milk can interrupt Mrs. Bogie. This kind of nuisance results in a decision. Buying a few Silverwoods milk bottles, the Bogies will operate a dairy service for cottagers. The milk is not pasteurized. Great care is taken to keep it clean and uncontaminated. Today, our laws would not have permitted it. First the milk must be processed though a hand operated separator. Some of the cream is taken off for butter; the rest of the milk still has enough cream to make it a rich milk indeed. Before the days of required pasteurization, cream was just allowed to rise naturally to the top. The bottles of milk are topped with a thin cardboard cap purchased from Silverwoods. If the family wanted to have cream for coffee they poured the cream off the top before they started to use the remainder of the milk. For homogenized milk, you shake the bottle, which turns out to be approximately two-percent milk. It is still enough to give Graham a milk moustache. Years later someone figured out how to make the milk stay mixed. When I was a kid, the cream just rises to the top.

Graham has a wagon with sides to make it into a mini-truck. Every morning before breakfast, I accompany Graham to the beach where we deliver the milk. Graham collects the money, making change where necessary. Graham has become a businessman without pay. All proceeds go to the family farm. Meantime, Mr. Bogie takes Graham and me for a walk to the north field. He breaks off a head of grain rubbing it in his hand, and says,

"The oats will be ready by next week." Then he turns to me and chuckles, "Bruce, have you ever seen a threshing?"

"Nope," I say. "But I sure am looking forward to it." Graham has been telling me all about it." The neighbours will help and we will see six teams of horses before we are through. I have been given a seminar on horses by Graham who explains to me, that male horses are colts, and females are fillies. Mr. Bogie's horses are both fillies. Peggy and Lilly are both girls. Maybe he gets more work done when a team of horses are female, "Hmmn?" (I understand this; it's like that at our house as well.) I now know, thanks to Graham, that racehorses are divided into trotters and pacers. However, we will see no racehorses tomorrow. Hackneys or Shires perhaps, but definitely not racehorses. These beasts of the farm are draft horses that know how to work. Awake at night well past bedtime, Graham has fired my imagination with the lore of Mustangs. Graham has a story book entitled Black Beauty, which I have now read. I am pumped, and the night before threshing, we can hardly sleep for excitement.

Graham and I are sitting on a cedar rail fence waiting for the parade. The chickens have been fed, and the morning milk run completed. Breakfast dishes are all put away, and the house is ready for six husky farmers plus their helpers, who will be hungry for lunch at noon. We can see the horse drawn wagons, as they make the bend on Bogie's road. Terrance Hunter leads the way with a team of chestnuts, pulling an empty wagon that could pass for a Conestoga, except the canvas is gone. There are hayracks protruding on either side. Loaded, these wagons will appear like giant Behomoths, pulled by horses which will seem to have shrunken to the size of Shetlands in front of the bloated wagons. Behind Hunter comes Wilfred Smith with his team and wagon. Next is Bill Cook. After him is Irving Hunter. George and Cree Freeman are next in separate wagons. Everybody knows Cree Freeman. From time to time, you can hear him singing a Wilf Carter song on radio, live from Wingham's CKNX. He has a terrific singing voice, and plays an electric Hawaiian guitar.

What a parade! The horses are panting and snorting, as though they too know that this is something special. Behind each team of horses, there stands a seasoned farmer, reins in hand, controlling the occasional mare that tries to browse on the high grown grass by the side of the road. No finer display by sixteen Clydesdales at the Canadian National Exhibition could have matched what these eyes witnessed that day.

An old fashioned threshing, courtesy Milton Antique Steam Association

The grand finale comes with Alexander Watson's threshing machine. It is being pulled by a big Oliver tractor. The tractor-threshing machine combination is the next best thing to a CNR 6000 steam engine. The thresher is more than a man made machine. It is almost something alive, with wheels and pulleys that set it apart as something with a life of its own. In wide-eyed fascination, I watch as the thresher is moved into the entrance of the barn. Next the tractor is aligned with the thresher, while the biggest pulley belt I have ever seen stretches out between the tractor and the thresher. Everything that moves in that thresher is powered by the Oliver tractor belt. Already there is a load of oats at the ready. Mr. Bogie, pitchfork in hand, is feeding the insatiable thresher with the oat bundles. Straw is flying into the mow. The oats are filling the near empty granary. It is Graham's job to stand by, dust flying everywhere, guiding the chute that directs the oats into the first bin. It fills in less than an hour. By now the other wagons are making their way to the neatly stooked oats in the field. Soon they will be lining up to disgorge their sheaves to the thresher. Next, Eveyln Bogie arrives with water to banish thirst. The sweat from the men soaks their shirts. They have now been in the hot sun for an hour. This is man's work and I am only a boy. Cree calls out,

"Someday you'll be big enough to do this too." I shrink back in terror trying to be anonymous. The men are laughing at me now. By noon, Act One of the drama closes for intermission.

It is time for lunch (dinner, remember?). The men are washed up, and file in for a snack. Roast beef with mashed potatoes and gravy is steaming and ready. I watch, fascinated, as the men load up their plates higher than I have ever seen. Wolfing down the food, they are soon piling up their plates for seconds. No magician's Act that ever disposed of a body that vanished can compare with this. The food disappearance that day is a sight to behold, and they haven't even started dessert. Two slices of pie times twelve men seems to suffice. They are sated for the moment. The miracle is that they can work at all, with all that food in their belly. They seem to have no problem with this, and at six o'clock, they will be back for a full course chicken dinner complete with more dessert. In retrospect, I'm not sure who worked harder, the men or the women. Mrs. Bogie did have help from the wives, who also ate, but only after the men were finished. I ate with the women.

Act Two of the greatest show on earth has come to an end. The wagons and their horses are on their way home. The whole drama will be repeated at Wilfred Smith's farm tomorrow. Six shows in six days, with the odd job here and there, and the thresher will fall silent for another year. All of this drama lasted to the mid-fifties, until some wiseacre invented the combine. That's when the loneliest profession on earth got even lonelier. How often have I thanked my lucky stars that I was born in time to see an old-fashioned farm threshing.

Modernity has made the world a poorer place.

My adventure is far from over. Mrs. Bogie has received a phone call from mother. Stratford is delaying school opening for two weeks. An outbreak of measles has to be contained. Its official: no school till September 15. We could hear the cheering all the way to Goderich. Mother has arranged for me to go to school with Graham for two weeks. With my extended holiday, I get to experience a one-room country school with Graham to show me the ropes. It is a scene right out of Anne of Green Gables. We are each issued a ten by eight charcoal slate, and slate marker by Mrs. Bogie (I had never seen these before). We walk a mile carrying our lunch bucket. I enroll with our teacher, Miss Dorothy Taggert. She explains to the class why this city kid is going to occupy a desk. This soon-to-be twelve-year-old meets all the kids. Grant Chisholm, I already know. His dad delivers gasoline and coal oil to the farms all around. I have ridden with him in his dad's truck. The rest are new. I have forgotten all their names except Jack Smith, who was the biggest kid in the class. He claimed that if you looked through the knothole on the boy's side of the backhouse, you could see the girls. I tried a look through that knothole, but couldn't see a thing. Some things never change; I think Jack Smith was a teller of tall tales.

"School days, school days, dear old golden rule days. Readin' and writin' and rithmatic, taught to the tune of a hickory stick," says the song, and I experienced it all in that little S.S. #5 Colbourne Township school. The parts I liked the best were recess and lunch. THE game, the best that was ever invented, 'Prisoner's base'!

The rules were this. Divide the kids into two lines. Everybody plays, boys and girls. Young and old. You have to take prisoners. This requires a taunter. Somebody quick on their feet to dare capture. I quickly take the challenge, but the trick is this, whoever is last to leave their line (the base) has the power of capture. But watch out for those who leave the baseline after you. In no time, I'm caught. It's confusing at first, but the kids keep track and nobody has the remotest chance of cheating. Whoever leaves the safety of the baseline has the power to tag a prisoner until somebody else has left his or her line after you. Whichever side captures all the kids wins the game. But if, reading this blows you away, there is one more rule. You can release your teammates. If you are a good sprinter, tag a teammate, before someone catches you. (Captured teammates are allowed to stretch out in a line, so long as the last prisoner has his foot on the opposing base line). Release a prisoner before you are intercepted, and you are home free to return to your base line, and start all over. Confusing? You bet, but it's the best game ever, once you get the hang of it.

I tried to explain all this to my friends and although we gave it a valiant attempt, they were too dumb to 'larn'. City kids think they are the smartest, but the city is where the population is the most dense.

Chapter 18

The Brunswick Street Battle

Eddie Marks has moved into the house two doors east of our place. Eddie wants an army, and Eddie has got panache. Eddie has organizational skills and quickly displays his leadership. We are all enlisted except Ted White who is more interested in his chemistry set than in playing soldier. Sinister plots are afoot. The kids one block east of us have organized. They are from now on 'the enemy'. To defend ourselves, we agree to enlist in Eddie's army, boys and girls. First thing we have to do is march. Left, right, step in time. Right wheel, left wheel, present arms, attention, at ease. We engage at Eddie's command. We have been militarized. We rush home from school and drill till we know how to drill to perfection. Soldier games replace cops and robbers. One shot and you are dead. You just have to lie there until the game is over. We hide behind trees, spying on the enemy, hiding behind trees, hoping we'll not be seen. If we are seen, terrified, we run home as fast as we can.

Now, it's always safe at the schoolyard; that's supervised. It's the two hours after four to suppertime that require vigilance. The army demands toughness of mind, so we learn to cuss. It wasn't really hard. There were plenty of roll models at school. Vince and I exchange cuss words. When we are angry, we know what to say, and how to cuss. It's all part of growing up but — how to break the news to Grandma?

One day I return from school and I tell Grandma,

"I heard a bad word at school today!" Breathlessly I wait for her reply.

"Well Brucie you will always hear bad words somewhere, so just don't pay attention to bad words." This of course is not the reply I am looking for; not to be deterred I enquire,

"Do you want to know what it was?"

"No Brucie, I don't want to know what it was," intones Grandma. Disappointed, I walk away and wonder how I can break the news some other way. Human nature being what it is; I don't have to plan on how to 'break the news'. It just seems to happen at a frustrating moment when I am angry. I let a few words slip out, and Grandma is shocked,

"Wherever did you learn to talk like that?" I sheepishly blame Vince, since he is not around to defend himself. Grandma rebukes me;

"Thou shalt not take the name of the Lord thy God in vain, for the Lord will not hold him guiltless." This is heavy-duty stuff, and Grandma has me scared. If I'm not careful, I might lose my salvation. I'm too old for supervised bedtime prayers, but I'm on my honour to say prayers. Faithfully, I have learned the Lord's Prayer which we say every morning at school. I can recite that to myself by memory in thirteen seconds (reverently in fifteen). Then just to be sure I recite,

"Now I lay me down to sleep, I pray the Lord my soul to keep.
If I should die before I wake, I pray the Lord my soul to take. Amen"

Next I recall how many times, I swore that day, and ask the Lord to forgive me. It will not do to go to sleep without things being tidied up, or I might not wind up in heaven (assuming I died in the night) but in that, 'ugh', other place. For the time being I am safe.

I turn twelve on Halloween and now I'm out of Cub Scouts. Vainly have I striven to become a Sixer. I have graduated to Boy Scouts whether I like it or not. While I could start all over again working on all the badges to reach the top, I decide that I will quit the Boy Scout thing altogether. Royce is a year younger than me, and has a year to enjoy being a Sixer and the honours therewith. I never did make the grade to Clarkie's level. I don't mind quitting Cubs, because now Clarkie can't boss me around.

Halloween is the best ever. With sugar rationing, cheap candy abounds, but my taste buds are not sufficiently developed to know the difference. I canvas the neighbourhood with my paper bag, wearing a magician's suit. It is made of black paper, and came from the Woolworth's Five and Ten. (Hard to believe that the mighty Woolworth's that had a store in every town no longer exists). At the Reeves, I am invited in, and given a thorough inspection. Lois Reeves is in high school, and wanted to make homemade candy for the kids. There isn't much, due to the rationing, but I am one of the favoured few (there were only twenty pieces). It is sweet and too soft to put in my bag, so I had to eat it on site.

"Delicious!" I exclaim. Lois is pleased. It is the best candy I ever tasted (Candy tastes so much better when you are young). I come home loaded, but on examination, I see I have a lot of apples. I eat all the candy within 24 hours, and I suppose, I ate the apples too. I don't remember them so much, but I talk of Lois Reeve's homemade candy to everyone I meet.

November passes quickly, and on a winter day in December, mother sends me to Thistle's corner store to get some sugar and a pound of butter. It's the closest store since Lloyd's Grocery has gone out of business. I have the precious ration coupons, but I have to go through 'enemy' territory. I'm not afraid because I have a legitimate reason for passing through 'their' territory. I arrive at the store safely. Mr. Thistle dips his scoop into a 100 pound bag that has three large x's imprinted on the side. His skillful eye is trained on a scale that is balanced with a lead weight that has 16 oz imprinted on the top. He carefully pours the precious sugar into a small brown paper bag until the sugar and weight delicately teeter-totter into perfect balance. The money and the ration coupons I now give in exchange for the goods purchased. Next, I begin my perilous journey home.

The snow is packing, and great for making a snowman. Or snow forts! I make an important discovery. The enemy is making a snow fort in Barry Knechtel's side yard. I am accosted at Barry's house on my return, but my paper bag with the butter and sugar guarantees safe passage. I have a reason for being in 'their' territory. Barry shows me the inside of the fort and points to the treatment centre. He says,

"Watch this." He then goes to his knees, and three guys join him, and suddenly snow is flying everywhere.

"That's what happens to someone who dares to break down the walls of our fort." I am impressed, and assure them that they will never have to do that to me. I give a full report to Eddie, who is equally impressed and says,

"I'll take that under advisement."

Christmas is coming. I pull my sleigh to the Waterloo Street market, and once again Grandma picks out the Christmas tree. It has to be full and thick. Grandma buys a chicken and other groceries. We load up the sleigh, and I pull it back over the snow packed sidewalk. I'm glad it's Christmas, because mother is obviously not happy these days, but I know she will not spoil Christmas with an angry outburst because she knows how important all this is to me. Christmas turns out fine. Spring follows winter and all the usual rituals take their turn, but there is one ritual that's wearing thin.

Me, Eddie Marks, Vincent, my bike, not fully man sized but shiny and red

With the coming of spring, we are all quite tired of being in Eddie's army. He comes up with a solution; we will meet the enemy on the lawn at the now closed Lloyd's store. We will pair up and have a fistfight to settle who is boss of Brunswick Street. It seems like a good idea, since it is Eddie who will have to face Donald Dunbar, the toughest kid on the street. That night I explain to mother and Grandma, that there is going to be a showdown fight at Lloyd's store. Grandma and mother are horrified. They refuse to let me go, in case I get hurt. I protest gang loyalty. I have no choice; I must go. I don't remember how I got mother to agree, but in the end, I prevail. Perhaps she thought it would be a good lesson to me, not to get into fights. The fateful day cannot be postponed. It is May 1944. At 7 P.M. we are gathered on the lawn at Lloyd's. We pair off and I get Barry Knechtel. We are not to start until Eddy gives the signal. Barry lands the first punch, and I go home crying. That dirty Barry didn't wait for the signal to start fighting. I was looking the other way. I cuss him out before Grandma. She is without mercy (Ouch, I should have known), I wince as I hear her recite,

"Thou shalt not take the name of the Lord thy God in vain, for the Lord will not hold him guiltless." Grandma puts the fear of God into me. Again, I have to count up how many times I swore that day. The number is growing, but it's good to know it is safe to go to sleep. Now as to the big showdown; I don't remember how the fight ended, because obviously, I didn't stick around to see. I guess everybody won. We were all so sick of the war games that from that time on, we decided it was more fun to be friends. Peace had returned to Brunswick Street. Frustrated and forlorn, Mars hung his head and cried.

One important detail needs to be recorded. When Eddie Marks called at my door, he had a trademark and would holler,

"Ooh-aah!" Before Eddie, we would approach the back door of our friends and call their names. For example, when I called on Clarkie, I would stand outside the door and call,

"Roy-ce!" One never knocked on the door of a friend; that was verbotten. You called the name. If he was inside, out he came. Eddie said to me,

"Why should I call your name? Every voice is different, you know exactly who's outside your door when I call 'Ooh-aah'. One could not resist that kind of logic, and so whether it was Clarkie or Johnny, we always called 'Ooh-aah'. The idea caught on quickly. Whether it was Johnny or anybody in anyplace, names gave way to 'Ooh-aah'. For all I know, the practice may have spread throughout the whole city. Everywhere I went and the friends I knew all wound up with the same calling card; 'Ooh aah'! Thank you Eddie Marks. In the year 2006, I read the story of Charles Mulli (Father to the Fatherless by Paul H. Boge). This wonderful citizen of Kenya, who cares for 1000 orphans, uses the same calling card we used 62 years ago, a fact which proves that the practice has spread all over the world. And to think — it all began in Stratford!

Chapter 19

The Best Year of my Life

June 1944 was the beginning of the best year of my life. First, I tasted fish and chips and actually liked them. Second, I met Jim Johnston (we usually called him Johnny) and John Butler. Third, I discovered girls. Fourth! Oh yes, the Allies invaded Normandy (yep, there still is a war going on). My childhood was happy, because I had lots of friends with great nicknames. First, there was Vince Schooley, nicknamed 'Gooey' because of his last name. There was Rabbit Herlick, Bummer Bolton, Buck Ward (his front teeth stuck out) Butter Butler, Alley McKone, Foo Pauli, Cats Schenck, Lakey Lakeman, Nick Knechtel, Whitey Whitehead, Spark Glazier, Murph Murphy, Willie Williams, Squirt MacDonald, and brainey Jim Madge who taught us all how to play chess, and quiet Les Palmer, who in later years got his name in the paper for saving a guy from drowning in the Avon River.

There were others too that defied being nicknamed, like gentle Doug Heath, who was the strongest kid at Romeo School. Since I was always scared of getting into fights, I liked to stick close to Doug. My mental image of Doug is a wintertime scene. After a snowstorm, there is always a pile of snow where Mr. Legg, the janitor, shovels the doorway. Seizing the initiative, Doug delights to stand on the top of that snowpile and shout,

"I'm the king of the castle, and you're the dirty rascal."
A dare like that invariably reaps a challenge and the kids respond accordingly. Led by Ralph Fryer, a bunch of us guys dislodge Doug Heath and Ralph now claims the snow pile. It is all in good fun and I don't remember anybody getting hurt. Now and again, by a stroke of good fortune, I claim the coveted spot for a few seconds. Boldly, I declare,

"I'm the king—." That kingly pleasure never lasts longer than two, or three seconds for a skinny kid like me; I am invariably bowled over by somebody else. Suddenly the bell rings and it's time to go inside. Just to top things off somebody calls out,

"Ashpile!" Next, everybody is in the snow, crawling on top of everybody else calling out, "Ashpile, Ashpile! Now it's Principal Pauli's turn, who, although he calls out for everybody to line up, cannot resist a smile. To any doubters who might now be wondering why we would call our little game "Ashpile" let me explain that in those days when every house burned coal during the winter an ashpile was a familiar sight. We all had our responsibilities and amongst many things to do each week, most of us boys had to carry out the ashes curbside for our parents. We all knew what an ashpile looked like.

The other great winter sport we played at Romeo School, thanks to an engineering flaw, takes place after a winter thaw followed by a freeze that always produces a glaze of ice where the snow pile stood. Now it's everybody on all fours pushing and shoving. We slide and laugh like a herd of buffalo, everybody having a good time till recess is over.

Doug Heath was the youngest of five brothers and except for Laverne, who was born physically handicapped; they were all athletic and physically strong. As a young grade eight neophyte that meant something to me. One day Doug invited me to his home after school to see a magazine he had found in the attic of his house. Its yellowed pages revealed its age but it was still legible. It was called 'Sunbathing' and was published by the American Nudist Society. The verbotten magazine was now hidden in the garage. After looking in all directions to make sure there was nobody watching, Doug fished this publication from its hiding place and showed it to me. Aghast but curious, I paged through that nudist magazine to see things I dare not speak. After about three minutes, Doug was getting nervous so he took it from me and carefully hid it away in its secret lair. Sixty years later I am E-mailing Doug about how I eventually became a Christian and a minister. Doug replied to say that he was now an Atheist and sent me a lengthy defense of Atheism. I think, "I know how that got started."

My advice to readers is,
"Whatever temptations come your way, be sure to stay away from nudist magazines or you may turn into an Atheist."

Not that I'm prejudiced against Atheists. They seem to be a pragmatic lot. Take my friend, Jim Jones. Years ago Jim ran a nightclub in the Florida Keys and loved to regale me with tough guy stories. Over the years he had lost a lot of teeth and what was left looked more like fangs giving him a mean look that reinforced his colourful tales. The truth is behind the façade there lay a decent sort of guy. The absence of those teeth and the tough talk made for a formidable impression. Knowing that I am a Christian, but wanting to be an honest neighbour, he flat out told me,

"I'm an Atheist." Seeing the dismay on my face, Jim softens the blow by saying, "Now don't get me wrong, I am not above offering a prayer now and again; it's just that I don't believe in God." I hadn't seen Jim for a few months when suddenly this nice looking stranger who bears some resemblance to the Jim I remember warmly greets me.

"Why — why if it isn't Jim Jones," I stammer, "But you look so handsome all of a sudden." As I continue to stare at him, I twig to the occasion,

"I've got it; you have a new set of teeth!"

"Yep!" says Jim, "You see, I've got this friend. He's a mortician who happens to work over at the cemetery. He's got himself a little business on the side. It took awhile before I could get a pair to fit but finally he found me a set of uppers. The tops fit perfect the first time I tried them on. Getting a set of lowers took longer. After several tries, I got the lowers two weeks later and with a little grinding, they fit just fine — only cost me fifty dollars." Talk about mixed emotions. I am shocked, but burst out laughing. In fact ever since when I think of Jim Jones I laugh. He amuses me. So as I said,

"Atheists are a pragmatic lot."

Getting back to our subject, I always liked Doug Heath and it seemed to be mutual. As one who lost most of the fights I tried so desperately to avoid at Romeo School, it was comforting to know that Doug Heath was my friend. Doug never picked fights. Why should he? He knew he was the strongest kid in the class (an enviable place to be) so nobody tried to get smart with Doug. We all understood the pecking order, and to be safe, we made our alliances accordingly.

The old two story Romeo School was placed in such a way as to divide the school yard between the girls and the boys. Girls got the East Side but the West Side was larger and reserved for the boys to give them more room to burn off their adrenaline by playing softball. One day Bob Whitehead was up to bat in a game of scrub and belted the ball so hard that it went sailing across Rebecca Street and right through Mrs. Hammer's front window. The poor woman was just enjoying a morning cup of tea when suddenly she heard an explosion so loud that she thought the end of the world had come. However, when she finally discovered the unexploded missile amidst the shards of glass, she came to the realization that it was vandalism (at least that's what she called it). This delicate state of affairs creates a problem for us, since it was incumbent for us to retrieve the ball if we are to continue our game. Ron Kelly is elected to be the peacemaker and with appropriate apologies asks for the ball so we can continue the game. He gets an ear full and with downcast eyes, Ron reports,

"She's not going to give us the ball." With a crisis like this, we lament our dilemma and appeal to Principal George Pauli. How we ever retrieved that ball is a complete mystery. I suppose after suitable apologies, and payment for repairs from public funds, (no wonder taxes are high) our baseball was finally returned. Mr. Pauli was most understanding, but pleaded with the kids not to hit the ball so hard. Since nobody had ever equaled Bob Whitehead's home run, the remark was quite obviously directed at the culprit. I can still see the pleased look on Bob's face as we all congratulated him on his worthwhile achievement, Mrs. Hammer notwithstanding.

With all my many pals, we could play just about any sport badly. The exception was John Butler, who replaced Archie Mulford as Stratford High School's best football carrier, and to boot, unbeatable in chess. John Butler was acknowledged by all to be the best Christian, even though he was a Catholic. Nobody could make John Butler swear and he never told a dirty joke. He was from a family of ten children raised by a widower father, who lived on Bay Street. John and his siblings were poor in this world's goods, but rich in character. Small wonder they all did so well. However, I do not wish to paint John Butler as a perfect kid, he was equal to the best of our shenanigans but always the gentleman. This we accepted with good grace since to be in John's circle of friends was our guarantee of safety against those wannabe bullies who didn't dare to mess with John, the strongest kid on Bay Street. Jim Johnston would have been just as good an athlete as John, but he was short. Which brings up the topic of my athleticism, or, what little there was of it. When we chose up sides for baseball, my crowning achievement was to be chosen second last, because that meant there was at least one guy worse than me, even if he was five years my junior.

There was no improvement for me when I played organized hockey. While Jack Ross played centre, I wound off playing bench despite the fact that I could skate. Stick handling with the puck was another matter.

To aggravate my self-esteem in athletic matters (or lack thereof) Jim Johnston had three sisters, who were good enough to make the Stratford Rotinettes fastball team sponsored by the Rotary Club. In my mind, I figured that getting a girl to like you meant you had to be good at sports. I'm in trouble already! Years later, Helen Haynes, also an athlete, who played senior girls fastball told me,

"You were the handsomest boy." If I had only known that, my life might have been so different. Alas, belated information is of no help. In the meantime, I could only envy guys like Bud Haviling, a terrific baseball pitcher, and wish I had been born of better stuff.

Concerning the subject of girls, Iceland melted in 10 months and I am introduced to 'vex' education. I refer to Eileen Johns. One day when the warm sunshine illumined her long flowing black hair, there she was. Gorgeous as CNN's Lynne Russel (before she dyed her hair red and went to work for the CBC) was Eileen. Eileen's dad owned a taxi business on Ontario Street, and she was at least five years older than my tender twelve. Of course, my romance with Eileen was pure fantasy, so I had to imagine in daydreams, how I was as strong as superman rescuing Eileen from danger. You can imagine my joy, when in the summer of 1943, her sister Muriel was vacationing at Bogie's beach, at the same time as I was. At least I could meet her sister. Muriel's great claim to fame was that she spoke fluent pig Latin. For unlettered readers, this is done by speaking English and mixing up the vowels so that the uninformed (guys like me), couldn't understand a word. All of which seemed to delight Muriel and her girlfriend and frustrate me.

Then there was Lois Vrooman with her long blond curls; I used to ride by her house after school on my bike just to see them again. She wrecked my affection for her the day she ruined her hair by getting a permanent wave. However, since I never told her about my addiction to her curls, not too much harm was done, if she even knew I existed at all. Then there was Anita Greenfield, a slender, statuesque beauty with flashing brown eyes and olive skin. That fire was put out the day her brother Rocky, our schoolyard bully, punched me for no reason at all, (names here are changed for my protection; Rocky may still be around). When Rocky looked my way, it took my feet three minutes to stop vibrating. Rocky punched a lot of guys, and had us all in terror including Jim Johnston. Thank goodness for Don Hutchison who kept an eye out for guys like me, or the schoolyard wouldn't be safe. To return to our topic, Lois Sewell was a class act all on her own. In grade 8 she occupied the seat in front of Patsy Stewart. Patsy sat beside me and was the smartest girl in the class. I was, however, in those days more attracted to beauty than to brains.

Now in the great beyond Pan whispers to Puck and Puck nods his head in agreement. These two have a bad habit of collaborating to make my life miserable. There's girl trouble afoot for me and I can't do a thing to defend myself. Shamed, my guardian angel turns in his resignation, but Gabriel refuses to accept it. I suspect he is as awkward about girls as I am. For example, I inveigle mother to give me a special birthday party and script the invitees including pretty Lois Sewell. Three guys and three girls! Royce Clark and Don Kelly already have their girlfriends, so I'm counting on Lois to get the hint. Naturally, Lois sits beside me for the meal. My reward for giving Lois my heart is speedily requited. From that day forward, she never spoke to me again, except for the day I stopped wearing groovy Corduroy knickers and exchanged them for long pants. I was so proud to wear those long pants to class in Grade eight. Not many kids in my class wore long pants. I can still see them hanging in my closet complete with a two button fly (zippers were a luxury yet unknown). Confidence wilts quickly under the scorn of a woman. Lois Sewell breaks her stoney silence.

"Look at Bruce, he's all grown up now, wearing long pants." she mocks. Women can be cruel! The gods of puppy love have no mercy and my guardian Angel is ignoring me again.

Pat Wilkes was pretty, and so I decided to fall in love with her, but that didn't work. Mainly, because she wasn't interested, and also because I was having too much fun with the guys. However, for the record, let it be known that I did like looking at pretty girls. I guess with all this girl watching, you may conclude as I did, "If God made girls this beautiful, it was my religious duty to admire them." I was entering the threshold of that enchanted ground, where I wanted to hang around after school so I could join the girls who were good at skipping rope, but would have been embarrassed to talk to any of them, one on one. I remember one day after school the girls had allowed the boys to join in on the secrets of skipping rope and I later said to mother.

"You should see Margery Litt skipping rope. She is amazing at double Dutch." I tried it once and that was enough for me. You have to be good to skip like that."

-o0o-

It was a hot day in June. Jim and I had just returned home from school. Next came a rendezvous with John Butler.

"Let's go swimming!" said Johnny.

"Where?" I reply.

"Behind the old swimming house at the park, I just found out about it," says Johnny.

"I don't have my bathing suit," I moan.

"Don't need it," says John Butler.

"What if somebody sees us?" I query.

"Nobody will see us, c'mon let's go."

With the heat of that sweltering day, I need little persuasion. We are off to the swimming hole, which can still be seen by the railroad trestle bridge, west of Romeo Street. We make our way down Snake Hill on our bikes. Soon we are behind the old swimming house, which is closed and in disrepair (it is now torn down). Murphy, who is younger, has volunteered to come along as lookout. Soon we are in the buff, and just under the sign that says, 'No swimming by Order,' we dive in. The water is delectable and warm. After about 15 minutes, Murph comes running,

"There's three girls walking down the railroad tracks; you guys are in trouble." Now, it's one thing to be arrested by the police for swimming where it is forbidden, but to be seen naked by girls would be the ultimate humiliation. We need no further motivation. Out faster than when we went in, dry clothes are on, over wet skin. We only need to put on our socks, when three older teen-age girls spot us. One of them says,

"You're not supposed to be swimming here, can't you read?"

"What makes you think we were swimming," we chorus.

"Look, we don't have any bathing suits."

"C'mon, your hair is wet. If we had come sooner, we'd have caught you red-handed." We shudder at the thought.

"If you know what's good for you, you'd better be out of here," says the stocky one."

"You're lucky the police didn't catch you first," says another.

We need no further persuasion. However, mounted on our bikes, once our backs are turned, we can hear them laughing. "At our expense, I thought." As we make our way home, we speculate on which would be worse, a life behind bars or to have been caught naked by three girls. We decide on the latter. We are not deterred from frequent visits to the old swimming hole. We have several close calls but never once got caught.

Hot summers and a fella's yen to swim leads to exploration.

"The swimming at Rosenor's gravel pit is terrific and the water's a lot warmer than at the Lion's pool. What's more, it's free." said Squirt MacDonald one sunny day. With news like that, we planned a bicycle trip north on Huron and then right to the gravel pit on O'Loane. For the unlettered, gravel pits are not supposed to have water, but every now and again Cupid's second job kicks in, and just for the sake of kids, he redirects those underground streams to gravel pits. This forces the road makers to look elsewhere for gravel and opens up a little touch of paradise for kids who love to use them for swimming holes in the summer and skating rinks in the winter. How we loved to bask in those warm-water gravel pits with no bathing suits, keeping one eye out for girls. Today the swimming holes we loved are gone. Filled in and covered over with a subdivision; those brick bungalows cover hidden secrets, which, if they could be revealed, are filled with the laughter of kids who lived in an era unlike any other.

The Tuer's farm on the northwest side of town also had swimming, but the water was not as clear as the gravel pit and every now and again one felt the fish nipping at one's toes. Today it has suffered the same fate as the gravel pit and is simply known as Matilda Street. Old man Tuer was okay with unknown kids swimming on his farm, but he could turn into a grouch when we forgot to close the gate to keep the cows in. I suffered one such verbal barrage that I will never forget. Farmer Tuer's lecture had its effect. I now have a great respect for cows.

Eventually we heard about the St. Mary's Quarry. Tales of its fabulous swimming were recounted to us by the older boys. We determined to be numbered with the jocks. It was an all day excursion riding our bikes for the two-hour junket to St. Mary's. After the usual ups and downs of the highway, riding into St. Mary's was fine because the town sits in a valley. The way we sped down that steep road into town was downright dangerous, and in those days, no helmets! It was the ride up the other side that was so demanding. We had to walk our bikes up the far side, but the prize was well worth the effort. On arrival, we ate our lunches and basked in the sunshine for the necessary half-hour wait before swimming. The common myth that if you swam before you digested your lunch, you would get cramps and drown, was believed by all. The water was indeed warmer than the Lion's pool but not as warm as the delectable waters of the Rosenor's. Thirty feet deep is what we were told, maybe deeper. Its size was immense and we revelled in the challenge. Since there was no diving board, with real difficulty we scaled the overarching cliff twenty feet up and plunged into the water below. After a day at the St. Mary's quarry, there was still the arduous ride home, 12 miles in all. Tired but happy we ate our suppers in our various homes bragging to our parents about the achievement of the day. Years later a wiseacre saw a good thing and bought the quarry, built a diving tower and charged admission. In our day it was free. Then things changed again and it is now owned by the town of St. Marys and available to the public.

In the end, the Lion's Swimming Pool won out over all other competitors. The reason was quite simple. The three metre diving board! The competition to master the jack knife gave way to ever increasingly difficult diving feats. Johnny and I never tired of working on our double dive. Johnny would stand on his hands at the end of the diving board while I grabbed his ankles holding them firm. Next Johnny would grab my ankles while we teetered precariously for a second before the plunge. The other dive we worked on was for Johnny to spring upward with his legs spread eagled apart while I in hot pursuit dove between his legs. He would land on my back and together like rider and horse we rode into the water below. We pretty well had these two dives down pat when someone trying the same thing got hurt. After that, we were forbidden to do any double diving. My abrupt departure from Stratford in 1948 ended my diving career. John Butler developed into a competitive diver but none of us ever caught up to the illustrious Bobby Easson who eventually competed at the Canadian National Exhibition.

The Gang: Vince Schooley, Jim Johnston, Allan McKone, Bummer Bolton, John Butler, Wilf Butler and me Murph Murphy (front).

Chapter 20

Brunswick Street War Hero

My buddy Jim Johnston has a brother, George. George and his St. Mary's buddy Johnny Aikens enlisted in the Canadian Royal Airforce when they were only eighteen. At the time George was sweet on Margaret Holleroyd. Margaret, like thousands of others, shed her tears knowing that a beloved boyfriend was off to war. The oft repeated separations spawned a spate of war songs that we loved to sing as we heard them over the radio. From a soldier's point of view, the song 'Don't sit under the apple tree with anyone else but me' was a favourite. From the viewpoint of the ladies, I remember a fun song written by Frank Loesser. How I laughed, when I saw Hollywood bombshell, Betty Hutton in a movie singing,

They're either too young, or too old,
They're either too gray or too grassy green.
The pickings are poor and the crop is lean
What's good is in the army,
What's left will never harm me.

They're either too old or too young,
So, darling, you'll never get stung.
Tomorrow I'll go hiking with that Eagle Scout unless
I get a call from grandpa for a snappy game of chess.

They're either too bald or too bold,
I'm down to the wheelchair or the bassinet,
The gravy's in the navy,
What's left will never save me.

I'm either their first breath of spring,
Or else, I'm their last little fling.
I either get a fossil or an adolescent pup,
I either have to hold them off,
Or have to hold them up.
The battle is on, but the fortress will hold,
They're either too young, or too old.

George Johnston and Johnny Aikens flew bombing missions over Germany in the War. George had the very dangerous job of tailgunner, flying in a four-engine Halifax bomber. For every tail gunner that survived the war, there were three who died. George was one of the lucky ones. Upon returning from a bombing mission early in 1943, his plane was shot down over Dunkirk. Once the aircraft was hit the pilot lost control. From now on, it was every man for himself. George and those who could, bailed out. The pilot and the navigator were killed in the crash. When George released his exit door, as he jumped, his boot caught in the jam. Plummeting quickly to the earth, George is dangling by his boot against the fuselage of the bomber that is now wildly out of control. Somehow, by an incredible rush of strength, he pulled himself back, freed his foot and jumped again. Altogether there were four men who parachuted free from the doomed bomber. George was one of the three who were captured. The assumption is that a fourth man was assisted by the French underground to escape and fight again. Having bailed out of an airplane that was lost, George and many others were now entitled to membership in the 'Caterpillar Club'. Have you ever watched a tent caterpillar ride his parachute to the ground in June?

1944, the crew of an ill fated Halifax Bomber, between the two officers, Johnny Aiken and George Johnston [without cap]

Before this last mission, George had paid for flowers to be sent to his parents and to Margaret for Valentine's Day. The Johnstons got the news that he was missing in action on Wednesday February 9th. The flowers arrived three days later on Saturday, February 12. The order of events played out as follows. Mrs. Johnston had taken the train to Bothwell to visit her mother. On her return, there was a wait at London that would lengthen things by an hour. Solution! Take the bus. Mrs. Johnston did exactly that. Meantime, a young man was on his bicycle with a telegram containing the news that George was missing in action. When Mr. Johnston answered the door and saw the telegram delivery boy he was already trembling. Wasting no time, he tore open the envelope and read the dreaded news. Standing behind him on her toes, fifteen-year old daughter Dorothy is following word for word. Immediately, James Johnston Sr. is weeping,

"My poor boy, my poor boy!" Seventeen-year old sister Kathleen was also listening in disbelief, tears flowing as Dad Johnston read the telegram again. My friend Jim Jr., now twelve, sat in stunned silence. Immediately Kathleen slipped on her coat and bolted through the door. Kathleen just needed to be alone for a while. Needless to say, there were many tears shed in the Johnston home and a great deal of concern for how Mrs. Johnston would take the news. Dad Johnston and Kathleen walked to the CNR Station where they were expecting Mrs. Johnston to arrive by train. Their efforts to cushion the blow for Charlotte Johnston were in vain. She was already walking down Brunswick Street as her husband was heading up Front Street to the train Station. When Charlotte Johnston failed to show up, they walked home again to discover Mrs. Johnston had arrived and was informed. She surprised her family by her Christian faith, and exhibiting an inner strength that comforted everyone.

"He's alive and he will come back to us," said the redoubtable Mrs. Johnston.

"But how do you know George is alive?" Dorothy asked. Her reply was short but memorable:

"Mothers just know!"

Two days later The Stratford Beacon-Herald carried the story under the caption, 'Flying Buddies Missing in Acton.' The first inkling of hope came in a letter from England written by George's flight commander only two weeks later. It was a personal letter written to the family. He had seen four parachutes open up from the stricken plane. The Johnstons now knew that four of the six-man crew had successfully bailed out. Early in March, nine weeks later, 'the unforgettable letter' arrived. To the relief of the family, the Red Cross confirmed that George had safely parachuted out of his plane. Captured by the Germans, he was now a prisoner of war. One of the ironies of the European war was the role of the Red Cross, which added a touch of humanity to an otherwise inhuman conflagration. Respected by both sides, the Red Cross included good people from every nation trying to make life better in what was an unspeakable tragedy. They were at work on George's behalf. Under their supervision, his captors had allowed George to write a brief note. With trembling hands and gratitude in her heart, Mrs. Johnston read these words.

"I am now a prisoner of war in Belgium. Parachuted to safety when our plane was shot down. Don't worry about me. See you after the war is over — Love, George."

Life in the POW camp was harsh for both prisoners and their German guards. George related how he actually felt as sorry for his captors as he did for himself. George and many others, including his guards survived on meager fare. Onion soup was their staple. George later related how the guys would pray that a stray bomb would kill a few horses so the prisoners and the guards could get some meat. There is no record of this ever really happening; it was just the longings of hungry men. Miraculously, after five and a half months, in a Red Cross prisoner of war exchange, George made it back. First to England and then after a long convalescence in an English hospital, he boarded a troopship to Canada in 1944. The long train ride home included a stop in Montreal to see his Aunt Maggie who phoned ahead to tell Charlotte the exact time George would arrive in Stratford. George had planned to surprise the family by simply showing up at the door. It was summertime and the weather was warm. Tipped off in advance, the whole family and a few friends were at the CNR Station to greet their returning hero. His sister Joan, was the first to see him,

"There he is!" (An unforgettable day to be sure) The stationmaster quipped, "The way that family attacked him with hugs and kisses, I didn't know whether to congratulate him or feel sorry for him."

In 1945, Flight Sargent G. W. Johnston R272572 volunteered for the Pacific War but, by then, hostilities had come to an abrupt conclusion. George was our Brunswick Street hero, and I was proud to have Johnny, his kid brother as my best friend. His had been an unimaginable nightmare, yet he had lived to tell the tale. Johnny Aikens who also had been assigned to the same aircraft shared with his buddy the same amazing story of near death, gruelling endurance, and survival. George and Johnny were lifelong friends, who like so many others, rarely spoke of their wartime experiences.

Well do I remember when I first met the handsome George Johnston; it was a Sunday afternoon after the Johnston family dinner. They were all still dressed in their church clothes right down to seven-year-old Tommy, who looked really cute in his two piece suit. It was the summer of 1944, and there was George Johnston, alive and well. It was just like Resurrection Sunday. He who had been feared dead was with us in the flesh and back at home in Stratford. Frolic was in the air. George was standing on the front porch swinging his seven-year old little brother Tommy back and forth as though he would pitch him right off the veranda. Of course he had him firmly in his grasp right under the arms. Tommy didn't seem to mind; he, along with the rest of us, was laughing, enjoying the occasion. The hidden celebration underlay every casual remark. George was home safe — and that's what mattered.

Later his story was told in The Stratford Beacon Herald. I remember reading the account and thinking, "That's my best friend's older brother." One statement George made was, for me, unforgettable. George had casually remarked to one of the German guards,

"I sure will be glad when this war is over." The German guard responded, "And so will we!"

When I read that, a revelation dawned on me. These German guards are human; perhaps the German people are too. Maybe the Germans are just like us after all.

Chapter 21

Minefields: Guys and Girls, etc.

Mother is on a tear against Grandma again. I have heard it so many times before, I have it memorized.

"You never taught me. I was ignorant of the world. It's your fault I made so many mistakes. You never told me what men are like etc., etc." This time it seems to be worse. Poor Grandma is trembling. Mother will not relent. Finally, I have had enough. It is bedtime. With pajamas in hand, I throw them into mother's face. I miss, they hit her chest.

"I can't stand the way you talk to Grandma; stop it, it's not true, she's not to blame for your troubles!" Grandma is relieved to have help. Mother is stunned at the boldness of her twelve-year-old son, but it works. We retire to our beds in silence. I think to myself, "To blame others for our own mistakes is the most destructive lie that a person can believe." In time, mother will be so convinced of this lie that she cannot be persuaded to the contrary, no matter who tells her so.

The next day is Sunday; mother asks me if I would like to have a hot chicken sandwich at the Mayfair restaurant at 20 Wellington Street.

"I sure would," I reply. So Grandma goes to St. Andrew's Presbyterian Church, and we leave a little later for the restaurant.

I like to look into the mirrors at the booth where we are sitting. They reflect in kind the same mirrors across the aisle. It seems to me that you can see through them indefinitely into infinity, because they reflect each other so perfectly. I wonder, if you knew the secret, perhaps you could travel forever through those mirrors. But then how would you get back? I shudder and decide to stay right here where I am. Pretty soon our dinner arrives. It is my favourite, white chicken, (I don't like dark meat), between white bread slices, and white mashed potatoes, smothered in rich brown gravy. I savour the meal. It cost 25 cents; that's 50 cents for the both of us and there is no tip. We never heard of such a thing in those days.

Photo taken by mom in 1946.

We are going for a walk by the Avon River with a visit to the Shakespearean Gardens. Mother has her Brownie box camera. She will take my picture, and we will stroll down the river. Today she has planned a surprise for me. We walk towards the old boathouse, which has long since been replaced, and rent a canoe. The price is 50 cents for an hour. This is a new experience for me and I am excited at the prospect. The attendant holds the cedar canoe tightly, while mother and I take our places. I get to paddle at the back, which means I do the steering. We quickly turn in circles and are clearly out of control. We laugh and try again until I get the hang of it. Soon we are paddling under the Waterloo Bridge. I sense the power of it all. We defy the murky depths, where last year, I saw a young man drown. The memory of his limp body lying by the paramedics, who failed to revive him, is still with me. He grew up on a farm south of Sebringville and was a friend of Harold Erb. His name was Eddie Appel.

Graceful swans glide by, accepting our presence as a matter of routine. I am thinking, "If I were a swan I could explore every nook and cranny of the Avon and all its tributaries." A swan's eye view would surely be a revelation. Soon we are at the Island, and pass under the arching bridge. I could go on forever, but mother reminds me that we are running out of time, and we have to return. We make for the lagoon, and squeeze our way under the footbridges. Soon, we're back to the Waterloo Bridge. The hour has gone too quickly. I beg mother to go again, next week. She promises me we will. It has been a wonderful day. We walk, chatting as we go up Coburg Street. The tennis courts are on our left and we watch a game in progress. Tiring of this we continue to Nile. As we make our way back home via Nile Street, a lady we pass happens to cough. Mother's face straightens!

"Did you hear that woman cough at me?" she questions. A loaded statement! I know only too well what mother means, and I firmly intend to disabuse her imagined insult.

"Mom, that woman was not coughing at you!" I sternly reply.

"She just coughed, and that's all there is to it." I assume mother's silence is assent. I don't even want to think about it. I dismiss it from my mind. I am not aware that mother cannot. The self-deception is spreading. Mother is helpless against her disease. She imagines that others, aware of her past, disapprove, and are talking

Later, I spill the beans with Aunt Elsie, imagining that this will be the first time that Elsie will have heard about mother's bizarre behaviour and tell Uncle Gordon. To my surprise my disclosure is not news. Children suppose that nobody can invade their private world unless they tell; which I am loath to do. On that occasion Elsie says to me,

"Your mother was a wonderful woman, kind and generous. I think her troubles all began with the divorce. She is so different from the person she used to be. The truth is, she is still in love with your father but that cannot be remedied." Elsie has told me this before but until now, it hadn't registered. This time it does and I remember how startled I am at Aunt Elsie's evaluation. "My mother still in love with my father!" The idea of it has never sunk in until now. Children are preoccupied with themselves. The adult world of tortured emotions is still ahead of them. I have just been given a window into a world that is prematurely beginning to open up to me. I didn't dwell on this revelation at the time. In later years, however, I have often thought about it. The complex world of unrequited love is a destructive force. It is a foreboding mystery. For the present, I postpone investigation.

The year is 1944. It has been thirteen years since the divorce. My father and mother have never so much, as laid eyes on one another. Sooner or later the meeting was destined to take place. It occurs in the most unlikely of circumstances.

"How would you like to go to the Canadian National Exhibition?" Mother's voice is cheerful. She loves to surprise me with special events. Later that week, we are on the train and heading for the C.N.E. There are extra coaches for the crowds that are making their way to the granddaddy of all Canadian Fall Fairs. From the station we take the bus and join the crowds of happy spectators heading for the Ex.

First we go to the midway, where once again my mother spoils me with all the rides I want to take. Finally, when at last boredom is beginning to set in, mother takes me to the Manufacturer's Building where all the things we cannot buy can be seen, but are still not for sale. With the war's end in sight, the manufacturing moguls, with an eye on the prosperity that is bound to come, are prepared. They have on display models of everything they intend to make for the commodity starved consumer. As we round the bend of one display, mother spots a sign that says Electrolux Vacuum Cleaners.

"Come on Brucie, I want to look at these;" as she points to the vacuum display. The friendly attendant who has his back turned senses a customer and turns around. The attendant turns out to be my father!

Totally unplanned and completely by surprise my mother and father meet after thirteen years. At age 39, they both cut a striking figure. After the initial shock, they politely chat while I listen. I finally get a chance to ask my question, which upon reflection I suspect was far from the thoughts that might have been on their minds.

"Why do manufacturers display their wares when it is impossible to buy anything they make in stores?"

My father explains to me that things will change after war's end. The burning questions that might have been on my parents' minds were never asked. Nor did those questions occur to me until much later. Afterwards, I asked my mother, what she thought after meeting my father like that after all those years? I wish I could remember her answer. It is gone from my memory. How I would like to ask that one again, but I can't; I can only imagine, but in my mind's eye, I can visualize two locks of golden blonde hair in mother's jewel box.

Eighteen months later, right out of the blue, mother receives a long distance phone call from Toronto. It is the unmistakable voice of Bruce Woods Sr. His new post war business, 'The Rock Wool Insulation Co.', has landed him a contract to insulate the Majestic Theatre, which is undergoing renovations. He will be in Stratford for two days with his crew of men. Could he take Bruce Jr. out for dinner? Mother agrees. Naturally, I am pleased to know that my father is now a successful businessman, and even hires men to work for him; just wait till I tell my friends. The day comes at last, and my father meets me at the Majestic. After the renovations were completed, the name was changed to the Avon Theatre.

Now mother always took me to the movies every Monday night; it was a ritual. I had never seen what was beyond those familiar walls. This evening at 6 P.M. was to be my baptism to the unknown. Dad, (it was so hard to call him that), took me up a back set of stairs. Soon we were making our way over the ceiling of the theatre.

"Stick to the gangplank," my father explained, "or you'll go right through the plaster, to the seats below." I shudder at the thought. I need no further warning.

The blower is on the truck outside. Long hoses connect one to another, until they reach the interior of the building. Rock wool, a by-product made from slag, the refuse of a Sudbury steel mill, is spewing out onto the hidden side of the theatre ceiling, disturbing the accumulated dust of years. The miserable job of guiding the hose is in the hands of a workman, with a facemask to shield him from the dust. I stand as far away from the racket as I can.

"We're late," says Dad, "We'll go to dinner, as soon as we are finished." Three hours later a very bored and hungry fourteen-year old gets to go to the restaurant with his Dad and the workmen. Dad is on a diet and orders a 16-ounce T-bone steak with no vegetables or potatoes. He seems to think this is good for his health, apparently it tasted OK, but I order my favourite, a hot chicken sandwich. Later, when I finally get home, mother asks me, how it went. I reply,

"Boring." For some reason, mother seems to be pleased.

-oOo-

Mrs. Goulding is one of mother's rich patrons. She informs mother she is on a committee that is organizing a teenage dance in the Blue Room on Market Square. Price is ten cents. I am excited because I love to dance. As a kid, I would pretend to tap dance, making a racket with my feet for the entertainment of mother's patrons. I also loved to ice skate. It was not enough for me just to ice skate; I had to speed around the ice surface faster than most. I guess you might say the fairy godmother of athleticism at the last minute, in a moment of compassion, had a change of heart and touched her wand to my feet. I was a passable athlete when it came to feet, and could high jump four feet. Later to my chagrin, I discovered playing hockey required more than ice-skating. I was a lousy stick handler. My feet, however — that is another matter.

The exciting day of the teen dance arrives and I am ready. Most of the girls that will be there are taller than I. I have solved this problem. I have made two wooden wedges for my shoes. Starting from nothing they thicken up till at the heel, I have gained almost 2 inches. They are impossibly uncomfortable, but I determine to manage. In the end, I ditch the wooden lifts. Too clumsy! I have a new respect for girls that wear high heels. I return from the dance and tell mother all about the good time I had. Mother smiles and says,

"I loved to dance." Astonished, that mother even danced at all, I reply,

"You mean that you used to dance?"

"Sure I did; remember I was young once, just like you."

"I suppose I understand." I reply, thinking, "Imagine, my mother out there dancing." My words do not match the incredulity that registers on my face. Seeing her son's disbelief despite my verbal agreement, mother astounds me even more by singing and doing a dance.

"Everybody do the Michigan Rag
Everybody likes the Michigan Rag.
Maine and Jane and Ruth, from Weehawken to Duluth;
Slide Ride Glide the Michigan.
Stomp, romp, pump the Michigan Rag;
That 'lovin' Rag."

Mother astounds her doubting son by standing up and dancing the Charleston. Her arms and legs are flying and her knees and feet are going every which direction. I am stunned at her performance.

"Wow, mom, can you ever dance." I exclaim. "Teach me how to do that." She tries to show me but I soon discover that I've got some learning to do if I want to dance the Charleston.

"If you can do that kind of dancing, mom, maybe you could teach me to Jitterbug. That's what all the kids are doing."

"I don't know how to Jitterbug," mother says.

"Maybe I don't want to learn how to do the Charleston; nobody dances that way any more, but would I ever love to learn how to jitterbug."

I retire to my bed that evening thinking that mother in her time must have cut quite a figure on the dance floor. "I'll bet she could learn the steps to the Jitterbug if she took the notion to try it." However mother's brief debut ends the same day it began. Perhaps it revived some forgotten memories of happier times that could never be restored. That's the last time I ever saw her dance. I put the whole thing out of my mind and think of nothing but the teen dance all week. And that's when they drop the bomb! The teen dance is a rousing success. In fact, it is so successful, that the Fire Marshall tells the organizers, they must cut down the attendance. The solution is to limit the dance to kids 14 and up. I am so furious at the rule that I determine to lie. The following week, the lady at the admission table asks my age.

"Fourteen." I reply. Alas, lying is not my strong suit and it must have shown.

"You're not fourteen," she says. Beside her, standing at her shoulder was the persnickety Mrs. Goulding.

"Bruce Woods, you are thirteen and you cannot come until you're old enough!" Mortified, head hanging, I descend the stairs to the street. Obscenities fly under my breath all the way home. When at last I make it through the door of my house, I cannot hold it in any longer. Grandma asks,

"Why are you crying?" I cannot help it. I cuss even in Grandma's presence. (Oh no, I should have known).
Grandma assails me,

"Thou shalt not take the name of the Lord Thy God in vain, for He will not hold him guiltless etc." I have a lot of sins to confess in my prayers that night.

On a Saturday night, from now on, I go ice-skating at the arena and stride to the rhythm of the Skater's Waltz. Those were the days when the disc jockey played decent music. I skate with a few girls, but it's not as much fun as dancing. However, poetic justice comes to my rescue; the following January, the Blue Room has a fire, and is no longer available for anybody. Now nobody gets to dance. Misery loves company. I think to myself, "If I can't dance, nobody dances." Now for all those suspicious minds, I'll have you to know; I had nothing to do with the lighting of that fire.

-oOo-

In summer we swim at the Lion's pool or, on Sundays, at the gravel pit just north of the city. In winter we swim at the YMCA. This winter, Butler, Johnny, Vince and I are on the way to the Y. The building (now replaced) is on Downie Street at St. Patrick, right across from St. Paul's Anglican Church, which is still standing.

We pay our dimes and open the door that leads downstairs to the pool. You can smell the chlorine. The hot vapour hits you the moment you open the door. The pool is only 20 by 40 feet and is heated by a tunnel connected to the CNR shops. The temperature of the pool is 90 degrees Fahrenheit (32 Celsius). It seems that in this case the problem is too much heat. The pool is always hot. We swim in the buff, without benefit of swimsuits; we only need a towel, no girls here. We pass the muscle guys, who are building beef. First, we have to take a cold shower. Then we jump into the pool, which feels like the equator. In this case, one has to adjust to the heat. The Lion's pool was always kept at 69 or 70 degrees (19 Celsius). In that case, you have to adjust to the cool water. No problems like that at the Y. After the swim, John Butler, who is the strongest of the four of us, grabs the water hose. (It is a rule that every half-hour we are to hose down the cement patio beside the pool, to prevent disease). We know what's coming, so we quickly do damage control. He intends to turn the hose on us, as soon as we try to leave the pool. Cold water against warm skin! John is only "obeying the rules," he says (tongue in cheek). Somehow the cold spray wanders a bit, and hits us broadside. We scream and run into the change room for protection. After the all clear, we re-enter the pool area, and try (now that we're dry) to push each other into the pool. When we tire of the horseplay, we dry off and dress.

Next, we make our way upstairs to the billiard tables. For a nickel you can play one game of spots and stripes. It's a good pastime to let our hair dry, before we go out into the January winter. The roads are snow packed smooth and great for hitching a car bumper and sliding on the snow pack. When it's time to go home, we decide that if a convenient car bumper is available, we will grab a ride. Luck is with us. There is a car warming up just ahead. We sneak up and take hold of the bumper. The driver doesn't seem to be in a hurry. This should have been our warning. Usually, when drivers see kids coming they warn us off; or take off quickly, so we can't hitch onto a bumper. Suddenly our cooperative driver guns his motor. Black smoke and oil comes belching out the tailpipe. Jim Johnston who is directly behind, screams. He is plastered with oil and smoke. Butler gets a bit as well. I am safely out of line, so I come off OK. The driver rolls down his window, laughs at us, and drives off. We fail to see the humour.

"That old crock of a car is burning oil," Vince says. "He did that deliberately — the bastard!" Our immediate concern is for Johnny.

He's got to face his parents. They won't be happy if he's ruined his coat.

The following day, we ask Johnny, "What did your parents say?"

"They were none too happy," but Johnny adds, "They did manage to clean my coat."

"Is that all?" we query.

"Nope," Johnny says. "They told me if I try that again, I will be in serious trouble.

We are all reformed delinquents. We never hitch a ride behind a car again.

-oOo-

February, 1945. Clarkie has asked me to his house party. The marvels of technology have brought us an invention that has surpassed the Victrola, which a few of us can afford. For ten dollars you can buy a 78-rpm record player and attach it to your radio. Records can be purchased for a dollar and you can have dance music for a house party. I am to invite the girl of my choice, and bring her along. The fortunate young girl turns out to be Loreen Jeffery, who sits two seats in front of me in grade eight. She lives in an apartment above Tamblyn's Drug Store on Downie Street.

My 13th birthday party - Loreen Jeffery on left, Lois Sewell in the centre, Royce Clarke in the foreground.

I'm dressed in the best suit and tie I own, and knock at her door at 7:15 P.M. We walk the two and a half blocks to Clarkie's house arriving at 7:30 PM. We dance to the latest records. There are lots of dance tunes; this is the big band era.

Clarkie has discovered a game. He gives the girls even numbers; the boys get odd numbers. He starts off the game by going into the kitchen, where the lights are turned off. He calls an even number. The girl who has that number goes into the kitchen, and they kiss. Now it is the girl's turn to call a number. She calls an odd number.

"It's my number." I exclaim. "Wow, I get to kiss a girl, and it's legal." I like this game.

External evidence, that I'm a normal guy. After a while, a light lunch is served, and it's time to go home. I say to Loreen as we're leaving,

"Yawanna have me walk you home?" She replies,

"If you don't want to, it's OK." I think, "Good, I'm not in the mood to walk the extra distance." Internal evidence that I've got a lot to learn. We say a friendly goodbye (I thought), and we go our separate ways. When I arrive home, I tell mother and Grandma all about the party. I mention in passing,

"I didn't bother to walk Loreen home." They are scandalized.

"Didn't walk the girl home," they chorus together,

"that's dreadful!" Grandma says to me,

"Didn't you call on her?" Mother adds,

"Where is your sense of honour?" I hadn't told them until about 15 minutes after I had arrived home, or perhaps I could have remedied the situation. By now she would have been home. By the time Grandma and mother chew me out, I feel about one inch high. That night, as I retire to my bed, with my fists, I pound the pillow. The next day at school, I try to be very friendly to Loreen. I get a chilly reception to prepare me for winter.

The winter of '45/'46, the 'let's go downtown' phenomenon hit Stratford. The idea was born in Detroit with the Zoot Suit. The Zoot Suit was draped at the knees and ankle tight above the shoes. A large gold chain hung from a belt loop to a pocket watch kept in your pants pocket. Clarkie and I both got Zoot Suits that year and would head downtown to show them off just like everybody else. Dressed up with flashy ties, we suppose we are the ultimate. We didn't have a chain and watch; that was too expensive. We walk downtown with our winter overcoats left unbuttoned and fedora hats tilted back, because that's the way it is done. The girls also flocked downtown wearing their best. Eschewing stockings, on the coldest day, there they were; bare legs in winter, because that was the style. We would congregate in chat groups at Wing's Café and order a Coke. After we had worn out our welcome at Wing's, we would cross the road and repeat the process all over again at Wong's Café, talking movies, the latest styles, and just hanging out. The idea was to see and be seen, and of course, talk to the girls. I guess Loreen Jeffery must have finally got around to forgiving me because I remember talking to Loreen as well as all the rest. After paying for expensive restaurant Cokes, we always saved a dime for the best bargain in town. A ten-cent butterscotch sundae at the Jumbo Ice Cream Parlour!

Chapter 22

Victory Day Celebrations, 1945

We all knew it was coming. Germany was in the death throes of defeat. We were listening to the six o'clock daily news. It was March 17 and in one last desperate attempt to defend Germany, Hitler had all the bridges destroyed that spanned the Rhine River. There was one exception. Drunk and in despair, the soldiers at the Remagen railroad bridge failed at their task. The bridge stood up for seven days before it collapsed. Enough time for the Americans to put four divisions on the East bank of the river. As we listened to the news that day we cheered. I remember dancing a jig to think that it had all been so easy.

By April we learned that the Russians were inside the Berlin defenses. The Allies were poised to link up near Prague. Every day in May brought us closer to V-E Day in Europe, especially when we heard about the death of Hitler. Officially V-E Day was June 8 but the news that Germany had surrendered came on Monday May 7. For those not glued to the radio, the signal came when the CNR shops blew the factory whistle at 2 P.M. McLagan's was not far behind. Next it was Kroehler's. A few church bells started up. Car horns were blasting. One by one, the factories were closing down, and the men were on the street, celebrating. I am now in grade eight. Our teacher is principal George Pauli. When he announced to the class that school would be released early, we had two reasons to cheer. The first was obvious, the second had more meaning. At long last, after five and a half war-weary years, the dreadful thing was over. True, Japan was still to be faced, but now their doom was sealed. We knew nothing at that time about the atomic bomb. Pundits were predicting one to two years to go. That would include Uncle Norman, who was due to be shipped west with his unit to Vancouver. None of this mattered just then. The big one was over, and it was time to celebrate.

With supper finished early, I team up with Jim Johnston to go downtown. We know that's where the action will be. Already the city has been rejoicing. Some are laughing and others are crying. As if by magic, the Boys' Band has appeared that afternoon, and has been playing. As we are heading downtown, a pickup truck slows down, and somebody hollers out,

"Jump in!" There is at least a dozen riding in the box and they quickly make room for us. We are shouting at the top of our lungs. As we close in on the City Hall square, we grind to a halt. People have spilled into the street. All traffic is gridlock. Deciding it is more fun to walk; Jim and I jump out of the truck and join the surging crowd. There are flags everywhere. No one is going in any particular direction, we just want to see how many kids we know, and greet one another with a cheer. Now the CNR Band has assembled and is playing. Somewhere the crowd is singing, 'Don't fence Me In.' A couple is dancing the Jitterbug. The young ladies are still in the majority, but the thought that the boys will be home again is exhilarating. They are to be found in happy groups chatting and laughing. They are sweater girls with their hair coiffured in pompadours. It is a general happy-go-lucky melee and everybody is having fun.

The party might have gone on all night, but at 8:20 PM. it starts to rain. A few brave souls hang around, but most of us decide three hours of revelry is enough, and head for home. Johnny and I part, because we both have the same idea. We want to share the fun with our parents. I jabber on to mother and Grandma for a half an hour. They listen with mature joy, as they take in the celebration through the eyes and mouth of one very happy 13-year old. Such a day has never been equalled in my memory from that time to the present. I slept the dream of a better tomorrow. Life had never been so good. Meantime, the Perth Regiment, was also having their own celebration in Holland. They were in Delfzijl by the Zuider Zee at war's end. Martin Gilbert in 'The Day the War Ended' writes quoting one war correspondent;

"We have been kissed, cried on, hugged, screamed at and shouted at, until we are bruised and exhausted. The Dutch have ransacked their gardens so that the rain of flowers which fall on the Allied vehicles is endless."

The one cloud on the celebrations was the treachery of Stalin and even some of the Canadian soldiers were ready, if need be, to take on the Russians. But first, we would need to defeat Japan. I'm not so sure about the Russians anymore. When they refused to help the partisans of Warsaw, I became suspicious of Communists. Uncle Gordon thinks Canada ought to become Communist, but I don't agree with him. Besides, what does Uncle Gordon know about Communism; he's just a factory worker. I think Uncle Gordon figures that if the Communists came to power he'd have more money. I told him,

"I think you're wrong."

Startford Communism got a boost in 1933 when the factory owners fought the workers over the coming of the unions. Unionism in turn thrived during the depression years. Capitalsim was deemed inferior to the ideals of Communism. Communism appealed to the poorly paid factory workers. In 1936 the labourers at Ballantyne knitting factory slaved at piece work. One man who just couldn't work as fast as the others actually received a cheque for three cents. Small wonder that Ballantyne's endured the strike that ended such abuse. In 1945 Stratford Communist sympathizers flourished for a while.

Mayor Waldo Monteith has proclaimed May 9th as a day of commemoration. In the Eaton's store window, prominently displayed, a sign reads, "And now shall mine head be lifted up above all mine enemies." It is a quotation from Psalm 27:6. Six thousand people pack into the arena (for hockey games 3500 is capacity). Nobody from our household attends. In the light of after years and maturity, I now realize, this was the event not to be missed. The combined choirs of all the city churches sang the 'Hallelujah Chorus.' Not even Billy Graham's giant crusades could match the enthusiasm of that choir. At age 13, I would not have been able to comprehend the importance of that service. With the experience of years, I know that the now lost art of congregational singing would alone have moved many to tears. People today are unaware that the acoustics for hymn singing in a packed arena is second to none. Those were the days when most people went to church, and tight-lipped men knew how to lift their voice in song. The commemoration service must have been a never-to-be-forgotten occasion. I'm sure there must still be a few people around, to attest to my hindsight observations. I'd like to meet one.

Chapter 23

Puppy Love

"If you and Bruce go to the movies, why don't you take your sister," says Mrs. Johnston to her son Jim. Jim rightly discerns that I won't care and he has earned a little extra spending money doing odd jobs. This is a rare treat for Joan Johnston because there was no money in the Johnston household for luxuries like the movies. This Thursday night the three of us go together. Joan has flaming auburn hair tied back in two pigtails that start above her ears. We pay our money to enter the Classic Movie Theatre. The price is ten cents plus two cents war tax. The movie is a detective thriller. Joan oohs and ahhs, as the heroine faces peril. The scary moment comes when she's in danger of getting herself killed. Suddenly, Joan grabs my arm with both hands. I think to myself, "She's touching me, hmm — what is this?" Now, all of this sets a few things in motion. I think, "Here is this girl grabbing my arm for no reason. Is this movie really that scary?" On the other hand, I am surprised at how nice it feels. It's logic versus emotion. Emotion wins the day. I look at her and smile. She smiles back. We make eye contact. I think; this "something or other that I've never felt before" is feeling kinda good. Gallantly, I take her hand. Suddenly, Aphrodite spots an easy target, mixes a potion, and gives me a drink. I conclude, "I've never experienced the like of this before." I squeeze her hand. Wow! There it is again. "Voila! What are these sensations I am feeling?" From now on, I am focused on soft brown eyes and auburn hair. Funny, I never noticed before, how on girls, pigtails can be so becoming. Forget the movie, this is more fun. I have fallen in 'like'. From now on, I 'like' Joan Johnston. After the movie, we walk home together. I hold Joan's hand, just like I did at the movie. I can detect a smirk on Jim, whose eyes are darting back and forth, from his sister to me.

On the way to the movie, we walked three abreast; Joan, Jim, and me. The order is different on the walk home. Now, it's Jim, Joan and me! I am talking to Joan. Jim might just as well have been somewhere else. Jim feels a little awkward at his sudden exclusion. Now there is nothing that can separate best friends except girls; however, our friendship survives, after all, Joan is 11 (going on 12) and I am 13 (going on 14). Furthermore, at that age you don't say much. For the next three years, the torch I carry for Joan Johnston will take the form of a furtive glance, the occasional wave of the hand, or the even rarer house party when I get to dance with her, or the ultimate bliss of a game of spin the bottle. Paradise when I get to kiss her, purgatory when its one of the other guys. However this is all in the future; for the present, I settle for the bliss of boldly holding her hand for the three blocks it takes to walk to my house. When we get to my place, I reluctantly release her hand, and say goodbye. Joan and Jim walk the last block to their house. I would love to know what they say, but I never find out. Neither of them can remember.

At home there are no inhibitions. The 'like' word changes to 'love', "I am in love" I exclaim to my astonished mother and Grandmother. I tell them all about it. One thing about our house is that there is no need for secrets. We can tell everything with impunity. I babble on about how wonderful it is to be in love. Grandma scoffs and says,

"You're too young to be in love."

"I am not." I protest. "I know how this feels, I am in love."

"Puppy Love," Grandma laughs. Mother laughs too. I go to bed that night feeling like its Christmas in June. Santa Claus has paid me a visit and left me a present like none other I've ever had. I dream of auburn hair and pigtails, and right there and then, I decide I will marry Joan Johnston. Yes, there can be no doubt. My vow to eternal bachelorhood is definitely in shambles.

I awake the next morning suffering from 'love-bite'. Puck and Pan are snickering as they inform Cupid of recent developments. After breakfast, I watch from the window for her to walk by. There she is with her girlfriends, Helen Haynes and Margery Schenk. Just as she passes our house, across the street, I race outside. I nonchalantly walk on my side of the street, and glance to my left. She was looking! She waves. I wave back. "She likes, me or she wouldn't wave," I reason. All is well with the world. At noon hour, it is time to walk home for lunch. I try the same logistics, walking across from Joan and her friends, keeping a respectful distance. She is wonderful. I watch her talking with her friends, wishing I could join them. We are approaching my house, but she still has not acknowledged my presence. She walks on, laughing and chattering away about something that's important to her. I am devastated. She didn't wave or acknowledge my presence. I have begun to ride the rocky road to romance, and already I am in misery.

"She didn't even wave at me," I wail.

"What on earth are you talking about?" says Grandma.

"Joan Johnston!" I am actually crying. Tears are running down my face. Puppy 'love-bite' is making a mess out of me. After lunch, I am at the window 'patiently' waiting in a hurry. There she is; I emerge and walk carefully adjacent to her in heart-beating anticipation. She looks my way and waves.

"She still likes me," I whisper. My heartbeat levels out; life is worth living after all. So goes my roller coaster life; it takes me a week to adjust. I resolve that, I simply cannot go on living like this I decide life is just one fool thing after another and love is just two fool things after each other. I will ignore Joan Johnston, I will put her out of my mind; I will be strong. It works — that is — until the next time I see her. Now the gods of puppy love are not very smart. Puck and Pan are no doubt to blame. When they are supposed to put the bite on someone, they often delegate their mischief to underlings who are even duller of wit than themselves. Such is the case that affects me. Audrey Murphy, Joan's friend, lives two doors east. These worthless gods missed the Johnston house by two lots east and put this blessing on Audrey instead of Joan, creating no end of trouble. While I've got the 'hots' for Joan, now Audrey has the 'hots' for me, which explains all those car rides that Mr. Murphy arranged. Now there's no ill wind that blows that doesn't bring some good. All our friends got the privilege of Mr. Murphy's car. Nonetheless this benefit granted; it was tiresome to have the confusion of all this puppy love stuff running amuck.

-oOo-

Manual training is a good diversion for me. I love working with tools and wood. The city is divided in half for manual training. Half go to Anne Hathaway School, the other half to the old red brick building adjacent to Romeo School. Miss Cameron teaches the girls home economics upstairs. Downstairs, Mr. James Skein is our teacher, a short roly-poly kind of man who divides his time between the two locations. He is not very good at instructions, blusters a lot,

but sets a great example. Most of us except Doug Heath, who is naturally smart with his head and his hands, can't figure out what he is driving at when he explains how to make a wooden windmill. In other words, the class just isn't getting it. In exasperation, old Jasper (our name for him when he can't hear us) chooses my project, and shows how to shape the windmill blade. First he claps my block into the vice. Next we watch in fascinating amazement; wood chips are flying as Jasper, deftly working his chisel, turns my wood block into shape. Magically, where there was only a wood block, a propeller appears. The kids chide me for being so lucky.
My windmill has caught up with Doug Heath's. Having a head start, we shellac our windmills while the other kids are just getting started. Next week, I will proudly present my windmill to mother. I never get the chance. In the night, June celebrates the passing of May with a four-alarm fire. It sweeps through the old manual training centre in minutes. The timbers are over 100 years old and burn quickly. Just like when 'Joshua fit the battle of Jericho', the walls collapse inward. By morning, there is only a smoking rubble of brick complaining from the heat, where the old building used to stand. This ultimate disaster takes Doug's windmill and mine to their graves. There is a rumour that the cause of the blaze just might be old 'Jasper' himself, and his stinking glue pot. He always had it heated with a flame that kept the glue hot, and forgot to turn it off. Serves him right for being such a cranky old man, but then, you must remember, it was only a rumour.

One day Vince says to me, "Woodsie, you walk funny."

"Whatja mean by that?" I anxiously reply.

"You walk with a spring in your step," retorts Vince.

"I don't get what you mean?" I'm getting concerned just about now.

"Watch me and I'll show you." I watch in horror as Vince, walks along bouncing up and down.

"You mean I look like that?"

"Yep, you look like that." Now I have to watch how I walk or I'll never get a girl to like me. Life is cruel. Just as I'm getting depressed about how I walk, I get a welcome reprieve. I discover that that spring in my walk is just what I need to catapult me up with the athletic kids I so envy. In preparation for the grade eight 'Olympics', our school gets a high jump set. I discover my legs. (Remember my dancing feet!) I'm one of the better high jump contestants. There are four of us who make the high jumping team. I revel in my newfound status. We assemble at the CNR baseball diamond for the competition. Our high jumping team does well but we are bested by others. We bring no trophies home to Romeo School, but I'm proud of my legs just the same. Four weeks later, it is summer vacation. I'm in shorts riding my bicycle, when I am flattered by a man who calls out to me and says,

"Hey kid, you got nice looking legs." When I told mother about the commendation, she said,

"If ever any man gives you a compliment like that, you ride away as fast as you can." Surprised, I say, "Sure mom." She didn't give me any reason. Grandma backs her up and warns me that such men are not to be trusted. I didn't think much about it; I just trust their judgement.

I get 90 % in public speaking. My topic is the silk trade. Mr. Pauli tells me, when it comes time to choose a career, I should consider something that includes public speaking. I query mother for a vocation that might interest me that involves public speaking. She wracks her brain and suggests that I could be the president of a large corporation. Mother has great confidence in her son. All sorts of professions occur to me, except that of being a minister.

-oOo-

Softball season is upon us. OK, I'm not good enough to play on the team, but I can cheer. My friend, Bob Whitehead, pitches for Romeo School. He is unbeatable. The showdown comes between Shakespeare and Romeo School. Romeo School wins the championship. We talk about it all the way home. The end of June has only one more test. Will I pass without having to try the final exams? Mr. Pauli reads the names of the fortunate. Surprised, I am listed among the elite. I never thought of myself as smart. I pass without trying. I am a bona fide candidate for high school. I have a little time on my hands while the unfortunate ones have to sweat it out in school writing their finals.

The gods of puppy love are still against me. I decide to read Anne of Green Gables. The heroine has flaming red hair. As if that isn't bad enough, Tom Sawyer is playing at the Avon Theatre. Becky is Tom's heartthrob. She is beautiful and also has red hair. I fall hard for Becky. I see the movie three times. I intuitively know that somewhere in the great beyond, the gods of puppy love have it in for me. So for a little relief, I turn to the comics. My favourite is L'il Abner; at least Daisy Mae is blond. She is always chasing L'il Abner in the Sadie Hawkins day race. L'il Abner is always trying to elude her. He's got it wrong. If I was L'il Abner, I'd trip on purpose to get caught, and feign sorrow. L'il Abner should be so lucky to have Daisy Mae chasing him. Nobody is chasing me.

Chapter 24

The Skeleton in my Closet Escapes.

The first two weeks in July, I go to Bogie's beach. Grandma tells me she wishes I wasn't going.

"Your mother is so much worse when you're not around." I can see it's getting to mother as well. I don't quite understand this, but it seems as though I am the only living person she is willing to trust. She misses me when I'm not around, and Grandma pays the price. I compose a song and sing it,

"Let's be happy, let's be gay. All the time that I'm away." I sing this song to both mother and Grandma, imagining that I can cover a wound with a band-aid. Both mother and Grandma are something less for my absence. Their reasons are quite different. It is a fresh reminder that in some incomprehensible way, I seem to be the glue that holds things together. However, when it comes to self-sacrifice, well — I'm just not there. At least not yet. If it's a choice between Bogie's and home, I go to Bogie's Beach, but this time things are different. I am to learn that growing up on a farm is more than just having fun. In the past year Graham has grown taller and stronger. The labour pool of hired help has dried up. The postwar boom is on and factory jobs are offering unheard of wages. Instead of the usual hired man, Graham is now his father's helper. I have no one during the day to hang out with. Graham is busy most of the time helping his dad. The time hangs heavy. I think, "I would be having more fun, if I was in Stratford with my friends."

To compensate for the boring days, Ethel Bogie tries to make the evenings interesting. We go to the movies. We visit their friends at other farms. One night Graham teaches me a fun song to amuse my Stratford pals. Apart from this, there is nothing very memorable. From now on the next time, I return to Bogie's beach, it will be for short visits only. To be a farmer, you have to be the kind of person who can handle loneliness; Graham is too gregarious for that. Graham's dissatisfaction with farming increases. Ultimately, he will spend a decade on the ships that ply the waters of Lake Huron.

I return from Bogie's beach to Stratford with a one-day layover. I'm off to Toronto to be with dad for a week. When I get there, I can't believe how much Pat has grown. She is 6 inches taller than I am, and has a boyfriend. I am intimidated. I feel inferior and outclassed. I think, "This is not going to be my best week." Quickly things get better. Dad has decided that its time for me to meet the clan. I am to meet all dad's brothers, their wives, and my cousins. By now I have sung my fun song that Graham taught me to dad and Phyllis. They have me sing it again for all the cousins. If only I could have had this kind of confidence, when I bombed out on 'Robin in the Rain.' I sing the following song called, 'I got but 50 cents.'

I took my girl to a fancy ball, it was a social hop.
We danced until the lights went out, the music it did stop
Then to a restaurant we went, the best one on the street.
She said she wasn't hungry, but this is what she eat.
A dozen raw, a plate of slaw, a chicken and a roast
Some asparagus with applesauce, and soft shelled crab on toast.
A big hot stew, and crackers too, Her appetite was immense.
When she called for pie, I thought I'd die, for I had but 50 cents.

You bet I wasn't hungry, I didn't care to eat.
Expecting every moment to be kicked out in the street.
She said, she'd bring her family round some day and we'd have lots of fun,
Then I gave the man the 50 cents and this is what he done.

He smashed my nose, he tore my clothes, he hit me in the jaw.
He gave me a prize of a pair of black eyes and with me swept the floor.
He took me where my clothes hung loose and threw me over the fence.
Now take my advice, don't try it twice, when you-got-but-50-cents.

The song proves to be a crowd-pleaser, and I get a round of applause. Kudos to Sam Devere, who wrote the song, 125 years ago. I sing a few more that Graham taught me with a similar response.

I have discovered theatre. Now that my ego has been reinforced, I prepare myself to enjoy a week with my half sister Pat, who seems more like my overseer, than a half sister. To make matters worse, she is clearly a beautiful girl. I steel myself to be led around by the nose for a week.

Pat patronizes me; in every conversation, I am supposed to feel like, "Aren't I lucky to be in this enviable spot." This feeling of privilege is a downer. We walk to her favourite store on Yonge Street. Some guys whistle at Pat; she treats them with contempt. To be associated with high class is a fleeting prerogative. I eye the old sandbox and think that those were better days. After lunch, Pat takes me downstairs to see her new toy. It is a billiard table, just like the one we play on at the Y. I can't believe such wealth is available to a single family. The new Capital Rock Wool Insulation Company is doing very well and is second in sales only to Johns Manville. Dad owns a Cadillac and a LaSalle. More wealth! Dad shows me his workshop. Every tool to fascinate a young boy is available in its appointed place (my Dad is neat freak) and some hang on the wall. I know a little bit about tools, because Uncle Gordon works in a furniture factory and has an electric table saw that he built all by himself. Except for the motor and saw-blade, it was painstakingly built from factory wood-scraps. Dad's table-saw has a steel top and is fresh from the factory. I feel like I'm in toyland. Within limits, Dad lets me play with his tools.

Pat invites me to play a game of snooker. Practiced from my times at the YMCA, I gladly accept the challenge. A guy ought to at least be able to match a girl at billiards. Alas, she takes me to the cleaners. I have not inherited my father's pool-shark ways. Pat has had a good teacher. She has had plenty of practice, and is more than a match with Dad. I hang my head in shame. I am as embarrassed as a nudist caught with his clothes on. Pat can make the ball spin or hook, or just about anything she wishes. I tell her,

"You could go into any pool hall, pretend you're a beginner, bet money and make a fortune." Pat laughs and passes me a Coke. She has cases of Coke and just about every soft drink that is made. She entertains a lot. Her friends come and go. Who wouldn't want to, with all that free soda pop available. I wonder how Dad can do it.

Sugar rationing is still around. I conclude money talks.

Pat has spending money. She can buy just about anything, provided it is within reason. So Aunt Marg thinks I'm spoiled? She hasn't seen anything like this, nor for that matter, neither have I. Before I return to Stratford, Dad sees the longing in my eyes. He has a surprise for me. He starts filling a six-quart basket with tools. The three sizes in Robertson screwdrivers go in. So does the hammer that I have been coveting all week. It's different from any I have ever seen. The handle is made of leather. I get a set of chisels, a pair of pliers and a coping saw to cut curves. Dad puts in a brace and bit, complete with drills from quarter inch to one-inch bore. Enough tools to delight a teenager's heart; and to get him started on some worthwhile home project. After the week is up (which didn't go so badly after all) Dad puts me on the train. Mother meets me in Stratford. I excitedly tell her all the things that Dad has purchased, now that he's so prosperous. I miss completely the constrained look on mother's face.

I have this surprise for Grandma and mother. I proudly show them my tools, and tell them from now on, when something needs fixing, they can call on me instead of always bothering Uncle Gordon. An hour later, we sit down for supper. I suddenly draw comparisons between our lifestyle, and the affluence I've just experienced. Our old green cupboard, where we put the dishes, seems shabby in contrast to the cabinets in Dad's kitchen. Their kitchen floor is straight, whereas ours is like a saucer, so helpful on washdays. Their kitchen table is modern with matching chairs, ours seems old and wobbly. They have an electric stove and fridge, luxuries that we can only think about. Dad's house doesn't need a coal stove for heat in the kitchen. His house is heated with a furnace that burns oil complete with a boiler. He has central heat complete with modern steam radiators. My adolescence has now made me perceptive. I see things, I never noticed as a child. Suddenly, my lower lip begins to quiver, the tears roll down my cheeks. I am about to utter words, that I have so often wished I could retract. Grandma has guessed, but dares not speak too quickly. Mother is concerned. She asks me,

"What's wrong with you, why are you crying?" I weep the

words,

"It's just that — it's just that — (more tears) — it's just that, they have so much, and we have so little." Mother bursts into tears. I could not have hurt her more deeply. Grandma remonstrates with me,

"You should be ashamed of yourself, after all your mother has done for you."

"I know it, Grandma, and I am grateful." I lament. "I really am."

Sadly, the damage is done. I know it intuitively right away. Mother's fragile health will only deteriorate. Grandma will pay the price. Later on that evening, after we've all gotten over it; I think, "I'm glad Grandma rebuked me in front of mom." It should be convincing to mother, once and for all, that Grandma supports her daughter, and loves her. She stood up for mother and affirmed her. She had the chance to boldly declare in front of me, that mother had done a good job of raising her son. It was the last great lost opportunity for mother to reorder her life, and here was all this evidence! Grandma loves her daughter and has demonstrated it with irrefutable proof. Can the daughter love her mother and forgive the imagined wrongs? Had mother seized the opportunity, love power might have snatched her from the abyss and given back her life. It was too much to ask. Wounded in the battle of life mother couldn't rise to the occasion. Conflict, the great forge of character, makes some and breaks others. As it was, it helped a little in mother's relationship with Grandma, but only for a while. Unfortunately, the kind of depression that afflicts mother represses all genuine offers of compassion, and fixates on the growing tragedy that will be one of her own making. The stage is set for an explosion. We don't have to wait long to feel the pain.

-oOo-

After the first edition of this book went to press, my step-sister Pat having read the book sent me this letter, however a word of explanation is now required. Disallusioned with my father she refused to call him Dad, choosing instead to call him B. L (short for Bruce Leigh). Now here is the letter,

Dear Bruce:

I am so sorry to have taken so long to answer your letter. I knew this would require a lot of time to write and say all the things I want to explain. Ross and I play golf five or six days a week. I play duplicate bridge five times a week. Mundane things like house cleaning and washing cannot be ignored. Time for myself is very rare.

I have so much to tell you about my life with B.L. and mom. You have the idea that we were a wealthy family. Nothing could be further from the truth. When I was very young (pre-school) we were like nomads. Never in one place very long. I believe now that the reason for this was running away from bill collectors. My first recollection was at age 3. We were in a few rooms in someone's house in Oshawa — then to Whitby to another shared accommodation, each lasting a few months. Taken to Niagara Falls for short time, I remember B.L. telling me that there were days he had one quarter to their name. During this time he was a vacuum salesman. Not the best of times to try to sell anything — never mind vacuum cleaners. Then we were on a boat (ice breaker) in Port Arthur (now Thunder Bay).

We rented a house there and that is where I started school. The house was very nice, a large house. That was where we had our first housekeeper at six dollars a month. 1935 was still tough times. Linda was so happy to have somewhere to live. The six dollars was a lot of money to her. Now I realize it was a lot of money to Mom and B.L. too. But they wanted to project an image of wealth. Image was very important to them. Everyone thought that we were privileged people; all my life, this was a façade. From Windsor we came to Toronto — (still running from creditors I suspect). Here, we (mom) managed to find a house in a very wealthy neighbourhood. Mom was on the radio then. She was making pretty good money. B.L. was having a tough time because Electrolux was made in England and the war was on and getting machines from England became impossible. I don't know what happened then. It seems to me B.L. got very sick. Mom's radio show was no more and they had to move again. Mom found a castle (yes really) for rent. They had no money for the rent, but somehow they made arrangements to live rent free for six months. Hopefully by then they would be financially on their feet. Unfortunately this did not occur, so they were on the move again.

They rented a duplex, but not for long; a few months and we were on the move again. That is when they rented the house on Bedford Park. That was the year I went to five schools in one year. Hence I was always the new kid in school which led me to be very shy and to this day still am.

I really do not know how B.L. got started in the insulation business. I think he sold it for someone and wound up owning it instead. All the furniture we had came from auction sales. My mom got all her clothes second hand. I don't remember her ever going to a clothing store — until my wedding. All our cars were second hand but of course, they had to be big cars. They had a reputation to uphold. Everyone thought we were wealthy but nothing was further from the truth. From "insulation" Mom investigated the storm window business and found that it could be lucrative and it was for awhile, until unpaid bills seemed to be overwhelming. A book keeper was hired to make some kind of order of the records and hopefully could implement a plan to overcome a messy situation. The poor man worked from dawn to dusk every day and I firmly believe he nearly had a nervous breakdown.

I would like to clear up a fact of my having unlimited amounts of money to spend. One dollar a week when I was a teenager was my allowance, which I had many chores to do to earn. Sometimes I would baby sit for my cousins for fifty cents.

Thank you for sending me your book. I would imagine that writing it was therapeutic. I hope so.

I met my father — when we were on our honeymoon. I saw him again when he came to Oshawa. He was an American and lived in Florida. I liked him very much. You grew up without a father and so did I (my real father). I did not like B.L. at all. I cannot believe that a man could abandon his son as B.L. did.

Michael and Toni (Dad and Phyllis' two children) did not fare too well growing up. They had some good times at the Island (Parry Sound) but not much time at home while Mom and B.L. eeked out a living. Consequently both married too young.

Not many happy times. Well I could go on and on but it is nearly Christmas and I have many chores to do. I wish you and your family a very merry Christmas and a Happy New Year.

Sincerely, Pat

What a revelation! Pat's letter to me removed the scales from my eyes. For fifty years I had believed the façade that my father was rich. The truth was that we were better off; in more ways than one.

-oOo-

I have my first job. Following in my father's footsteps it is in sales. I deliver the Star Weekly. After I had sung my fun song to Dad's family members, my Uncle Stewart introduced himself to me.

"I'm the circulation manager of the Toronto Star," he announces. "How would you like to work for me in Stratford selling the Star Weekly." This is the humble beginning of that thing called initiative. The sales genes run in the family. I get a route delivering 18 Star Weeklies. My profit is five cents per paper; if I sell a Liberty magazine for five cents, I get an extra two cents. I canvass for more customers and build the route to 24 Star Weeklies and 10 Liberty magazines. My profits soar from 95 cents to $1.40. I keep the job for five months, until Vince gets me in with him at the Standard Drug Store on the corner of Ontario and Downie. We work with our bicycles, delivering the phone-in orders. I get to know every street in town, with a map in my head that stays with me to this day. My delivery job is after school and all day Saturday. I make $4.00 per week.

I should have known better. Mother has been on a tear ever since I got back from Toronto. Not safe to invite company, but a momentary lapse of discernment eludes me. I invite Jim Johnston in for a game of monopoly. As we make our way upstairs, I can see mother's agitated frame of mind on her face.

"Excuse me Jim, I have to go downstairs for a moment." I race into the living room and look mother dead in the eye,

"Johnny and I are going to have a game of Monopoly, Mom, don't embarrass me. I mean it." I am as stern as my 13 years will allow. We start into the game, but I can hear mother talking to Grandma in all too familiar words. I try to ignore what's going on downstairs. I am getting more uncomfortable by the moment. I wish we were somewhere else. We have barely started the game when suddenly even I am taken aback. Mother is screaming like I've never heard before. My immediate vision is mother with a knife in her back.

"What was that?" Jim exclaims.

"You'd better go," I grieve, "I'll explain all this later."

Jim is down the stairs in a bound, with me right after him. Outsidc thc kitchen, I say,

"I'm needed inside; I'll see you after supper."

I storm into the living room. Mother is in tears, but my only thought is the shame I feel. I am ferocious in my condemnation of mother. This is the worst moment of my life. Our dark secret is out. Jim is only a kid. He will tell. The word will spread. The world will hear. Our reputation is forever ruined. The loss is irretrievable. How can I face my friends? It is the most hopeless feeling, I have ever known.

Another supper in silence. The atmosphere is surreal. I waste no time in finishing my meal. I am out the door. How do I explain all this to Jim Johnston? Will he really understand? Have I just lost my best friend? The end of the world has come, but perhaps I can explain. All I can do is try. I slowly make my way down Brunswick Street. I come to Johnny's house. I call expecting to see Johnny. I am surprised. Mrs. Johnston comes to the door, and does the unheard of thing. She smiles and invites me in. Mrs. Johnston is a Baptist and a good Christian. She proves it now in a profound and memorable way. I sit at her kitchen table, and she tenderly asks me,

"How are you, Bruce?"

"I'm okay, I guess."

"I just want you to know, that you are always welcome at our house," says Mrs. Johnston. "If you ever need any help of any kind, you can always ask, and we will be here to help."

The sense of relief is overwhelming. At crisis moments like this, children can get it all mixed up. Self-blame and loathing, in these situations life can be devastating even if it defies logic. Yet kids can do just that, and self-destruct to their ruin. It is a defining moment; Mrs. Johnston gets it right and conveys to me without too many words the understanding that all is not lost. I am my own person. I have a future. Mrs. Johnston is a saint and I appreciate it. Jim and I go out to play. We don't even talk about mother. I am relieved. Fifty-seven years later, in preparation for the writing of this book, I ring Jim up on the telephone and rehearse the events of that fateful day, when my dark secret was at last exposed, and ask him if he remembers it all. His reply was a revelation for me. He said to me:

"Well Bruce, in all deference to you, your secret was not so secret. We all knew that your mother had had a tragic life. It was well known that your father had left her for another woman. We felt sorry for her and for you, because it was also known that she still loved your father. Her mental distress over her sad life was understood. We observed that it had affected her emotionally. So Bruce, I was not as surprised as you might have thought."

A revelation to me! All these years, I had thought that that particular day of crisis was an announcement to the world. I had imagined that all my sleight of hand had kept the neighbours from knowing mother and Grandma's mental anguish. The emotional trauma, I had felt that day had misled me to believe my own deception. In my mind, up till then, nobody knew. In fact, the truth was that everybody knew, and sympathized with genuine compassion. So mother had not been as unreasonable as I thought. People had whispered her tragedy, and the information by word of mouth had made its way through the grapevine. She had discerned rightly. People were talking. However the great deception for mother was that she imagines it to be slander. The truth lay elsewhere. It was compassion that people felt. The misreading of this genuinely intended sympathy was to destroy her reason. She misinterpreted the facts to her ruin. I always told myself that when I grew up, I would bring about her cure. It was an illusory vision, but for the time being, it sustained me. Eventually, I would learn that a healthy mind accepts responsibility for past mistakes. When the mind gets sick, it blames others for the things that go wrong. In time this sleight of hand becomes reality. From now on the real world is out of focus and the delusion becomes a tragic substitute for authentic living. The patient gets worse and cannot cope.

Chapter 25

V-J Day Celebrations

Wednesday, August 15. Mayor Waldo Monteith has declared a day of celebrations. Japan has surrendered. Uncle Norman won't have to fight the Japs. That's a relief. We have been following the Japanese war in Life magazine. We are overjoyed to know there will be no more pictures of dead soldiers and ferocious battles. It's time to celebrate. I read in the paper that there are to be swimming competitions, canoe racing, and a parade. I want to try my hand in the acquatics. I try to convince Johnny to join me in the competitions. He is not interested, but will wait by the river to watch. There is a crowd that turns up at the river's edge to see the festivities. Many are friends that Jim and I know. Johnny and I part at the fort. I expect to see a swarm of kids, who have responded to the Mayor's call. So far there are only three: the unbeatable Bobby Easson, Ray Richards, and me. The time for competition draws near. Where are the kids? By 10:30 A.M., it is apparent that nobody else is going to come, and the show must go on. We swim out to the raft with the diving board. We pull ourselves out of the water and shiver on the edge. A loudspeaker booms out that the competition is about to start. Ready, get set, go. The three of us dive in. The only competition is between Ray and me. Bobby gets 50 cents for coming first. I get 20 cents for second.

Once again, the MC through the loudspeaker booms out, "The diving competition will now commence." We swim back to the raft. The diving order is as follows, Bruce Woods, Ray Richards and Bobby Easson. By now, I'm starting to feel my confidence. This is a celebration, so why not do a little grandstanding for the benefit of the audience. I walk out on the diving board, and take a bow. There are a thousand or more people watching; and they are in a festive mood. The bow draws a laugh. I return to the diving derrick, pause, and run out on the plank, (the plank was not a bona fide diving board and is very springy, a little item that I had not considered). I bounce for all I'm worth, and spin madly out of control, arms and legs flailing the air. The crowd roars in laughter, at my expense. I surface coughing and spitting water; my mortification is complete. "Bruce, you dunce, why didn't you test the board first?" I moan. I was the guinea pig. Ray has taken notice, and adjusts accordingly; he takes a clean dive. Once again the unbeatable Bobby Easson takes first prize. Now he's up to a dollar. Ray gets 20 cents. I slink away trying to be invisible, when (horrors) a reporter from the Beacon Herald calls the three of us for a picture. I am trapped. Not only am I humiliated, my shame is about to be immortalized in film, (and — shudder) to appear in tomorrow's newspaper. The reporter writes in his notebook the names of the three divers. In vain do I protest,

"Could you change that to swimmers?" I plead.

"Sure." says the reporter.

I don't remember the canoe races or the parade. I can only think of my humiliation. There is one thing left to mourn. I ask Johnny,

"Was your sister in the audience?" He replies, "Yep!" Twenty cents is poor compensation for my shame. Jim reminds me to be a good sport.

"It was so much fun." he says, and gives me a rerun on how much the crowd laughed at my exhibition.

"Thanks a lot!"

When I return home, I tell mother and Grandma the sad tale of my mortification. No sympathy here! The next day the newspaper is full of pictures, and stories about the grand celebrations of V-J Day. In horror, I see the picture I dread. There I am for the world to read. I see the by-line, "In the only diving and swimming events of the day, Bob Easson was declared the winner in both. His opponents were Ray Richards and Bruce Woods." The 'Champ' is pictured with the two runners-up on the diving platform in the centre of the river. Mother says,

"We should cut that out of the newspaper and keep it." I say to mother,

"No thanks that's a picture I want to forget." Sixty years later, I pay the Stratford Archives $5.00 for a poor quality photocopy. Time has made me able to laugh at myself. As the saying goes, 'Learn to laugh at yourself, you'll never run out of material.'

Back to V-J Day. Later that evening I have recovered from my humiliation and Johnny calls for me after supper. We are going downtown where there are more celebrations. The streets

1945, Uncle Norman is discharged

I thought my cousin Janet was so cute
With war's end she gets her daddy back

surrounding city hall are packed with happy people. It is dejavu of V-E Day with a little more planning and a beautiful evening to boot. Some events are spontaneous but most others are planned. There are people who are standing shoulder to shoulder to watch anything and everything. One scheduled event is a barn dance. We watch in fascination as a band takes the stage and starts to play. The fiddler is sensational and everybody is tapping their toes. There are some that know exactly what to do when the caller sings out,

"Allemande left and swing your partner round." This is all new to me; I don't know a Virginia reel from a Clog dance. I had never heard of a Cakewalk in my life before this, but I watch in fascination and try to imitate the dancers with my feet. Suddenly, a stranger I've never seen before says to me,

"Wanna dance?"

"Sure do." I reply, and next thing I know this older lady has me as her partner and furthermore, she knows her stuff, even if I don't (feminists don't be smug, I know what you're thinking). I get hopelessly mixed up. I'm going left when I should be going right. I bump into the next couple and throw them off pace. Soon the crowd is laughing. This time I don't care, I'm having too much fun. Finally my partner has suffered enough and says to me,

"Better take some lessons kid, you've got the heart, but you have to practice." I dutifully agree and melt back into the crowd. Johnny says to me,

"Nice try Bruce, but you've got some catching up to do."
We hang around for at least an hour and watch one novice after another, get things wrong. By a process of elimination the pros take over and the clodhoppers settle back to watching. The professionals show us how it's done. While I am fascinated by their skill I especially notice the disparity in ages. Old and young who are experienced are having the time of their lives and so are we, even if we're only watching. Nobody wants to go home.

The exhilaration is delicious and we savour the moment till at last around midnight, the crowd begins to thin out, and it's time to go home. Back at our house, I tell mother that I want to go to a barn dance and learn how to do all those steps. I never seem to get around to it. When I retire to my bed that night, I think, "Embarrassment or no, this has been a good day. I don't know when I've had so much fun." I pull the covers up to my smiling face and sleep the dream of a whole new world that will never have another war again.

Potatoes! I cannot close this chapter without mentioning them. The 1944 crop had been dismal and we were peeling and eating the most miserable shrivelled up thumb sized potatoes you ever saw. Some folks had given up completely and were substituting bread for potatoes. In those days we never heard of rice. I shall never forget the happy day the new crop arrived in the summer of 1945. I was in a lineup with hundreds of others waiting my turn to buy potatoes for Grandma at the Dominion store. Two bags per customer was the limit. August 1945 put an end to the great Ontario potato famine. I learned that year not to take anything for granted, even the lowly potato.

Chapter 26

The Soap Box Derby

I have been eyeing my six-quart basket of tools, and considering how to use them when suddenly I get the opportunity. The Optimist Club under the inspiration of Harry Langdon, decides to sponsor a kid's Soap Box Derby. The idea was birthed in Akron, Ohio, where it all began. In the window of Dave Simpson's Dry Cleaners is a homemade four-wheel crate, built by Keith Pauli. It is named "D for Donald" for a Lockheed Hudson bomber flown in the war by Keith's brother-in-law. We know Keith by his nickname 'Foo.' Somebody had called him crazy Keith. Eventually, he got 'Foo' short for fool. Keith was a little like the mad scientist or eccentric inventor, a pretty smart kid who inspired us to match wits. Keith was the son of Charles Pauli, a butcher who ran his own store under the name of Pauli's Meat Market at 31 Ontario Street. The Pauli's house was on William Street with access to the river, convenient for punting and other fun river activities. A great place, for a 'mad scientist' to live, and practice his dreams. He and his friends build punts for the Avon and for extra fun used the Waterloo Street hill to race their wagons. A sort of embryo for the coming of the Soap Box Derby.

Ken Ferguson, president of the Optimist Club, Harry Langdon, and Dave Simpson are friends. Mr. Simpson, a former mayor of the city, has his dry cleaning business on Downie Street. These civic-minded men look for opportunities for a celebration to help kids. When they discovered the Akron Soap Box Derby, they brought the idea to Stratford. This special event had this rare advantage; it was the first public event after war's end. The spirit of celebration is strong within the hearts of Stratford citizens. Anything public at this juncture will succeed in drawing a crowd. So, to promote the derby, Keith was encouraged to build a Soap Box Crate. The finished product was put on display in Dave Simpson's store window. For citywide participation, the Soap Box Derby couldn't have come at a more propitious moment.

Signs accompany the display in the window encouraging the kids of Stratford to build their crates, and have them ready for the race on Labour Day. How I admired that crate; inspired, I think, "I could build a crate like that." In all, 16 entries are submitted, and I am one of them. I appeal to mother for the cash to buy the wood and the hardware. Mother, who denies me nothing, provides. Fortuitously, the neighbours across the street had put an old baby buggy out to the garbage. Quickly, I take possession of the buggy, and strip it down for parts including a leather-upholstered seat. I am soon at work using my new tools. Dad has calculated correctly what a kid needs. I use all of the tools for the job. My plan is to take the buggy wheels, complete with axles, and attach them to my crate. The axles on my crate are wooden two by fours. Front axle is four feet wide; back axle is three feet. I will attach the buggy wheels to the axles. The wheels are on a narrow rod of spring steel that needs to be sawn in half and attached to my wooden axles. However, I am soon to learn that spring steel is tough; my hacksaw won't even dent those rods. I abandon the plan in favour of the wheels from my wagon. I buy 3/8th inch iron rods, and have the blacksmith cut them to appropriate sizes. Voila! At the expense of my wagon my racer is well on its way. An orange crate from the grocery store is my main body; I streamline it with a little help from Uncle Gordon. I'm bending the rules here; I'm not supposed to get adult help. I cover my crate with oilcloth purchased from Duggans, and paint it yellow with a wide red stripe at the top. Beautiful! If looks count for speed, I have this race in the bag. Even the puppy love gods are pleased.

Johnny, me, Bummer Bolton, Vince, my crate is under construction

Labour Day is the great occasion. The Optimist Club have set up a carnival with several booths in the park. They sell widgets, gadgets, hotdogs, and pop provided by the Stratford Bottlers with the trademark, 'Kist.' (Small town bottlers of soda pop eventually become extinct. They cannot compete with the majors like Canada Dry and Coca-Cola). The crowd starts to gather. By the time I get to the assembly area in front of the square at City Hall, there are over three thousand people who have gathered to see the parade. Participation is always the key to the success of any event. The Optimist Club has not been sleeping. Kids, both boys and girls, have been invited to participate. Tricycles and bicycles can enter the parade, provided they have been decorated for show. Prizes for the best presentation add incentive to get in on the fun. Kids come in clown suits, others pull their wagons. (In today's lingo, mini-floats.) The destination is the carnival at the park. The planning pays off handsomely. The whole town shows up. The next day The Beacon-Herald reads, "several thousand" gathered for the event.

The Boys' Band led by bandmaster E. M. Brett starts the parade, heading north on Downie Street, and we are lined up in procession after the band. Next come all the kids' tricycles and bicycles. Proudly I sit in my crate and Vince Schooley is my pusher. Foo Pauli is the guy to beat. I turn up my nose at Moe Brennon's crate. It looks like he threw it together the day before the race. It has buggy wheels like the ones I spurned, (unbeknown to me, Mercury has taken a shine to Moe or I might not have been so confident). We come to a halt at the shell bandstand by the river. The drum and trumpet band of Squadron 19 Air Cadets takes over. The parade moves on up Cobourg Street, finishing at the top of Snake Hill in Queens Park. The race is announced. The crowd lines the road. Of course, we soapers are the main attraction.

The big event is about to start. We match up two by two and wait for the signal. The pusher gives us our start; after that, we're on our own. I finish behind my competitor. I hide my disappointment; I'm out of the race. To heighten my chagrin, Moe Brennan is coming down the hill like greased lightning. His crate is narrow. It's only as wide as a pair of buggy wheels. Foo Pauli does better than I, and comes in third. Later Foo says to me,

"Moe's crate didn't look like much, but boy did those buggy wheels go." I think about those discarded buggy wheels I had and muse, "Mercury, where were you when I needed you? My crate is so sleek and shiny." Apparently, Mercury is not impressed with sleek and shiny.

Moe Brennan gets $25.00 for first Prize, Foo only gets $5.00 for third. The gods of puppy love smile, and decide to give me a break. I didn't know it going in, but there is a consolation race for losers. I get another crack at the prize money, and come in second. I can't believe my good fortune. I win $15.00; Foo gets more honour, but I get more money. I am as euphoric as an immigrant in heaven. I get compliments on how good my crate looks. Since all of us have no evidence left except photos, get a load of my crate.

My crate was the sleekest entry in the parade [so I thought]

"Mom, look!" I exclaim. "You got your investment back. It cost you $15.00 for me to build my crate, and I got $15.00 in winnings." Mom lets me keep the prize money. I am grinning from ear to ear, 'A profit is not without honour'. I have great plans for next year's Labour Day race; so does Keith Pauli. The difference between Foo Pauli and me is this, he delivers. I'm having too much fun to execute my plans.

In March 1946, Keith Pauli loses his dad. Charles Pauli dies of a heart attack at the age of 46. The Pauli Butcher Shop on Ontario Street closes. Elizabeth Pauli sells their home, and moves to a smaller place on the corner of Avon and Avondale. Keith Pauli's superb location on the river passes into the hands of strangers. I think, "That punt Foo Pauli built will not have water access." How I admired that punt. It really was the inspiration for my own, the one I built the following year. Harry Langdon feels the pain for the loss of his friend, and especially for Keith, who is now fatherless. Harry has an idea. Now that the war is over, ball bearing racing wheels are available in Akron. Harry imports the wheels and sells them to Keith at cost, for $20.00. Keith insisted that he pay for those wheels. He wants no sympathy because of their recent misfortunes. The racing wheels were the first to show up in all of Canada. Keith builds a new crate. This one is sleek, and is mounted with the Akron imports. For twelve months, I hardly think about the race until the appointed time. If you 'snooze you lose.' I enter my crate in the 1946 race unchanged and underclassed by all the new entries. Keith has unveiled his new racing cart; it's a beauty, and I get this premonition. "Foo Pauli will win for sure." Ken Ferguson is in charge of the race, which this year is on Erie Street. A racing ramp has been built at the top of the street. The ramp levels the playing field for all entries.

The attendance is phenomenal. We are all excited at the prospects and the prize money. The coolest cat in the race is Keith Pauli. He knows what lies inside those racing wheels, which are considerably larger than the wheels on my crate. His pusher is his brother Ken. In the parade, I am astonished how his crate rolls with so little effort. There is no doubt in my mind, "Keith is the guy to beat". We rise (literally) to the occasion. The view from the top of the ramp is great. Even scary! Erie Street is lined with spectators on both sides of the street with excited fans that have turned out in droves to see the extravaganza of the decade. We race two at a time. When Keith's turn comes, he is out of sight. Incredulously, I watch as his crate rolls and rolls and rolls. He is the clear winner.

What was that gentle rush of wind? Charlie Pauli, were you watching from somewhere else? Ken Ferguson gives a wink to Harry Langdon, who has tears in his eyes. Keith wins first place and the prize money. Not only does he have the best crate in Canada, he has the prize money of $25.00 in his pocket. He has made a profit of $5.00 and everybody is glad. Our derby days are over. Once you turn 15, you can no longer compete. Those were the rules of the competition.

Chapter 27

Shenanigans

The time has come for confessions. This has to do with my life of crime. We often like to walk at night down Cat's Alley. It is one of the few alleys in the city. Running from Brunswick Street south to Douro, between Bay and Front, it provides a wonderful view of the back yards of residents. It is a great place to play hide and go seek. It is also a great place to raid gardens. One day we decide to steal some carrots. We could ask our parents for carrots anytime and they would provide. However, stolen carrots are better by far, and provide some adventure in the bargain. John Butler, Johnny, and I slip unobtrusively under cover of night to a neighbour's garden. The prized carrots had been located earlier by daylight. Now the carefully planned theft proceeds. Allan McKone has been excluded from the plans for his own protection. He lives too close to the proposed theatre of operations, and might squeal. Besides, his parents go to church every Sunday and that makes inclusion of Allan risky. We should pull the job off without a hitch. With two or three carrots apiece, we rub the dirt off in the grass, and proceed to eat at least one each. I suspect we wantonly threw the others away. I don't quite remember.

Emboldened by our easy acquisition of carrots, and only mildly repentant over those discarded veggies. We decide that the next job will only be to elicit a little bit of excitement. The plan is simple. We get a cardboard box and carefully attach a rope to the corner. Again, under cover of darkness, we place the box carefully at a neighbour's door. Not any neighbour will do. It has to be someone with a veranda about three or four steps high. This gives us a place to hide. With all in readiness, we place the box at the door, ring the bell and duck just out of sight. The action proceeds something like this. First the porch light goes on. The lady of the house looks out and says,

"There's nobody here." Then she notices the box. Bending down to examine the box is the point at which we pull the line, and the box moves at the speed of rope. The lady screams. We grab the box and run. Composure regained, the lady exclaims.

"Damned kids!" The penultimate pleasure is when we laugh about it, and tell our friends.

It's September and the plums are ripe for picking. We decide to raid the neighbour's plum tree, and grab a few carrots in the bargain. Once again under cover of darkness, we make our foray into the Schmidt's who live at 217 Albert Street right behind where Barry Knechtel lives. Things are progressing nicely and Johnny has just found a good picking perch in the tree, when suddenly, we are discovered. Mrs. Schmidt rushes out with a broom, and we scatter, leaving Johnny to fend for himself. He's desperately trying to navigate his way down the plum tree, when suddenly the angry woman starts applying the broom of learning to the seat of understanding.

"I'm trying, I'm trying!" cries a terrified Jimmy Johnston, and bails out the quick way to the ground. We are all running scared now for fear we will be identified, and have to face our parents. Discouraged as a devil caught doing a good deed, we repent. Having tried a life of crime, we decide to go straight. We never raid any more gardens, and we don't climb neighbour's trees without permission.

We do climb fences. The Stratford Nationals is our home baseball team. The Intercounty League includes the London Royals, our bitterest rivals. Our heroes are pitchers Bobby Fischer and Earl Craig. The National stadium (built by who else, the Canadian National Railroad) is still in exactly the same location on Norfolk Street. When championship games are played, we can squeeze 4000 into the stands. Most games have lots of empty seats. The kids all get in to see the game the same way. We park our bikes at the fence where the rush seats have a roof conveniently located 12 inches from the fence. We scamper onto the roof and then drop to the seats below. Hundreds of kids never pay to see a baseball game. Our Babe Ruth is Irish Miskimmons. Every time he hits a home run you can hear the cheering as far away as Brunswick Street.

A little east of the stadium is the obstacle course of the Perth regiment. It is now occupied by Steed Transport. In our day, after the regiment was disbanded, the kids of Stratford would enjoy the challenge of climbing the ramparts and swinging on the ropes just like the soldiers of the regiment did when they were in training. I guess there were enough accidents and broken arms to eventually bring the city fathers to action. It was summarily torn down and flattened. From a kid's point of view, we were sure it was the action of a spoilsport who had a grudge against kids having a good time.

For shenanigans, I am envious of Al MacDonald. He seems to outdo us. Our friendships overlap, so even though I didn't hear of it till afterwards, I report it now so that my readers can understand the historic events that shaped the destiny of Stratford. Let me identify the culprits. For starters, there was Bob Hesson, Orval Steinburg, Ron Mulligan, Evan Pike, Barry Knechtel, Murray Dunbar, Bob Herlick, and Al. This list omits the ones obscured by failing memory. The Lion's pool always closed at 9 P.M. That's OK for a normal summer evening, but when you have a scorcher on your hands, a fellow has to swim. The guys decide to take a little swim after dark around 10 P.M., so swim suits will not be required. First, they climb the fence. Pretty soon there are 12 boys having a perfectly decent swimming party without benefit of swimwear or paying. That was when the police showed up, and spoiled everything.

A shining flashlight on the pool alerts the guys that the jig is up. Grabbing their clothes, they hop the fence to make their getaway. Alas, by a 'shriek' of luck one poor chap panics and discovers he is on one side of the fence with his clothes on the other (by the pool). Choosing the logical course of action, he is last seen 'streaking' past St. James church and hiding in the bushes. I can't identify the guy because in the darkness no one could quite remember who he was. The following day the felon refused to 'fess up', so to this day, the nudist cannot be identified. It is commonly reported that a group of bystanders (who later that evening were standing outside the police station just chatting) couldn't figure out why there was such laughter inside the station, as has not been heard for some time. It caused them to laugh too even if they didn't know what the big joke was.

Brief histories are as follows. Bob Hesson joined the Canadian Navy, and became the Navy heavyweight champion in boxing, no doubt a prerequisite for keeping order on ship. Of all the friends I knew, Royce Clark was the first to marry, and the first to divorce. He sped that up by enlisting in the army.

"When I volunteered to go to Korea in 1948", he said jokingly,

"I joined the heroic 10,000 man Canadian Brigade to fight the Communists; of these 9,999 were running away from home troubles." Al MacDonald, of course, as many will know, was employed at The Stratford Beacon Herald, and consequently made himself more knowledgeable on the affairs of Stratford than Lutzen Reidstra of the Perth Archives. Bob Herlick became a detective and worked for the London Police force. After these brief biographies, memory fails me. I guess most of them did fine except for poor Vince Schooley. The last time I saw him alive was on the front lawn of Aunt Elsie and Uncle Gordon's house. Vince was telling me about his sister Barbara's wedding.

"She was beautiful, stunningly beautiful." I was amazed that this gangling kid I remembered could be so lovely, but then that's what happens sometimes when ugly ducklings grow up to become beautiful swans. Vince and I were discussing what mattered in life. By this time, I was getting quite religious and I said,

"I have decided that from now on I'm going to live for God, even if it costs me." Vince replied,

"That's all well and good Bruce but you have to look out for number one." How Vince died is too sad to tell here; I think I'll keep that for later. Jack White, Vince Schooley, Mac Ross and Jim Madge all died a premature death; when you're young, you cannot conceive of such things.

Oh by the way (to resume my story), the puppy caught me again. It all started so innocently with a game of hide and go seek. Sure enough, it's all about Joan Johnston and the 'crushes' she inspired. I think to myself, "Now's my chance to hide with Joan Johnston, under the pretext of the game," but Gordon Glazier spoils everything. There are three of us hiding together. "Maybe later." I think. No dice! Every time a new round of the game begins, there are three of us every time. The tormentors do it to me again.

A word about Gordon (nicknamed Sparky) needs to be said. He liked Lois Candler. In grade 8, we all knew that he liked Lois, and that the feeling was mutual. Spark Glazier showed his affection for Lois by teasing her. Now a little bit of teasing is all part of puppy love, but there are limits. Gordon never seemed to know his limits. Eventually 'like' turned to 'hate'. Now Lois Candler hates Spark

Glazier, and for good reason. (I add my own evaluation of bad manners).

Sparky was greedy. He never shared anything with anyone. Working at Thistle's grocery store (and Sparky was always working), he came into a package of Wrigley's chewing gum in June of 1945. With the war over, such luxuries as chewing gum had not been seen for three years. Sparky (who is as strong as an ox) chewing the first piece, flashes the remaining four pieces in my face and runs away. Soon, a gang of kids are in hot pursuit.

"C'mon Sparky, share the wealth; let us have some of your gum." Sparky is now chewing two pieces of gum, and unwrapping the third. We are closing in but Sparky eludes us all. Even when we catch him, he's too strong to overpower. In the end, we despair, and Sparky is chewing five pieces of gum. With Sparky's character now explained you can understand my deep concern, when he takes a shine to Joan Johnston. There we are hiding for the umpteenth round of the game, and I am not very happy. To exacerbate the situation, Joan grabs Sparky's arm (just like she did with me when we were at the movie show a year earlier) and says, "C'mon, we are going to get caught."

Jealousy, ah, cruel jealousy, makes a beast of a man. There she is making my life miserable again. My altruism comes to the fore. I think, "Joan Johnston, Spark Glazier is definitely not your type." I quit the game and go home. I say to myself, "This is not a good day." The next day I make an entry into a textbook entitled **Britain and the Empire**. It is my history book, on the flyleaf, I inscribe immortal words for posterity. After drawing a heart next to the affectionate original, I inscribe on the second heart, B.W. hates J. J. As an afterthought, just in case things change, I add the words, "while we don't like each other."

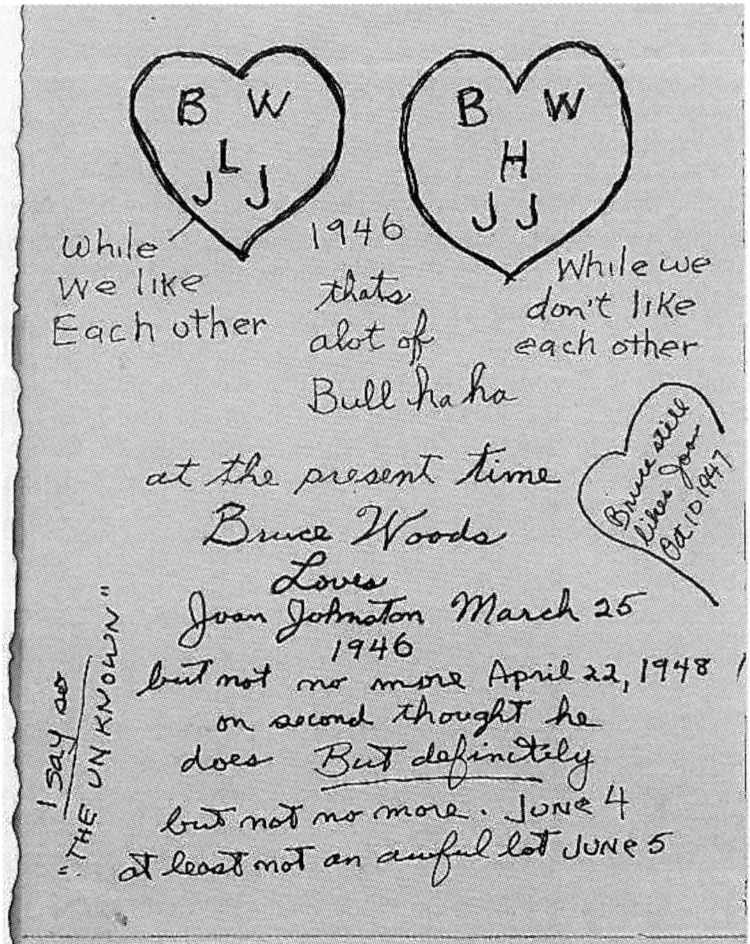

I am of the opinion that puppy-love is akin to Chinese torture. For the uninitiated, Chinese torture as explained to me when I was young is that someone ties you up and tickles your feet until you can't stand it. The sort of thing a kid might be curious enough to try since tickling can be such fun. Puppy-love is also explained in history books (mine) provided you can interpret the graffiti. Take for example Britain and the Empire written by E.L. Daniher and published in 1939 by the Copp Clark Company. This was my textbook in grade ten when I was at high school. I must have purchased it second hand, as there are notes in pencil made by its previous owner. I added a few of my own. It went to John Butler after me and finally was bequeathed to his sister Rita who kept it for over fifty years. Somehow it made its way to Dorothy (Johnston) Landers who in turn gave it to me. I have photocopied the extraneous notations for your reading which while failing to define puppy-love, nonetheless illustrates it.

My explanations as best I can interpret is this. (1) The two hearts illustrate the ambivalent nature of our subject. I suspect the annotation "That's a lot of bull" was added by John Butler at a creative moment of inspiration. (2) The unwritten literature on our subject is my fluctuating emotions, which in a scrupulous manner I painstakingly document off and on as moved by the Muse, who sometimes is open to romance, that's why I added the words, "at least not an awful lot." To verify this legal transaction with fate, I dated it June 5, probably in 1948. (3) The other contribution that says, "Bruce still likes Joan" is in a handwriting I cannot recognize; I therefore attribute this statement to an impartial scribe and it now begs the question for scolarly identification. (4) There is one more ponderous statement that plunges us into the world of mystery. It simply says, "I say so," and is signed by the "The Unknown." Further investigation into the matter explored is in the hands of our readers. Three cheers for puppy-love; may it never perish from the earth. In other words, if I had to suffer so should you.

Puppy Love Pandemonium Photo

Audrey Murphy has engineered a Sunday swimming outing at Embro, July 14, 1946. What I don't know is that she has a crush on me. Mr. Murphy loads nine of us kids into his new Studebaker and takes us to Embro Park.

Audrey arranges a picture op, putting herself in front of me and putting Joan Johnson as far as possible to the right. Oblivious of this, I am preoccupied with my heartthrob, Joan. Meanwhile, I have become self-conscious of how skinny I look, which is why I wear (inappropriately for the occasion) a sports jacket. I imagine that I have now improved upon my anatomical shortcomings. Eventually Audrey gives me the picture. Obviously I still have something going for me, because this photo hints that my affections might be better placed with the girl that is closest (i.e. herself). Such is the paradox of puppy-love and teenage insecurity.

Puppy love is not the same as dating. Dating means kissing; in puppy love you write notes. Having written a few and received a few, I submit myself as an authority on this topic. I regret to report to you that I have forgotten all those notes except one. Billy Murphy gave me a note that had no signature. I share with you its unforgettable contents.

To 2-18-21-3-5 (Here's how it reads)

I am sorry to tell you that I don't like you anymore so I hope you understand that from now on we're just friends. Find yourself another girlfriend.

signed, 10-15-1-14

Who is 2-18-21-3-5? Suddenly, I get it. The numbers correspond to the alphabet, 2 equals B, 18 equals R, etc. This is written to me. As I read this note, my spirits fall. Whoever this mystery person is, she doesn't like me anymore. I wonder immediately, does this note comes from Joan Johnston? I apply the same decoding method to 10-15-1-14; it spells Joan. I am crushed. Now, I wonder which is less painful, jumping in front of a car or taking gas. Fortunately, I did neither or you would not have been able to read this tragic tale. I have loved and lost; it's enough to make a man eat worms. One week later I discovered it was a forgery penned by — you guessed it, Audrey Murphy. (I wonder was it Puck or was it Pan that put her up to all this mischief.) All of which goes to show that it was wise on my part to write in my history book "At the present time, Bruce Woods loves Joan Johnston but not no more" (dated April 20) whatever that can mean. Some few days later I write, "On second thought he does" (this entry was not dated). My recollection is fuzzy. Perhaps somewhere along the line Joan must have smiled at me because, I emphasize my uncertainty by writing, "But definitely" (added shortly afterwards but not dated). A little later I add "But not no more"; perhaps Joan had ignored me when we were playing tag or some such game like hop scotch; at any rate, I take pains to document this entry (June 4). Then with magnanimous heart, I write "At least not an awful lot," a phrase, which illustrates my inherent forgiving nature (June 5). All this weighty stuff within a 24 hour period of time! Just what really took place between April 20 and June

5 now eludes me. I will leave my reader, fed by their own variety of experiences, to imagine. Most of you at one time or another have probably been through a torturous bout of puppy love and can commiserate without any help from me. If this is too confusing, just look at the page from my history book provided for your edification.

Sunday afternoon and Russell McIntee is coming home from teaching his class at Ontario Street Baptist Church. He has a habit of asking me to come to Sunday school. He reminds me of Charlie Michie, who was my Sunday school class teacher, for the year I went to the Congregational Church. Of course, I don't want to go, so I always politely decline Mr. McIntee's invitation. It is another pleasant Sunday afternoon and we are playing baseball when the guys say to me,

"Here he comes again, Bruce." I make a hasty exit to the storage shed and hide. With Mr. McIntee out of the commons playground, it's safe to come out and resume our game. At this point, I decide on a little mockery of religion. Singing in a falsetto voice and perversely looking for a cheap laugh I belt out a few lines,

"Jesus loves me this I know, for the Bible tells me so." I reap the desired response; a surprised Vince Schooley exclaims,

"Woodsie, you crack me up, I didn't even know you ever learned such a song." Johnny laughs too, but John Butler just turns and looks the other way. Later that day, I review my histrionics and think, "Bruce, you crossed the line." From now on, if I decide to play the joker, I will restrict my material to off-colour stuff.

Unbeknown to me my guardian angel, crestfallen, routinely reports the events of the day to Gabriel. He's inexperienced like me and is feeling inadequate for his task. Gabriel's eyes twinkle, and if you were glancing at just the right angle, a wry smile can be discerned on his otherwise solemn face. It's as if he knows something that my guardian angel has missed. He shows little emotion. Meanwhile my angel does his usual daily chores and despite my fluctuating emotions, I sleep well, oblivious of what is happening in my other world.

Chapter 28

Stratford High

I shall never forget the wounding of my knee. The pain was excruciating. I am a normal fun loving kid playing a game of tag at Uncle Gordon's house. I am chasing Bobby, my cousin, along the side of the house on the jagged cement pieces of old torn up sidewalk that make up the path beside the house. Oh Yeah! I should slip on the one that protruded like some ancient but jagged Stonehenge from the past. Next thing I know, blood is spurting from my leg; as Aunt Elsie holds the cold wet cloth-compress tightly to my kneecap. When the bleeding eventually stops, she pours iodine on my wound.

"The flesh is torn so badly," she says, "I think it needs stitches to close the wound." I shudder to hear her words and imagine the worst. The pain is so intense that I get no sleep that night. I think, "This is what it's like to be wounded in battle." The war in Europe has been over for three months but I think of our Canadian soldiers who are still far away in Europe recovering from their wounds. I didn't get those needed stitches and I pay the price for my fears. It took five weeks for my knee to heal just in time to take in the Fall Fair.

The annual Fall Fair is a celebratory event. The rides are a nickel and mother has given me a dollar. Johnny and I walk a mile to the fairgrounds on the north side of town. Our pace quickens as we hear the sounds of the midway. The Caterpillar is my favourite thriller because once we are seated, the canopy covers the circular track while we whirl around madly, going nowhere. The Fall Fair is really a time for farmers to display their produce and livestock. Even the lowly pig can win an award and every housewife that bakes a pie or cake gets into the competition. Its great stuff for kids too who longingly gaze at the delicious looking food and wish they could abscond with the prize winning dessert for an illicit feast. I remember vowing to myself, "When the day comes that I can afford to buy candy and delicacies like that, I will surely gorge myself on all that is forbidden to me now." Life is so unfair. At last, now that I can afford it, sweet things have little appeal.

The fair has many exotic smells and exquisite sights. Red candy apples tantalize the eyes. Pink candy floss tests the palate. Then there is the Freak Show where one can see a sailor who is tattooed from head to foot. The fat lady beside the midgets beckons us to go through the funhouse where, after it's over we are tempted (provided we pay 15 cents) to see things we dare not tell our mothers. Johnny and I count our quickly diminishing cash and decide on prudence. We still have to visit the hot dog stand and we can't begin to afford all the rides that are offered. We were rewarded when we heard the older guys (who could afford 15cents) muttering,

"What a rip off; not worth the money!" O the wonderful fall fair where the 'grandest and the damnedest' can be seen and experienced on a single day! Additionally, there is always the privilege of exchanging glances with the girls who are there for exactly the same purpose. The 'test of strength' bell is always an attraction. It is great fun to watch the strong guys pit their muscles against the hawker who will give them a useless doll if they can ring the bell with the sledgehammer. There are plenty of red faces to go around the-would-be-jocks, that is, until Gus showed up. I never got to know his last name but everybody around Stratford knew the gentle giant who was as strong as an ox. Achieving recognition is easy in a small city. When he took the sledge in his hands, we all knew the hawker was going to lose his doll. How we laughed when he rang the bell again and again to the place where we thought he was going to destroy the rig and the hawker protested that he had seen enough.

There was one temptation, however, that still beckoned. Over supper that night I pled with mother to give me four nickels more so I could go to the gambling booth.

"Mother" I intoned, "I feel lucky; just let me go back with four nickels and I know I will come back with a dollar." Perhaps it was because she thought it might teach me a lesson, or perhaps it was because mother just caved in to my persistent pleadings, but right after supper, once again, I was on my way to the fair. I go straight to the gambling booth and lay down my nickel on a three to one return. The attendant spins the wheel and promptly I win. I now have 35 cents. I should have walked away but the thought of winning a dollar is so alluring, I cannot resist. You can guess the rest of the story. Nickelless, I tramp the sights of the fair wishing I had my original four nickels. The fall fair has lost its allure. I can live without it for at least another year. Later that evening when I return home, shamed, I tell my mother,

"I shall never gamble again," and I never have. Not even a lottery ticket.

I'm in grade 9 and Mr. O'Leary is my home class teacher. A likeable guy, he is balding and has middle age spread. He lives around the corner from me on Nile Street. Mr. O'Leary teaches French. I soon discover that languages are not my forte. I am fated to do badly in French. Later, I will continue to do badly in Greek and Hebrew. Latin was impossible for me. I dropped out after two weeks, and took typing instead from Maggie Mitchell. Geography is my favourite subject because geography is where they make history to which I have now aspired. My good news story about High School is, — that in the athletic competitions, anybody who is 13 doesn't have to compete with the fourteen-year olds. With most of my competitors out of the running in the high jump, I tie the high school record by clearing 4 feet 4 inches. When I return home, I exhault in my newly achieved Olympian status. In my other world, Mercury gives a report to Zeus who laughs me to scorn.

The tormentors of puppy 'love bite' are at it again. I am riding my bike down Brunswick Street and slip off the seat. I suddenly scream in pain, (in guy language, as I have previously explained, its called 'cracking your nuts' or to be more sophisticated, it's that most vulnerable part of the male anatomy that, metaphorically, we call the 'family jewels'). I'm on the lawn rolling in pain. Suddenly, my worst nightmare descends upon me. I look up, and who should be coming by, on her bike? None other than Joan Johnston. She says to me with genuine concern,

"What's wrong with you?"

"Nothing," I protest.

"You don't look like it's nothing," she replies.

"It's nothing, just leave me alone." By now my face is red.

"Sure there's nothing I can do to help?" Joan replies.

"Nothing."

"Doesn't make sense to me, but if you're OK, I guess I'll be on my way."

My relief comes not from the cessation of pain, but from the comfort that at last Joan has departed. I think, "She has brothers, she knows." I cannot face her for a month.

Joan Johnston has a friend that walks to school with her every day. (That is until grade 8 when the boundary line was redrawn and Helen had to go to Juliet Public School for one year.) Alas, the kid population has so dramatically declined that Juliet school was torn down in 2003, and ever since Romeo Public has been in such mourning that they don't even return phone calls. Helen Haynes and Joan Johnston are always together. They decide to give each other a permanent wave. The Toni is in. Competition for mother's business begins in the most innocuous way. Helen's hair responds well to a Toni. She looks in the mirror and is pleased. Tomorrow, it's Joan's turn. For Joan Johnston, the Toni is a disaster on the order of 'Anne of Green Gables' green hair. Joan's hair is thick and full, so when the Toni has dispensed its magic, Joan is wearing an Afro, twenty-five years before people knew what an Afro looked like. Horrified, she threatens to quit school.

"I can't let people see me this way," she cries. Mrs. Johnston is prosaic. Joan goes to school. Later that week, when I see her, I cannot believe my eyes. Joan looks the other way. She's not in a talking mood. It takes a year for her to look normal again. It looks so awful that for a while, it breaks the spell. Maybe, I like Pat Wilkes better. Nope, the scars of puppy 'love bite,' will not go away. I go to see the movie, 'Meet me in St. Louis'. The heroine is Judy Garland. I fall in love with Judy; she has red hair. I'm in trouble; Joan Johnston's Afro is slowly growing out. It's a Samson and Delilah story in reverse.

My Uncle Ross is Dad's brother; he has returned to civvies, after his release from the Air Force. Uncle Ross pays us a visit. He has a model airplane of the famous Spitfire with "Myra" neatly lettered on the fuselage. I covet that model airplane, but Ross ignores the obvious and takes it with him when he leaves. He tells us how he was stationed during the war on Ascension Island, in the Atlantic, 800 miles off the coast of Africa. Bombers destined for Britain, with a limited flying range, made the circuitous route through Brazil, and then to Ascension. From the airbase at Ascension, they flew to

North Africa. From North Africa they flew to England. There were 8000 men stationed at Ascension in 1943. All crowded on an island with only 36 square miles and a single tree. Ascension was where Napoleon was to be banished; however, at the last minute; he was switched to St. Helena. Ascension was regarded as too desolate. Uncle Ross said,

"The place was so barren that some of the men lost their minds." Years later Ross told me, near the end of the battle of the Atlantic, the Germans, in a desperate gamble to snuff out Ascension attempted a commando raid. Loading 200 men on five submarines, they were to attack by night. They were easily detected, and destroyed by aircraft. Commandos and submarine crews met a watery grave. I suspect that kind of information was something he would sooner forget, a truth, which explains why he waited 50 years to tell me.

The teen dance has started up again at City Hall. Now that I'm 14, I am no longer persona non grata. I pay my dime and I'm in. Joyce Bossence is a good dancer. Every time they play 'In the mood' I ask her to dance. We hit it off. To my mind, it's just a lot of fun. I learn later on, that she reads more into it than I did. That's what 'puppy love' is all about. Designed by the gods to make kids miserable. Somebody tells Richard Schmidt that I'm flirting with his girl and trying to take her away. It's the last thing on my mind. How do these rumours get started? Richard takes me outside and roughs me up. He's stronger than I am, so his girlfriend Pat never gets an invitation to dance from me. Sure glad that one is over. I guess the thing I remember most from the teen dance are the songs. Sixty years later and I can still hum the tunes. The Hit Parade is always in our minds and the words of the songs can be purchased in the Hit Parade Song Sheet with the top 100. My favourites are; 'When They Begin the Beguine' and 'Stardust'. I love to sing the songs in the kitchen when nobody out there is listening. I never miss listening to the Lucky Strike Survey on our radio to keep me informed which song is on the top of the Hit Parade. I guess Lucky Strike cigarettes wasted their advertising dollars on me. When I finally got around to smoking, I always bought Sweet Caporals or Player's Mild.

Danny Coughlin is a pretty good singer, and sometimes acts as M.C. at the teen dance. He sings a few songs and we listen. I think he could make it in the big time. Danny eventually did a stint at Nashville. However his greatest claim to fame comes through TV from CKCO, Kitchener, where he hosted The Treehouse Show for kids. Danny is as close to a celebrity as you can get to be in the hometown scene. He was often in demand for special appearances. The program was syndicated and sold in Canada and also in the USA. Years later, I even brought him to Hamilton for a Sunday evening gig. Danny was a Stratford boy through and through, and he made good. He often spoke of how Gene McLelland of Nashville fame stole his song, rewrote a few lines and published a hit called, 'Put your Hand in the Hand of the Man Who stilled the Water'. Danny's song was remarkably the same. If indeed the story is true, Danny "wos robbed". That song sure did the rounds, and made a lot of money for Gene McLelland. I don't think Danny ever got over that disappointment. Makes me wonder if the whole episode hastened his death, but he's in heaven now, so maybe he doesn't care.

Chapter 29

Army Cadets

The war is over but the spirit of patriotism is strong. I am standing at the Avon River and I see a gang of Sea Cadets rowing a long white boat complete with a dozen large paddles. I watch in fascination as they glide by and say to myself, "Now that's the life for me." I enlist in the Navy. There are a hundred of us who have all been similarly, and patriotically, inspired. We march around in a vacated store facing Ontario Street, hear stories about battles at sea and long for the day when we can get to paddle the long white boat. It's my third time attending Sea Cadets, when our leader announces that he has something important to teach us. He has two pairs of boxing gloves in his hand and enthusiastically says,

"Today we are going to learn about self defense." I cringe at the thought of fighting a battle I am sure to lose and try to look invisible.

Observing the circle of kids, our Captain chooses Bev Crawford, a husky kid who leaps to his feet with enthusiasm. Next he looks squarely at me cringing in fear and utters the first death threat I have ever heard.

"The other contestant will be Bruce Woods." I feign enthusiasm as our leader explains to us the art of self-defense. I think to myself, my best defense is to run, but I am ashamed to admit it. Now I am facing my adversary. I remember when I had to fight Barry Knechtal. History repeats itself when the bell sounds and its 'fists first' while I'm just thinking it over. Bev lands a punch squarely on my nose which bleeds profusely. Needless to say, our leader is alarmed and stops the match. He sends me home with encouraging words to return next week. I decline the invitation. My patriotism is spent. Others can paddle the boat. I quit Sea Cadets for good. I will be automatically drafted for Army Cadets when I enter grade 10.

January 16, 1946 was as cold as a polar bear's living room. The weather was not exactly suited to the warmth in the hearts of the Stratford citizens who were anxiously waiting at the CNR station for their sons and husbands to come home. The day was special because the Perth regiment had completed their tour of duty in Holland and Germany. They had missed Christmas 1945, but at long last they were home. The Trans-Atlantic journey was made on the Queen

Elizabeth to New York City. Monday, January 14, they had arrived and set eyes on North American soil. Wednesday, January 16, they detrained in Stratford.

The once proud 900 strong Perth Regiment that marched in Stratford four years earlier was still proud when 833 men boarded ship in Halifax, bound for England. They eventually numbered 1047 as they completed their training in England. Their fate was to fight with distinction in Italy in some of the bloodiest battles of World War II. Theirs was no ordinance job behind the front lines, which for so many made the overseas junket a hazardous, but not necessarily dangerous, job. No advance training can prepare a soldier for live combat. Like many other front line regiments, they had to learn the "little tricks" on how to stay alive the hard way, while too many others paid in blood the inevitable price of inexperience.

The million men that were in the Canadian Armed Forces averaged 4.5 % fatalities. For regiments like the Perth, it was more like 25%. The war in Italy was a ferocious bloodletting in which Canada's citizen army engaged Hitler's professionals. From their disastrous beginning at the Riccio River and Ortona to their "spectacular performance" cracking the Gothic Line, the Perth Regiment distinguished themselves as one of the finest fighting units in the Canadian Army. They ultimately wound up squaring against the elite 1st Parachute Division of General Richard Heidrich and won, earning respect and fear from one of Hitler's most renown Divisions.* Rerouted to Belgium in February, they waged their final battles in Holland. After Germany surrendered, they were stationed in the Dutch City of Sneek.

Attrition had claimed nearly 50% of their number; European graves claimed 261 more. Of the original regiment, a battle hardened but weary 367 deployed for the very last time on the snowy grounds of the Stratford CNR Station. The tumultuous welcome the loyal citizens of Stratford gave these worthy veterans hid from my eyes

*The inspiring story of the Perth Regiment and their fame as a fighting force is recounted in Stanley Scislowski' book **Not All of Us Were Brave** published by Dundurn Press, 1997.

the horrific price they had paid for our freedom. It was only many years later that the full import of their sacrifice came home to this naïve teenager now many years older and wiser. Despite the bitterly cold weather the same crowds that cheered the Perth Regiment four years earlier once again lined the same Downie Street to receive home their "special" boys. The final staging area was in front of the City Hall. Stratford native Lieutenant-Colonel Maurice Andrew gave the last order,

"Company Dismissed." It was just that simple, and now it was over.

Breaking ranks and reuniting with loved ones and families, the Perth Regiment melted away while the frozen snow remained until spring. The price of war is paid by the young. The aftermath is the loneliness of the women, whose lot in life, is to fend for themselves and to remember with sadness the missing faces at family reunions. It took time to comprehend this dreadful truth. Had we really considered this at the time of the V-E celebrations, we might have declared a fast of mourning. Providentially, we were spared that knowledge until much later. Perhaps it was for the best.

Two years later, the spirit of the military establishment has been emboldened by the cold war. Furthermore the 'Commies' now have the atom bomb. All male students in Stratford High that are not in Air Cadets or Sea Cadets are to get an update in patriotism the military way that was sagaciously called 'Inspection'. We are all to be Army Cadets for a day. I am pleased to know that our instruction will be given during gym period, because, now for a little while, I don't have to play basketball pretending to enjoy the game that favours the athletic. As for 'Inspection' as such, we were to soon discover the day was more of a pain than a pleasure. In contrast to the hardened faces of the Perth Regiment we saw two years ago in January, Stratford will witness her innocent teens taking a stab at pretending to be soldiers. The high school kids will wear those old army uniforms in June complete with rifles and go on parade. I suppose the grand event is to inspire us kids to think patriotic thoughts and imbue us with a warlike spirit. It is the brainchild of the military establishment to challenge kids like me to consider the virtues of the military life. If we could have penetrated the great beyond, I'm sure Mars and Apollyon would be congratulating one another with appropriate speeches and toasts to the follies of war.

For the first time in my life I get to handle a 303 carbine and march around the gym. The rifle is unbelievably heavy and hurts my shoulder. I think that those soldiers who had to carry these things all over Europe deserve a medal just for lugging these rifles around, let alone shooting bullets at the enemy. We are challenged to go to the armoury on Waterloo Street and take up target practice. This is fun for the jocks but I'm not a jock. I decline the invitation. In fact, I am soon to learn that I can avoid carrying that heavy gun altogether by joining the Red Cross medics. In a burst of patriotism, I volunteer to carry a band aid kit to help the wounded and congratulate myself that the only thing I have to carry on parade is a small metal case that holds less than a pound of first aid equipment.

There is a price tag for my rifle exemption. Now I have to learn first aid, which means I stay after school for the instructions. Alas, just as you think you've beaten the system, they exact a price. I think about the day I asked my guidance teacher about a future in the army and doing three years at the Military Academy in Kingston. I seriously thought a career in the army might be a challenge, but the trouble is now that World War II has been fought and won, there won't be any more wars. I can still hear Mr. Malcolm's words.

"Never fear, Bruce, as long as men inhabit the earth, there will be wars." My dreams of a world with no more wars are shattered.

Parade day is Friday, June 18, 1948. Classes are cancelled. Every kid in high school is involved: the guys to participate, and the girls to watch. A week beforehand we are to be issued our uniforms. We find out that they are winter wear made of wool. Meantime, this year, summer has arrived early. Previous experience has rendered disclosure. Coach Ray Sinclair knows exactly what to expect. The combination of wool uniforms and kids standing at attention for a half-hour in summer weather is a recipe for sunstroke. Half of our Red Cross unit has been preempted for the work of stretcher-bearers for those who are bound to faint. Since they take the bigger guys for this job, there are still fifteen of us in possession of our little metal case to succor the wounded should the need arise.

Knowing in advance what we are in for, I pray for a cool rainy day.

June 18th turns out to be cloudless with a weather forecast that predicts the temperature will be hot and humid. Apparently, army prayers have clout. We shed our light summer clothing for the wool army uniforms while the grumbling begins. Kids in grade nine are exempt. The grade ten kids have to participate; however, they can march with wooden replica rifles. The rest have to lug around the real McCoy. Al McDonald and three of his buddies swipe four of the wooden replicas when Mr. Sinclair isn't looking. Lining up in our predetermined places, we look like the Perth regiment reborn. The similarity is, of course, a resemblance only and as everybody knows, looks are an illusion. Coach Ray Sinclair is too smart to be fooled by illusions. He spots the four grade eleven malefactors with the wooden replicas. With appropriate expletives, he orders them to exchange them for the real thing. If looks could kill Coach Sinclair would be awful sick, if not completely dead. Parade day begins with a march past the Army brass assembled on a platform located on the high ground near Birmingham Street. After we have returned to our formation, we hear the command, "Company at ease."

We are standing erect and motionless in the sunshine and are squirming with the heat. Nobody is listening to the speeches made by important people in praise of King and Country. It's worse than 'a boring sermon in church'. Our faces are facing the platform. Our ears are completely tuned out. Our minds are groaning, "When is this thing going to be over." Ten minutes into the charade the first student bites the dust. Somebody calls,

"Stretcher-bearers." The first of 17 hapless students earmarked for ignominy is carried off the field. The speeches drone on and suddenly I am starting to feel queasy. I get this sickening sensation in the pit of my stomach. The day is bright but I am unfocused and darkness is crowding in around my eyes. My knees begin to buckle; the heat is unbearable and has taken its toll on my strength. I am now engaging in a dance with the shifting ground that won't stay still.

"I must not faint, the shame of it, I'm not even balancing a rifle — I must not faint — I must not —.

Through the gathering fog I hear a distant command, "Attention! Right wheel! Comp–any march!" Instinctively, we stomp our left foot and wheel on our right. The words are far away but they come like a life preserver to a drowning man. It's all I can do to navigate the earth, which is reeling under my feet. Somehow, deep within the reservoir of human courage, resolve, and the fear of ridicule, I manage to stumble one foot ahead of the other. Slowly stamina returns. By the time I get to the platform of dignitaries I am a sweating drone bee staving off death, but at least I'm on my feet. We are now heading up Birmingham Street with thirty to a platoon led by several Sargent-for-a-day jocks pre-chosen by Coach Sinclair for their muscular appearance. In other words, because these guys looked like Sergeant Major material, they get to be important.

Don't ask me what Sergeant-for-a-day David Forbes said to Private-for-a-day Bob Collins, but a scuffle breaks out between them right on parade while we are supposed to be looking our best. Mars and Apollyon are about to have their little tea party spoiled. Out of character to be sure, they rush their aid to the call for intervention. Before Bob and David come to blows, they decide not to break up the parade with a fistfight, fall in line, and continue to march. Meantime, Scooter Lennon, (one of the four wooden rifle-cheating malefactors) takes the notion to defy Coach Sinclair. Walking off at the spot closest to the high school, he returns his rife and goes home. The rest of us march up to Erie Street and then back to the football field. When we finally hear the command,

"Company dismiss." I stagger up the hill to the front door, surrender my Red Cross kit and uniform. Smiling at our Coach, I say,

"Thanks, Mr. Sinclair." — I lied! As I give up my outfit, I mutter under my breath, "Underwear from hell on the hottest day of the year." I am relieved to see the end of inspection and ponder the virtues of being a pacifist, which I suppose is not exactly what the Army had in mind when they dreamed up this special occasion. Just as I make my departure, school friend Muriel Bellamy says to me,

"Whatever was wrong with you on Parade, you looked white as a ghost." I stammer a reply that I can no longer remember and resolve whatever the future holds I shall never be a soldier.

Somebody must have complained. There are no more Army Cadet days and I finish my high school having long forgotten how to dress wounded soldiers in battle.

Chapter 30

Growing Pains

Vince thinks I ought to take up smoking; I agree. I've been thinking about it myself, and have decided that it would look good to smoke. Clarkie thinks the same. He saw a kid riding his bike smoking a pipe, and noticed how mature it appeared to see a teenager smoking a pipe. What could possibly look better than a boy smoking his pipe while riding a bicycle? I tried that for one day and nearly choked, so I opted for the easy life. Cigarettes are readily available because the Schooley's have opened a little booth on their property and sell candy, ice cream, and cigarettes. We are finished with picking up butts and relighting them in the garage, out of sight from prying eyes. I buy from Schooley's Booth a package of Sweet Caporal cigarettes. I can smell the tobacco as I open the foil paper. Carefully placing a cigarette in my mouth I run to the mirror to see how I look. I light the cigarette, admiring myself in the mirror. I should have taken a picture.

This devil–may–care kid has to learn to inhale the smoke; otherwise, you are just puffing. I light up and take a deep drag. Vulcan rallies to my aid and vainly tries to help. I choke and my eyes start to water, while Vince looks on and laughs. Self-immolation aside, I smile at Vince and rasp the words,

"Boy that sure tastes good!" I work at this slowly, and within a week with blackened lungs and several choking sessions, I have arrived. Vulcan gloats over another convert and I inform mother and Grandma that now I am just like any decent self-respecting grown up. I am a smoker with all of the benefits thereof such as bad breath and sizzled taste buds. Uncle Gordon tells me how to save money smoking. You buy the tobacco in a can and roll your own. I tried this once. The result was so miserable that I conclude, "Might as well roll up tobacco in toilet paper", besides, it wouldn't look good to have anything but a proper cigarette in you mouth for people to see. I have a worthy objective; I wish to qualify for the arena smoking room. The Stratford arena allowed smokers to enjoy their addiction in the smoking room. That's when between periods at a hockey game we got to inhale multiple cigarettes all at once. The smoking room was always crowded with guys puffing their nicotine. I can still feel the exhilaration of that room, blue with smoke, knowing how great it was to be all grown up and mature like everybody else.

-oOo-

It's summer in Stratford. A new adventure calls. We hear its great fun to swim off the Waterloo Bridge. To make it even more appealing, we hear the police have placed the bridge off limits to kids who want to swim there and dive off the bridge because the river is polluted. The challenge is appealing. Bathing suits already on, we wear light clothing, and ride our bikes to the bridge. Johnny, Butler, and I, are soon in the water having a great time. We are encouraged; we got away with it. However, after a few times some weeks later, the inevitable happens. We have just had another thrill of a lifetime. We have climbed to the railing; precariously balanced ourselves on the narrow railing, and then with a good push plunged into the water 15 feet below.

"Here come the cops," Johnny laments. The police car slows down and we hear,

"Hey you kids, out of the river. There's no swimming allowed." Looking a little sheepish, we gather our things, dry off, and dress. It's a wonderful achievement to be kicked off the bridge by the cops. We celebrate with a butterscotch sundae at the Jumbo Ice Cream Parlour and tell Jimmy Barr, our server, all about it.

Butler, Johnny, and I have never been kicked out of anything except the river. We are good kids. Still the idea of being kicked out of anything for being bad has appeal. The opportunity comes along the next time we go to the Classic theatre on Ontario Street. The Frank Sinatra craze is riding high. The girls go nuts at the crooner's concerts and sometimes even faint. We are at the show watching a movie that stars the singer and (boys will be boys), we are turning up our noses at one of his torch songs. Suddenly, we come up with a bright idea. Conspiracy is afoot. After a quick conference we decide to scream every time Sinatra sings a love song (I assure you, envy has nothing to do with this). In no time the usher is at our side telling us to cool it. We agree. The truce is temporary. The next time a song is crooned, we feign a swoon and scream. Our usher returns and gives us an ultimatum. Just what we wanted! We wait for the next song Sinatra sings, and we are at it again, reaping the desired harvest.

"Out of your seats!" The usher commands. Music to our ears! Our usher takes us to the door shouting,

"And don't come back again." We are on the street laughing and congratulating one another. It is an exhilarating feeling to think that we are bad enough to suffer such ignominy, and can hardly wait to share our good fortune with the guys.

The dissolute life of the troublemaker is now our pursuit. Our guardian angels are in disarray. Clarkie has just told me that you can get drunk for a few seconds, if you stand under the exhaust fan of the Windsor Hotel. The thought of it is so intimidating that not even the most rebellious of our number is willing to try.

"Okay," says Clarkie, "if you are scared to give it a try, I will lead the way." With heroics like this who can resist? If Clarkie goes first, and survives, we will follow suit. The crucial day comes after a swim at the Lion's pool. It is a warm summer day in August and we arrive at the Windsor, breathless in anticipation. The patrons are in the bar and having their usual beer and cigarette. Bravely Clarkie steps up to the wall right under the exhaust fan. He breathes in deeply and exclaims,

"I can smell the cigarette smoke and the fumes from the beer." In anticipation of this profound experience, we await Clarkie's existential high. He walks away and reels a little to the left and says, "There – I was drunk for at least a minute!" Gallantly, I'm the next to give it a try. I wait for the intoxicating moment, but nothing happens.

"You must have used up all the fumes, Clarkie," I disappointedly say, "I can't feel a thing." Next Johnny gives it a try with the same result. Finally John Butler tries as well, but nothing happens. Clarkie says, "You'll have to wait until another day. Maybe only the first guy gets the best crack at getting drunk for a moment, but it sure feels good while it lasts."

The next day, we try again. This time Clarkie is not with us but we are game to go, even thought Clarkie is absent. No luck. None of us can get drunk.

"I think Clarkie was just play-acting," says Butler.

"Yah," says Johnny, "I'll bet he was just pretending to put us on."

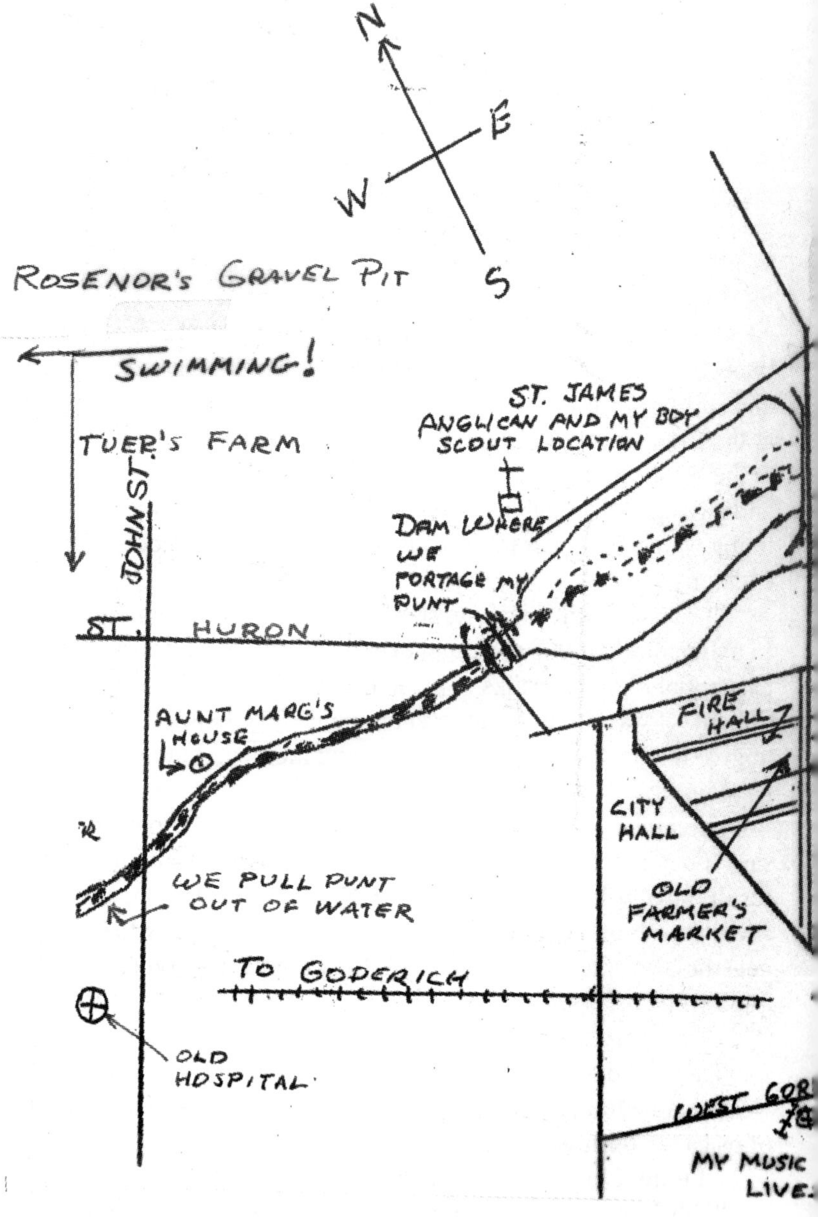
N
E
W
S
ROSENOR'S GRAVEL PIT
SWIMMING!
TUER'S FARM
JOHN ST.
ST. JAMES
ANGLICAN AND MY BOY
SCOUT LOCATION
DAM WHERE
WE
PORTAGE MY
PUNT
ST. HURON
AUNT MARG'S
HOUSE
FIRE
HALL
CITY
HALL
WE PULL PUNT
OUT OF WATER
OLD
FARMER'S
MARKET
TO GODERICH
OLD
HOSPITAL
WEST
MY MUSIC

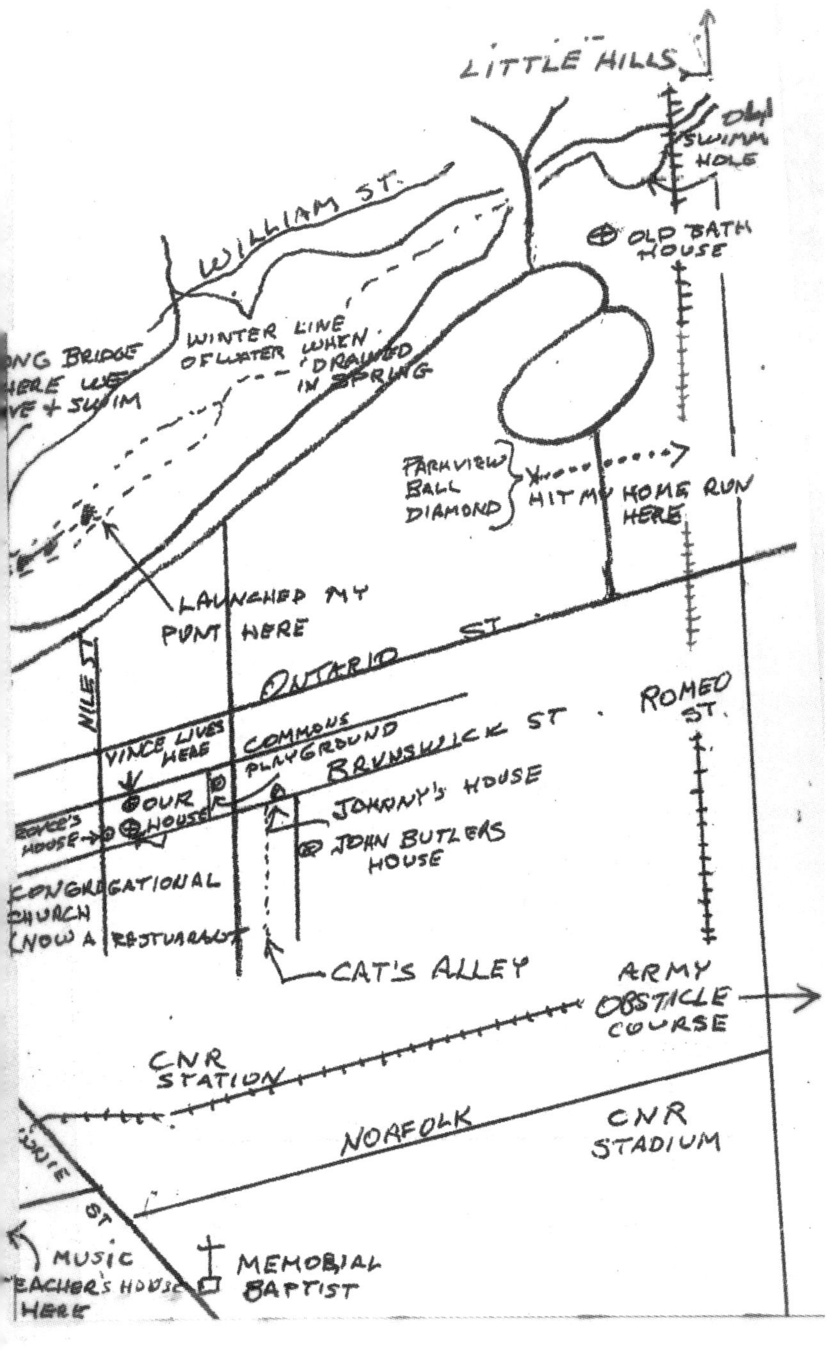
LITTLE HILLS
OLD SWIMM HOLE
WILLIAM ST.
OLD BATH HOUSE
WINTER LINE OF WATER WHEN DRAINED IN SPRING
NG BRIDGE HERE WE VE + SWIM
PARKVIEW BALL DIAMOND
HIT MY HOME RUN HERE
LAUNCHED MY PUNT HERE
ONTARIO ST
NILES ST
ROMEO ST
VINCE LIVES HERE
COMMONS PLAYGROUND
BRUNSWICK ST
OUR HOUSE
JOHNNY'S HOUSE
JOHN BUTLERS HOUSE
HOUSE
CONGREGATIONAL CHURCH (NOW A RESTUARANT)
CAT'S ALLEY
ARMY OBSTICLE COURSE
CNR STATION
NORFOLK
CNR STADIUM
ST
MUSIC TEACHER'S HOUSE HERE
MEMORIAL BAPTIST

On this conclusive evidence, we soberly agree. There will be no drunken orgy for us. We just give it up as a bad adventure and decide not to believe Clarkie's wild stories anymore. The next time I see Clarkie I tell him we know he was spoofing,

"No way," he protests, "try it again at night when there are more patrons at the hotel." I have become an unbeliever. We have better things to do at night than to bother about getting drunk for a minute.

Chapter 31

Boatbuilding

It's an adventure story that began in the spring of '46, and takes two years to run its course. I have to skip ahead of my tale and then pick up where I left off. I am eyeing the dam that keeps the Avon River looking like a small lake in summer. As the spring runoff rushes over the dam, I watch in fascination at the lower Avon, as Neptune and Poseidon violently churn the rushing stream it never is at other times. At the moment, the Avon River is limpid and shallow but below the dam it is a torrent. I think, "What an adventure it would be, if I could rent a canoe and ride those turbulent waters." Of course the Stratford Canoe people would never agree to that, because it is too dangerous. I am ignorant of the annual drowning records of those that pit their strength against the frigid spring runoff. I make up my mind: "I will build my own boat and ride the floodwaters of the Avon, next year." There is consternation in heaven, my guardian angel has just fainted. I am oblivious of the many sad stories of springtime boating mishaps. Kids are totally innocent of hidden danger.

"Mother, think of the fun I could have; Uncle Gordon will help me build it." Mother agrees. (Did she ever disagree with my nutty schemes?) I make the proposal to Uncle Gordon.

"If your mother is crazy enough to pay for it, I guess I'm crazy enough to help you build your boat." Uncle Gordon has at last recuperated from a sad industrial accident, when he cut off three fingers of his left hand on a table saw at Preston Noelting's Furniture factory.

"Twenty-seven years I worked at that factory without an accident, and I have to do something as stupid as that," Uncle Gordon used to say.

The skeleton of my new craft is taking shape like the bones of a whale. Soon, we are putting on the skin, which is made of Masonite. Getting the nose right is a little tricky. A piece of canvas spread over the skeleton completes the work. It is painted green. Summer has arrived and now we are ready to launch. Johnny is my shipmate. We have made a little pull cart with the buggy wheels I never used for that first Soap Box Derby crate. We are about to give my craft its baptism. The placid Avon invites us. Johnny's up front; and I take the back. We push off for our maiden voyage, dipping our paddles into the water, and moving nicely just like when we rent a canoe. My punt has surpassed my wildest dreams. Foo Pauli, eat your heart out. Then simultaneously, we both cry out,

"Our feet are getting wet." Johnny complains,

"This thing leaks like a sieve." It's all we can do to turn the punt around before the whole thing sinks to the bottom. Water is squirting everywhere. Now we are laughing as we make for the riverbank. We scramble out and turn the craft sideways, dumping the water.

"I don't think you're as good a boatbuilder as you thought," says Johnny. I ruefully agree and wish I knew an Indian (after all, they invented the canoe). Deflated, we haul our craft back home. I thank Johnny for the effort,

"There's gotta be a way to fix this thing. We'll try again after I figure it out. I need an expert."

Jack Rutherford is my expert. Jack is a year younger than I, and is also building a punt. I go to see Jack, who recommends a black pitch for the seams that leak. I apply the pitch, which is like tar. I figure to give it eight months to dry. We will try the venture again, but not till the spring of 1947. Mother's caper to Vancouver/Calgary (more of that in a later chapter) had nearly sabotaged my boat building career; however, with that adventure out of the way, I am ready to navigate the mighty waters of the lower Avon.

Easter comes late in 1947. There is still some snow around, and the water is flowing fast from the snowmelt. The placid Avon below the dam is boiling with the runoff. Poseidon rubs his hands with glee. The moment of my adventure is now ready. Johnny and I have the week off from school, because it's Easter. Monday we are ready. Just after lunch we make our way to the Avon via Nile Street. Lake Victoria looks more like a deflated millpond (they always let the water out after the winter, leaving only a limpid stream about 20 to 40 feet wide). We drag my boat to the edge over the muddy river bottom. We gingerly launch the craft, and with great relief, find that the punt doesn't leak. We frequently touch bottom with our paddles, but the spring runoff is strong and we are moving fast. Our hopes are soaring as we make our way past the old fort to the dam. Time to portage. We carry the boat around the dam, carefully placing it in the fast flowing water. We are having such a great time that we fail to notice that the pitch, which has had 8 months to dry, is still soft and sticky. We are already stained with black streaks on our pants, but are having too much fun to notice. We leap to our stations. We are off with a rush in the foaming water. We whiz past the little island that shares the Shakespearean gardens. The high school flats are to our left. We swoosh under the St. Vincent Street Bridge, and are approaching the John Street Bridge, when it occurs to me,

"Paddling back against this raging water might be hard work." I suggest as much to Johnny, who has been thinking the same thing.

"Maybe, we ought to test our strength against the river." I say. (Poseidon frowns.)

"Good idea," says Johnny. Already we are past the hospital, so we paddle up to the nearest overhanging tree, and cling to the shore. The effort against the current is hard, but we get the craft turned around and jump in, paddling for all we're worth.

"It's no use," shouts Johnny, "We're going backwards" (in today's world, we'd be a candidate for America's funniest home videos). At this rate, we will be outside the city limits and lost! I think to myself, "Bruce don't panic!" This is not the moment to lose nerve. We have to decide what to do. We make for the water's edge, and tie the punt to a tree. Time for a conference.

"Two grown men could never paddle against that current," laments Johnny.

"You're right," I admit. "But how are we going to get the boat back home?"

"Don't ask me," says Johnny, "I think you are stuck; we'd better pull the boat up on the edge of the riverbank and walk home."

"Never," I declare. "Before I do that, I'll jump into the water and pull the boat back with the rope; the water may be fast but it is only two feet deep."

"The water is too cold for that," says Johnny. I know the water is cold, but it's my boat and I'm afraid to leave it by the riverbank for fear someone will steal it and reap the engineering breakthrough that I have pioneered. I resolve to brave the cold, and pull the boat back to the dam with the rope.

"I'm not helping you," says an emphatic Johnny.

"I'll pull it myself," I declare.

"Go ahead, I'll bet you can't do it," Johnny retorts. The gauntlet is thrown down. I rise to the challenge, and jump in the fast flowing water, towrope in hand. I pull the boat against the water easily because there's no weight in the craft. I make about 20 feet, before the chill water freezes me to the bone.

"Can't do it," I admit, "the water is too cold." Defeated, I haul the boat ashore. Johnny is dry, but I am soaked from the knees down and shivering.

"We'll have to walk home till I can dry out," I admit. I think.

"I hope it's still there when I get back," This is 1947 with Communist espionage in high gear. I can just see some Commie stealing my punt for my engineering secrets and using the information against us in the race to build a better boat. In those days, we are loyal Canadians and on our guard against Commies who could conceivably be hiding behind the very next bush. I slog along with Johnny the shortest route home. We trudge past the high school down St. Andrew Street, and after another 20 minutes, we are home.

"How did it go?" says Grandma.

She had been a skeptic from the start. I relate the sad details of my voyage. After I thaw out, I still have work to do. Sorrowfully, I walk to the river, retrieve my cart, trudge back to the hospital and load the craft on the cart. I am home late for supper. Exhausted, I sleep well while Grandma gets the tar off my pants with turpentine. My craft is stored in the garage, never to sail again. Beaten once by Poseidon, I am not one to take things lying down. It takes me twenty-five years, but I challenge him again with my homemade plywood sailboat and win. Our contest is a draw.

Chapter 32

New York City 1946

Mother has been reading a lot of books on health. We have to eat Dr. Jackson's whole wheat bread because she doesn't want me to consume the white poison. She has also been reading about the benefits of drinking carrot juice. She is buying carrots by the bushel and grating them (by hand) into piles of roughage. She has a cloth for straining and puts the roughage into the cloth. She squeezes until the clear carrot juice comes out. Making that stuff is labour intensive. I think, "Secretly, she is glad that I don't like carrot juice." Dr. Jackson has a retreat centre for health fanatics. Mother reads all about it, and decides that she will take a pilgrimage to Dansville, N.Y. That's where Dr. Jackson collects health nuts and brainwashes them, to support the eccentric industry that promises good health for twice the price of normal food. She is sure I will like it. I have my doubts. The bribe is that after a week in Dansville, we will go to New York and see the big apple. There is, however, an ulterior motive.

Things are not good at home. The tension between mother and Grandma has intensified. My presence is Grandma's defense, but I'm often out with my friends. In fact, the home tensions drive me out, especially when I've had all I can stomach. Tonight, there is a hockey game between the Stratford Kroehler's and the Galt Terriers. Our usual strategy to get into the game is this: we skip the first period until all the paying fans are seated. After the period is over, the fans gather at the concession booth (adjacent to the foyer) for a coke and hotdog, or other snacks they might wish to buy. We hail one of the fans pleading poverty, and pretty soon we have someone on our side who understands our lack of money, and a kid's desire to hook into the arena and see the game for free. Once conscripted, our fellow plotters gather a few friends. Just before the second period when stub-taking time comes along (proof that you have already paid) they crowd around Mouse McEwan and turn in their stubs. Now Mouse is no fool; he sees this sort of thing at every game but is helpless to stop it. You might say, our fellow conspirators, form a line of scrimmage. Then Johnny, Vince, Clarkie, Butler, and I make a dash for it. Mouse McEwan cusses us up and down, and threatens to catch us, and throw us out. He never does. We see the next two periods of the game for free. Thus we are ardent supporters of our local hockey heroes, and root for the home team. What we don't contribute in finances, we supplement with cheers. Flick, Roth and Flanagan! We figured they were the best hockey players ever born, and how we loved to cheer for them. I'll bet when they were kids they hooked into the arena just like we did. Years later, I wonder if Mouse McEwan didn't do exactly the same thing when he was a kid. We always managed to hook in free when there were empty seats. We never succeeded in hooking in when there was a sellout crowd.

I'm excited about the game, because Stratford won. I'm ready to tell mom and Grandma all about the game; however, when I return home that night, mother is crying and making threats. She shocks Grandma and even me with her language and antics. She never ever struck Grandma. Words are her weapons. Poor Grandma! She is paying a high price for the avalanche of abuse that mom dumps on her. Grandma's palsy gets worse. I go to bed that night trying to figure out what mother means when she said, "I might as well walk down the street naked, the way people look at me." I put these things out of my mind and think about the fun we will have next summer when we play Tin Can Cricket, a new game introduced to us by the erstwhile Bummer Bolton.

Bummer Bolton is a good sport. He accepts his nickname without complaint. Legend has it that Joan Johnston, in a moment of inspiration, called him 'little bum', because Bill Bolton was short and skinny. Whatever the truth about the source, somehow from that day forward, Bill Bolton was called Bummer. Bummer Bolton's ears stuck out so distinctly that one wondered on a windy day, if he wouldn't be able to fly. I suppose one of the reasons Bummer is so good natured about his nickname is that he possesses a good self-image. He is good at every sport and especially at road hockey. My memory of Bummer Bolton is a kid who in summer always had a baseball glove in his hand. In winter, he traded that glove for a hockey stick, and, with tennis ball in hand, is always organizing a game of road hockey. Once the snow pack sets in, he trades the tennis ball for a puck and stick-handles his way through the rest of us to score goal after goal. The only time Bummer isn't on the street playing hockey is when he is working at Thistle's grocery store. He tells us all about his new invention, that he's sure we'll love, called 'Tin Can Cricket.'

It is now springtime. The slightly depressed pathways of the Commons were made by pedestrians who liked to cut corners, walking home from work. The pathways made a perfect bowling alley for a tennis ball. Next we set up three oilcans liberally supplied by The Waterloo Street Cities' Service Gas Station which we would bowl over with the tennis ball. Of course the batter (who stands in front of the cans) is attempting to hit the ball out of the park. The bats are the creation of Mr. Bolton who made them. Everything is supplied on the cheap but the reward was lots of fun. Once again in 1946, the growing conflict between teens and tots became all too apparent. Getting ahead of my story, a year later in 1947, the Optimist Club hired Margaret Brooks who had just changed her name to Wade by marrying my cousin Frank. Margaret Wade, who eventually became Deputy Mayor of Stratford, was our playground supervisor. We had no idea why we needed a playground supervisor but accepted our lot because Margaret was a diplomat. Margaret used to smile at our games and soon endeared herself to us kids. It was her job to protect the little people from guys like us who supposed all others beside ourselves were intruders. Little did we know it was our days that were numbered. Margaret especially took a shine to Vince Schooley's red hair and blue eyes.

"That kid had the reddest hair, I've ever seen!" she laughed. In 1949, the Optimist Club took action by putting in hills for kids to climb and adding new equipment that ruined the baseball diamond. By this time we had become older teens and more interested in jobs than play. The teens who came after us had the problem. The little kids had won the day.

Vince had the reddest hair.

So, as I was saying, mother is talking about New York again. She tells me what a great city it is, and that we ought to visit the place as soon as I'm out of grade nine. This was the plan. First we go to Dansville where she is scheming to convert me. She hopes to make me as enthusiastic about granola as she is, or, in other words, to become a health nut. Second, we will be moving to New York to live happily ever after. I figure that going to New York might be OK, so I'm agreeable. I am now set up for mother's grand design. Mother, who reads every movie magazine in sight, tells me that if you want to make it in Hollywood, you have to start in New York.

"Wouldn't you like to be a movie star Bruce?" I hear this so often from mother's lips that I don't hear it anymore, even when she says it. Mother had already sent my picture to somebody in Hollywood, figuring that that was all it would take to make me famous like Jack Benny, or, if not a Hollywood star, someone humbler like Prime Minister Mackenzie King. She dreams of starting a Beauty Salon in New York. That's how to be rich, and who knows, maybe even famous. The whole thing strikes me as unrealistic, but the trip to New York sounds Okay, so mother makes the plans and I just go along. Just what Grandma would do with her breadwinner in New York is none of my concern. Mother has told Grandma that she needn't worry. She is going to make so much money in New York that she would keep Grandma by sending her a monthly cheque.

Mother has saved up enough money for the trip; so, late in June, we're off to Buffalo. We change trains, and take the Lackawana to Dansville, home of Dr. Jackson's retreat. The retreat centre is a rude awakening for me; everybody there is old. We check into our hotel room and eat downstairs in the restaurant. The meal is the healthy sort, the kind of meal kids don't like. Dr. Jackson Jr. leads us in a song in praise of orange juice. The guests sing enthusiastically but I cannot help myself. I am laughing at the guests, who in my mind are a little bit crazy. I'm beginning to wish I were somewhere else. After supper, I am bored and tell mother I want to walk downtown and see if anybody my age lives in Dansville. I can tell that the United States is different from Canada right away. The streets are broader and the houses are bigger and built on large lots. I make my way downtown. I see a bunch of kids and realize I'm an outsider. They are laughing and talking together. They have obviously grown up in Dansville and feel right at home. I do not. There is nothing to compare to a summer evening just hanging out with the friends you know. I decide there's no future here, so I walk on alone, and look into the store windows. The shopping area of Dansville is almost as large as what I am used to in Stratford, so I figure that the two cities must be about the same size. Feeling like a total misfit, I decide to walk back to the retreat centre. When I arrive, I ask the lady at the reception desk about geography, my favourite subject. Next I get around to my big question.

"What's the population of Dansville?" I ask the clerk.

"About 4000." she replies. I am surprised,

"Dansville appears to be as large as Stratford and we have 18,000 people in our city." I exclaim. The clerk rearranges her face and replies, "I wouldn't know about that." I tell mother all about my findings, and ask her for a reason why Dansville is posing like a city, when it is only a town. Mother has no explanation for me, and tells me I should go to sleep and, if I like, after breakfast, I can go swimming in the pool. I warm to that idea and so I retire for the night.

The following morning, I am making my way to the pool. "Good," I think to myself, "There are only four people sunning themselves by the pool; I don't have to share the diving board." I boldly walk right up. I have it all to myself, a luxury I would never enjoy at the Stratford Lion's pool. I pause, and then take a good spring, diving straight into the water. Shock! Who put the ice cubes in the water? I knife my way to the ladder, and pull myself out of the pool as fast as Tarzan. My elderly audience is smiling.

"How do you like it?" they ask.

"Freezing!" I reply. "What's the temperature of this water?

"Sixty degrees," (fifteen Celsius) they reply. "Dr. Jackson keeps it cool for the good of our health."

"Torture, you mean!"

I have had enough. I march back to our room; finding mother, I protest,

"Get me out of this crazy place." The rest of what I thought and said is unprintable. Mother understands me and checks out that very day. We are on our way to New York. In retrospect, I think mother knew all along that she had made a mistake and was only too glad to accommodate me.

We have taken the night train to Hoboken, New Jersey, so we arrive early in the morning. We finally get a look at Manhatten across the river from the Jersey side and we just knew we're in New York when we 'hoid the woid' of the baggage men. Even the fowl of the air seem to 'choip like a boid'. We catch a bus to cross the bridge to the city. The Hudson River is bustling with boat traffic. I had no idea that New York was an ocean port. Ships of every flag can be seen. We finally arrive at lower Manhatten in the theatre district, lugging our suitcases and looking for the cheapest room we can rent. Mother is shocked at the prices. New York is overwhelming to us country yokels. After arrangements are made, I lug our suitcases up a steep staircase to a decrepit room with a double bed. The bathroom is down the hall. I can see that mother is a little bewildered by it all. I get the distinct impression by her lack of enthusiasm for job-hunting, that she won't be looking for work in New York. Meantime, we decide to see the city.

We do the tourist thing. The guided tour through Rockefeller Centre comes first; we take in a concert that features the Rockettes dancing girls. We go to the top of the Empire State Building. The Sky scrapers are impressive. There is a place, where you pay 50 cents and record your voice. We jabber on about the glories of visiting New York, and get a cheap recording to impress our friends back in Stratford. We are in awe of the architecture. Grand Central station is a wonder to behold. The central library is beautiful. We do the Island Tour on the boat. We visit St. John's Cathedral. However, most of the time, we go to movies. One in the morning, one in the afternoon, and one at night! Oftentimes, there are celebrities who perform after the movie. One such celebrity is Dinah Shore. She sings an off-colour song, 'Roll me over in the Clover and Do it again'. I am embarrassed and mother can clearly see it. It would not have been a problem for me if one of my buddies had been my companion for the show, but to sit there with you mother —
Out of the corner of my eye, I can see that mom is feeling guilty that she has brought her son into this den of iniquity. Imagine, mother subjecting her son to the blatantly provocative temptations of the city. After it was all over and we were on the street, mom says to me,

"I'm sorry for bringing you to that!" Now is the time for a bold face. I fancy myself as a 14 year old man of the world, and tell her,

"Forget it mom, I know the score." As we hurry down the street, I spot a sign in a store window, "Pornography for Sale, 50% off.

"Look mom, a bargain. Just what is pornography?" Mother replies,

"Never mind, it's nothing that would interest you."

I shrug my shoulders and think, "Oh well, what does it matter; we don't even own a pornograph. Come to think of it, none of my friends owns one either."

After a week of movie going, and seeing the sights of New York, we admit that this has ceased to be fun. We buy our tickets home to Stratford, and board the train. Mother is actually glad to be back in Stratford and I agree. Grandma tells me mother is extravagant, wasting her money on a trip to New York. I shrug my shoulders, and half-heartedly agree.

"At least, I got to see New York," I say and head out the door to look up Johnny.

The summer of 1946 is passed in this order: in the morning we play Tin Can Cricket; in the afternoon, we swim at the Lion's pool, and learn how to perfect our diving skills. Sometimes there are 20 guys in the lineup. But at least the water is a civilized 72 degrees. At night, we play baseball until it's time to go to Queen's Park and watch a softball (fastball) game. Our favourite is always, when the Rotanettes play. Johnny's sister, Dorothy, catches at the plate. I am amazed at how well these girls can play fastball. It's intimidating because I'm not the athletic type, but I do enjoy watching the game. The senior team is sponsored by Kroehlers. Jim's two sisters are on the team. Kathleen plays second base and Dorothy catches Greta Harmer's sizzling fastball. Eventually, Joan Johnston, Audrey Murphy, and Helen Haynes (kids I hang out with) will advance to this level, leaving me in the dust. I seek fame in other pursuits. I read books, play chess, and work on my boat.

Girls from the Rotanettes ball team Joan Johnston 2nd from left. This picture was taken by coach Bunny Fryer. Unknown to the coach, someone had hit a foul ball which was heading straight for the camera. The girls are Ellen Salter, Joan Johnston, Vera Moss and Betty Blom.

Chapter 33

A Wing Like a Chicken

I am standing in front of the hall mirror with my bathing suit on, and in consternation I am examining my physique. I quit going to Sea Cadets because they made me put on boxing gloves and fight Bev Crawford. One bloody nose, a bruised ego, and I was finished. No wonder I lost that one. Look at me — I'm a scrawny kid. The torso and the arms are too thin. From the neck up things aren't too bad. Helen Haynes confirmed that. From the waist down the legs are not too bad. I can beat Royce or Vince in the hundred-yard dash and high jump better than they can. It's Vincent's statement that has me worried. He said the other day,

"You know Woodsie, you throw like a girl." All we were doing was playing a game of catch. I protest saying,

"What do you mean?" Vince tells me,

"You look awkward when you throw a ball." Vince is my critic. He tells me that I walk funny, now he's correcting my throwing arm. It's good to have friends. I think of the Lifeboy soap ad. "Even your best friends won't tell you." Vince is not impressed with dignified propriety. He never flatters anybody, especially me.

This new revelation is damaging stuff. Playing ball is what we do in the summertime and when it comes to sports, reputation is social currency. I have a problem to solve. At the Commons, I watch in horror as one of the girls throws a ball and wonder, "Is that how I look?" Not all the girls throw like that. In fact, most of them throw a ball like a guy. But the revelation is cause for consternation. I have to resolve this quickly. That's why I'm looking in the mirror. The torso is only passable, but plainly the arms are too skinny. When mom wants to take my picture, I run for a suit jacket. I look at the Charles Atlas ads. They say, "I was a 98 pound weakling, but now I'm the champion body builder, etc., etc." I ruefully admit, "Bruce, there's no hope for you. You are skinny." As of yet, there is no fast food industry to solve the problem. How am I going to get a girl to like me when I'm this skinny?

It's not that the kids would deny me a game of scrub. There's no issue here, but a sandlot league has been formed for the summer of 1946. There are four teams: Bud Haviling's crowd; the kids Al MacDonald hangs out with; Rocky Greenwood's team (I figure no one would dare to say no to join his team or he'd punch them out); and then there is our team made up of the kids that play at The Commons. The Commons is our sacred territory, or so we think. It is a field surrounded by Albert Street, Front, and Brunswick. We have our regulars. They are: Bummer Bolton, Vince Schooley, Willie Williams, Jim Johnston, Allen McCone, John Butler, Royce Clark, and me. After that we have the guys that only show up if something else hasn't come along. We never seem to be able to muster nine players. This is good news for me, because I never have to face the problem of being cut from the roster.

We have a different problem. Seven guys (our usual number) cannot play nine. So we import two players from the north side of the river. Jack White and his good friend Mac Ross, who is the best pitcher around. It was Vince Schooley's idea. Now we have great games (because we win most of them) and everybody seems to enjoy themselves, but we have no coach. I suggest my Uncle Gordon who is nicknamed 'Lum'. I have an ulterior motive. I want him to work on my arm. The kids are agreeable and Uncle Gordon gives his OK. Lum calls for a practice to see his new team. I'm throwing the ball to Johnny with my uncle watching. Gordon is smiling and says,

"That kid's got a wing like a chicken." Mortified I plead with him to help me improve my throw. Vainly he tries to straighten out my arm. But it is useless. The chicken wing will not go away. Finally he decides to teach me to throw side arm. I'm still as wild as ever and my distance actually decreases, but it helps to disguise the evidence. He puts me in right field where I can do the least damage.

My problems persist. I strike out too often and when I get a hit, I'm lucky if I can get to first base. Then I come up with my own invention to improve my game. It is a gamble, but I decide I will create my own bat. It will be heavier than most and it will be made of solid oak which Uncle Gordon conveniently borrowed from the Preston-Noelting Furniture factory. Now I need a lathe. School is out for the summer holidays so I arrange with our manual training teacher to come into the high school when he's there. Its summer hours but we come up with a suitable arrangement. I bring my square piece of oak and he shows me how to mount the wood on the lathe. I am turning out my own bat. Vince Schooley gets interested and he joins me in the quest to build a better bat. With the lathe chisels, we slowly turn our oak until we are beginning to see the fruits of our labour. They are heavier than most and the first time we bring them to a ball game the kids turn up their noses, and call it a war club.

"Too heavy," says Mac Ross who is a good hitter. "With a bat like that you have no control." The guys are not interested in using my war club. Meanwhile, I continue to strike out and in general am thankful that the team seems to be able to win despite my mediocre showing.

I decide that maybe I'd be better off using a regular bat, but I am determined to give my own precious bat one more try. Our next game is at Queen's Park. After the usual warm-ups, we are progressing nicely into the game when suddenly the bases are loaded and there are two out. Lum calls out,

"Woods, you are next to bat". In terror I realize that it's my turn to face the pitcher. I can hear the booing already before I strike out. The pitcher tosses a fastball and I meet the ball with my war club. A mighty crack of the bat tells me something good is about to happen. (Hey there Apollo, if you're there, did you see that?) The ball sails over Parkview Avenue and is out of sight. I drop my war club and race to first base.

In my excitement I fail to touch the base with my foot. In fact I miss it by two feet. I am running for all I'm worth, forgetting that with the ball out of sight, I have all the time in the world. Suddenly the guys are shouting,

"You missed first base, go back and touch first base." I stop dead in my tracks and turn around to remedy my error.

"Keep going," say some of the others, "you're fine". Now this is what you call a breakdown in communications. Half the guys are saying one thing, and the others are saying the opposite. Three times I change directions and three times I don't return to first base. I finally run to second and third base and then to home plate, but Vince screams,

“Go back and touch first base.” I race down to first for one last effort, but the fielder has at last retrieved the ball. My non-athletic guardian angel can’t help so it’s up to Mercury who never gives me a break.

“You’re out!” cries the ump. Charley Brown like, I hang my head and trudge to the bench for my glove while I ingest my self inflicted ‘gripes’ of wrath. Later, a smile creases my lips. Not all is lost. I drove in three runs and we won the game. I decide to retire my war club, while its reputation is still untarnished.

> How life treats us can be a mystery. Mac Ross and Jack White made our baseball team into a winner. Mac Ross, who was playing junior hockey at age 19, died in a tragic automobile accident on the way to Kitchener. Jack White, who was good enough to play pro hockey, died when his hockey career ended at age 40. Alcohol!

Chapter 34

Vancouver Here We Come

I tell mother I'm ready for more travel, my style. I want to hitchhike to Bogies' Beach. I've never hitchhiked before, but I want to try my luck. Mother who always is concerned about the safety of her son meekly protests. I easily break down her defense. After appropriate warnings to be careful, she phones and finds a good reception. Mrs. Bogie tells mother there will be no cost. She's glad Graham will have some company. Farm life for a 16-year-old boy is dreary; Graham has been complaining that he will never be a farmer. He's got his eye on the ships that ply the Great Lakes. I walk to Huron Street and wave at Clarkie. He's got a summer job working at the City Service Station on the corner of Huron and Mornington. Royce sees my suitcase and calls out,

"Running away from home?" I laugh and remember.

"No Clarkie, I'm hitchhiking to Bogie's Beach."

"You're lucky," says Royce. "I have to work." Then he shows me his hands — raw from changing tires — and gives me a demonstration on how he does it. I am impressed and remember how Clarkie, Fonzi-like, will next be talking about his girlfriends. He does not disappoint me. I tell him,

"Well Royce, while you make all this money to spend it on girls, I'm going to be poor and just have fun."

"Enjoy yourself," says Clarkie, "but when you grow up, you watch and see; you will be just like me."

"Perhaps," I reply, "but for now I'd sooner play than work the way you do, just so you can spend it all on girls."

I wave goodbye to Royce and, (standing beside my suitcase) stick out my thumb. It is unbelievably easy. The second car I see pulls up and takes me the first twelve miles to Mitchell. I thank my driver and start again. In minutes I have a ride to Seaforth. Once again, I'm thumbing the last twenty-two miles to Goderich. In no time, I have a ride. One hour and 15 minutes and I am in Goderich. I actually beat the train. Fifteen minutes later, I'm in Dunlop. I am three miles from Bogie's Road, but here my luck runs out. One half-hour later, I walk inside the Dunlop Mill, and ask, if he will phone the Bogies and tell them how close I am. I could walk it, if I were not lugging a suitcase.

Mr. Bogie is at the farmhouse when I call. Ten minutes later, he arrives with Graham and picks me up at the Mill. We swap stories and enjoy six days together. Again, the time hangs heavy. Graham has to help with the hay. When the hay is ready and the weather is good, you harvest hay; with rain as the enemy, there's no time to waste. When the week is up, I go into town with Mrs. Bogie who has shopping to do. I hitchhike home. It was all so easy.

Now that I've become a veteran hitchhiker, I'm ready to go again. This time the trip will be longer. I want to go to Toronto and visit my dad. Then I'll strike out for Tillsonburg and stay with Uncle Norm for a few days. They have a four-year-old daughter, Janet, who is cute as can be. I figure I'll be gone for a week. I'm off on my new adventure and in three hours, I am in Toronto's Union Station. I catch a streetcar heading north on Yonge. In transit, an older lady gets on the bus and looks at me. Feeling uncomfortable, I look away but out of the corner of my eye, I can see her standing at my seat.

"Mind if I sit beside you?" the pleasant stranger asks. I do mind, there are plenty of seats on the streetcar that she could have taken, I think, "Why does this woman have to sit beside me?" Raised to be polite, I say,

"It's Okay by me." After an awkward silence, she strikes up a conversation with this unwilling passenger,

"Are you from Toronto?" she asks.

"Nope," I reply uncomfortably.

"I'm not either," the friendly lady replies, "Toronto is just too big. So where do you live?" I can see that I'm stuck with an unwanted conversation so I decide to make the best of it and reply,

"I'm from Stratford."

"I know somebody from Stratford."

"You do? Who's that?"

"Her name is Ethel Woods; she lives on Brunswick Street." Nonplussed and surprised, I reluctantly admit,

"That's my mother."

"Well isn't that just a wonderful coincidence," she enthuses. "God must have arranged this meeting." I really don't see what God has to do with all this. The only thing I am thinking is, "Lady, you are making me feel very uncomfortable." I am now wishing I was somewhere else, but she has me trapped. Then she continues,

"I met your mother in church years ago and I have never forgotten her."

"We don't go to church anymore," I reply.

"I'm so sorry to hear that, my name is Helen Westurn. Will you tell your mother that we met on the streetcar; I'm sure she will remember me." I shrug my shoulders and tell her I will.

"Do you know what I think?" says my friendly stranger. After an awkward silence, I reluctantly rasp,

"Nope."

"Well, let me tell you what I think. I think God arranged this meeting and that he wants me to tell you something."

"Yeah? What?"

"I think God wants you to be a follower of Jesus Christ just like your mother used to be and I think God sent me here to tell you that." To be polite to this total stranger is taking all the grace I can muster. To be preached at is more than my mature teenage years can handle.

"Maybe," I unwillingly reply. "I get off at Bedford Park. So since my stop is coming up, I guess I'll have to go." Helen smiles and says goodbye. Meantime, I am relieved to be away from the clutches of my over friendly missionary who had explained to me that she had spent many years in China and was returning to Japan. I have no intention of accepting her advice and am grateful to forget every word that she had spoken. I make no mention of my encounter to my father but later when I returned to Stratford, I did tell my mother, who, although she remembered Helen, promptly dismissed the matter.

In all, the journey to dad's house took four hours. I get a good reception from Dad and Phyllis. I notice a photo of Phyllis taken twenty years later sitting on the mantel. She obviously was a looker in her day. She has since put on weight and doesn't look trim like my mother does. I think, "Mother has done a better job of aging than Phyllis." I contemplate the awkward feelings of talking to a mother and a stepmother in the brief interlude of twenty-four hours. I've grown six inches since they last saw me. At last, I'm taller than Pat. However that doesn't help me in snooker; we play a game and I am skunked. Pat is still the Queen of green. I relate to the family my success story about the Soap Box derby, and tell them how I used the tools that dad gave me. I outline my new plans to build a punt, so I can navigate the Avon River at will. After I have sufficiently impressed them all with my exploits, all five of us sit down for supper. I say all five because Dad and my stepmother Phyllis have a new baby boy. His name is Michael. So now I can say, "I have a brother and a sister". It's just that I don't get to see much of them. Twenty years later, Michael will do well. He married Helen Beattie. They are as poor as church mice. However, Helen's brother and Michael are into stock car racing. Together they develop a special racing engine called Beattie and Woods. It turns them into successful businessmen. But that's another story.

Pat has a girlfriend whose name is Lois. For some reason they seem to be taking too much time while I am waiting around before we are to go to a dance. I decide to tiptoe to the bedroom door to listen to their conversation. With my ear to the keyhole, and with widening eyes, I am hearing things that I ought not to know.

"Wow!" I think, "Imagine that! Girls are as curious about guys as guys are about girls!" All would have been well, if I had been smart enough to settle for partial information. Alas, curiosity gets the better of me and I linger at the keyhole until I am discovered when suddenly they open the door. That's when I learn that it's is better to remain in ignorance than to have forbidden knowledge. Red faced Pat is furious and in no uncertain terms tells me so. In five minutes flat, I have worn out my welcome and I am feeling very uncomfortable. We didn't go to the dance. The poet says, "Silence is golden". I suppose that is a reasonable proverb, but there are exceptions.

Still uncomfortable in Pat's presence, the very next day I am 'out of here'. I want to hitchhike to Niagara Falls, and then proceed on to Tillsonburg, grateful that I will not have to face Pat for at least another year. After a suitable farewell, I'm on my way. I have to make one hundred and fifty miles in a single day, plus time to sightsee in Niagara Falls. This is before the days of four lane highways, so the going is slow. I make it in time for lunch. I settle for a hot dog, the cheapest thing on the menu. I walk past the gardens to get a good look at the Canadian Falls. I now make a discovery. It's all very good to go touring but it's not what it's cracked up to be when you have no one to share it with. The clock is ticking, so after two hours I figure I need to move along. The hiking is not so good and the rides are short. It takes me till six o'clock to make it to Dunnville. For supper, because money is scarce, I eat my second hot dog. Time is against me; when I get to Canboro, it's getting dark. I wonder, "If I have to spend the night here, maybe some farmer will let me sleep in his barn." I can see a barn in the setting sun and decide that's my last resort. Night has fallen, and just as I'm about to give up, a kind motorist pulls up and says,

"How far are you going?"

"Tillsonburg is my destination," I reply.

"That's where, I'm going," he says.

"You're in luck." His wife laughs.

"We saw you and your suitcase and figured, young as you are, it would be safe to give you a lift."

Needless to say, I am relieved. I tell them about my idea to sleep in a barn if I had to. They tell me, they are glad for me that they decided to give me a ride. I am grateful. One hour later, they take me to Aunt Jean and Uncle Norm's front door. When they answer the door for this urchin, I'm grinning from ear to ear. Aunt Jean says,

"Well of all things, look who's here. Have you had any supper?" Music to this traveler's ears! I reply,

"Not very much." Jean makes me a late supper of fried potatoes and the all familiar wiener. As a hungry teenager, I make no protests. Wieners are good. Now it's time for music from Uncle Norman's player piano. I carefully select a twelve-inch scroll with tiny rectangular puncture holes and insert the scroll into the player piano. It's March Militaire by Franz Schubert. Next, I start pumping at the two foot paddles and soon I am watching the keys magically depress and listen to the music as the pneumatic pump inside the piano responds to my efforts. I am a concert pianist pounding out the unfeeling notes of a masterpiece.

"With a contraption like this, who needs to take piano lessons." I glow. I am oblivious to how mechanical the music sounds. After three fun filled days in Tillsonburg (Doing what? Swimming everyday! What else?), I don't have to hitch hike home. Norm and Jean have decided to visit the family and accommodate their guest. The last leg of the journey is easy. The following September for English class, I submit my first piece of journalism, it is entitled, 'Hitchhiking across Ontario'. I have now become an author with original material. I get an A for my masterpiece.

Grade 10 in high school gives me a chance to choose my first elective. I select my favourite subject, geography. My home class is with Miss Margaret Baldwin, who teaches French and Gym class. She's OK, but neither French nor Gym are my thing, even if they would let me compete with the girls. I like Geometry though, and especially my teacher, Mr. Burnett. I'm fitting in quite nicely at Stratford high; however, there are rumblings that will disturb all this. Mother is at Grandma again. I hear her say,

"I'm leaving Stratford, and seeking happiness in the West where I belong." Oddly enough, mother is not thinking off Camrose but Vancouver. She has read about that great city and is now convinced that a future awaits her far far away. First she has to convince me that leaving Stratford, and moving to Vancouver is in my best interests. Reluctantly, I go along with mother's plans. Anything to solve this depression problem of hers is worth a try. Mother's last nest egg is an insurance policy that is to mature December 15. Depressed people, I am to learn, make desperate decisions that will not wait.

Mother borrows at the bank against her policy to get the money by November 1st. She has $300 plus $150 she has saved, and my agreement. We're off to Vancouver at a dismal time of year. I say a fond farewell to my boat and wonder if I'll ever see it again to fulfil my dream. Fate is kind to me; the following spring I get to fulfil my dream, but I've already told you the story.

To this young 15-year-old, a train trip across Canada seems like high adventure. The travel bug that vaccinated me the day the policeman nipped my plans to run away will not be denied. To save money, we will travel coach, and sleep on our upright upholstered seats. We pull out of Toronto at 9 P.M. It's too dark to see much, so we try to get some sleep. I am awake at every station; the conductor's call sees to that. Early morning light brings us to Cochrane. Tired and bleary-eyed, mother takes me to the dining coach for a good breakfast of bacon and eggs.

Northern Ontario is a vast hinterland of scrub pine and stubby trees that fills the languid horizon hour after hour. The monotony and tedium of the journey sets in quickly. The occasional break in scenery comes with welcome relief and turns out to be man made. They are the towns and villages. I am surprised that there are heroic northerners, who have built in this forsaken land. In my opinion, a northern town is where people gather out of necessity. They all seem to look alike, bundled up in their winter coats, and they are tough, just like the landscape. The most exciting thing that happens the first day of our journey is nightfall. Mother caves in to our weary bodies, and decides to purchase a lower berth. At last we have got a 'nest' and 'some rest' heading 'West.' We are finding out the hard way that none of this is very satisfying, especially in November. We share the birth for a fitful sleep. If people thought that this was a lack of propriety, that idea does not occur to me. We wake up the following morning approaching Winnipeg.

November 6, 1946, we have a 40-minute layover in Winnipeg. Mother and I decide to see the downtown metropolis of the great Prairie City we have so often heard of. Leaving Union Station, we walk up Main Street. The wind is biting. After three or four blocks, we arrive at Portage. By now we are shivering with the cold. We take a quick look inside a few stores, including Eaton's and Simpson's, the two biggest retailers of the times, and then head back for our coach. Having seen all that the big city has to offer, we settle down to an uneventful train ride to Yorkton. Bedtime, exciting bedtime, breaks the monotony. Sleep, the balm of the bored, does its work. When we arrive in Edmonton it is morning, and mother has arranged a day pass. A twenty-five-year old dream is about to be fulfilled. She wants to see her beloved Camrose. Alas, there is no bus, at least not one that fits our timetable.

Mother is determined. We really can't afford it, but she hires a taxi to traverse the fifty frozen miles to Camrose. Four inches of newfallen snow has made the main street look cold and dreary. The delightful town of mother's memory is barely recognizable. However, some buildings are the same. Mother is heartened. Next we drive to the house that mother called home for 10 years. We pause for a few minutes. I ask mother to see if the people will let us go in, and look at the house of mother's childhood dreams. The outside is smaller than she imagined and run down. We knock at the front door while the taxi waits, but there's nobody home. At last mother tells the cabby to take us back to Edmonton. We return in an hour and have just enough time for lunch before we board the train. This fruitless junket has cost us $30.00.

"I can't believe how the town has changed," says mother. "It's nothing like I remember." Another dream is dashed. I'm sure the world needs dreamers. It's the stuff of progress. However, there is a difference between dreams and fantasy. Mother has trouble discerning the difference. We board the next train at 2 P.M.; our destination is Jasper and we are there by 4 o'clock. We are in time to see the mountains in the setting sun. This is the only significant scenery in this whole trip worth remembering. Night falls quickly, and the cloud cover rolls in. It is dark in the Rocky Mountains. We sleep our way through the grandeur that eludes our eyes, because mother just had to see Camrose. We awake at morning light in Hope, British Columbia, which is shrouded in fog. It is raining.

A lady who had boarded the train at Hope tells us about herself; she is from Winnipeg. We tell her she must be glad to no longer live in that frigid city. She demurs and says,

"I have lived in Winnipeg and I have lived in Vancouver, and I can tell you, with all that rain, I have shivered more in Vancouver than I ever did in Winnipeg." Encouraged by this augury, we arrive in Vancouver two hours later. It is still raining and damp. We now have to retrieve our suitcases and my bicycle, which has traveled with us. We check them at the station till we decide where we will live. A bus to the downtown drops us off at Granville Street. It is a 'drismal' day. Mother's solution to a dilemma is always the same. We did it in New York; we do it again in Vancouver. We take in a movie. At five o'clock mother decides we have made a mistake coming to Vancouver; we will go to Calgary. Calgary is now the illusive golden pot (I guess it should be the pot of gold at this very elusive rainbow's end); however, I'm closer to the truth with the pot.

A quick supper at the station, and we board the train to Calgary. Once again, we are going through the mountains at night. So much for scenery! Perhaps we were spared more despair. Leafless trees and rain leave only the evergreens. We've seen enough of that already. Calgary is the end of the line. Mother has enough money to pay for a week's rent at Mrs. Greenburg's Tourist Home. Necessity is the mother of enterprise. Mother gets a job at a beauty parlour. The wages are a fraction of what she'd be making in Stratford. It's work or starve. We are stuck. After delaying two days, mother insists that I register at the local high school. Reluctantly, I walk to the high school alone. I am amazed at the size of the building. It dwarfs Stratford High. I present myself to a friendly secretary who registers me in my homeroom and escorts me to my class.

Now it is my dream that has shattered. Till now, I had faithfully followed mother's foibles, without complaint or doubt. I believed her fantasy world without a single challenge to her vacillations. Despair rushes over me like a mighty riptide. Reality comes home to me with a horrifying disclosure. Mother has been deceived, and her madcap schemes are divorced from real life. The journey to fortune and happiness has been a fool's errand. The dream has become a nightmare, and I am trapped with no way out.

Chapter 35

The Revelation.

"I'm not going back to that high school," I tell mother. Mother is shocked; she can read the mood of her very disillusioned son. I have just removed the last of mother's house of cards. She knows she has made a dreadful mistake in coming west and she is worried; however, she is not quite ready to admit it. Keeping face, she protests and tells me,

"You will like it if you try to adjust."

"I hate it," I emphatically declare. "I don't know what I'm going to do, maybe I'll get a job, but whatever I do, I'm not going back to that high school."

Mother wilts; she knows that she has led me to a dead end, but she bluffs.

"So what's wrong with the school?" Mother enquires.

I list a long string of complaints, none of which make sense. The reality is that I miss my friends. I am homesick, and I am fed up with the life of a gypsy. Mother had always talked a college education as the number one priority for me. My talk of quitting school is alarming her. She sees that my attitude is the end of her dreams for me. No high school, no university! She fears for my future; the truth is, I am her future and she will do whatever it takes to get me back to Stratford. She tries to placate me with promises that I know she cannot fulfil.

It takes me a few years to assess my mother's complex personality. However, two things I understand: mother loves her son, and mother lives to see that her son will succeed. As I reflect upon this, years later, I know how much she loved me. It is my underpinning. The fear of rejection is never one of my concerns. This present crisis cannot separate us. With forlorn hope, we make our plans. Mother will make enough money to get us both back to Stratford. It actually might have been possible, if mother could have found steady work. Unfortunately, she has to manage on part time. We have a single electric plug-in burner in our only room. The bathroom is shared with others at Greenburg's Tourist Home. To save money, we eat cheap. I cannot look at canned Deviled Ham to this day. Deviled ham sandwiches becomes our staple for supper. When mother is at work, I walk the streets, fearing that the truant officer will pick me up for vagrancy. I read a few books but I cannot concentrate, I think of Stratford continually; and count the days till I can return.

We keep outrageous hours and the nights are long. There is plenty of time to talk. It is the talk that redeems the waste of this fruitless trip. Although I am only fifteen years old, at last mother begins to reveal to me things till now withheld. It is as though, lacking a counsellor, mother confers upon me the privilege (or was it a cry for help from her disordered mind to the only person she trusts anymore). Step by step, the revelation will perforate my world of youthful innocence. I will relate them in sequence, although I'm sure she did not tell me these things in logical order. Nor did I make sense of what she revealed until much later. I was unprepared for much of what she would say. I am shocked at what she told me; things I could never have revealed until after her death. I am free to relate them now in the hope that it will benefit some naive child, who, forewarned, will escape potential tragedy.

Mother tells me how unhappy she has been living in Stratford. She is in reality trying to rationalize before her disillusioned son this abortive western junket. Mother is speaking,

"I had a happy childhood in Camrose, but from the minute we moved to Stratford, I was homesick for the West." (With the lights out and lying in bed in the midnight hours, mother recalled to me many stories of her happiest times that for the most part I have now forgotten except her tale of hiding in the tall grass that grew six feet high. My memory must begin as she related her years in Stratford.

"When I graduated from high school, I got a job in a business on Downie Street," Mother rasps. "It was an office job that required typing and filing orders." She pauses for a minute; obviously, this is difficult for her to tell her son.

"I was wearing a blouse and skirt and doing my job, when the boss's son came into the room and stood behind me. Suddenly, he was under my blouse and grabbing at my breasts. I screamed, and ran around to the other side of the desk. He pursued me, but I managed to keep the desk between him and me. A few minutes later, his father returned to the office, and the son promptly left. That's why I quit that job."

I have come to realize that pretty girls can have a problem with admiring men. Beautiful women, beware. There is a fine balance between being stylish or provocative. Pretty girls are safer when they dress modestly, especially if they are naive. A beautiful woman is especially vulnerable. (I must be careful here, as I tell you this story. I find it actually possible to wind up hating men.)

Rape! A woman's worst nightmare happened to mother when she was nineteen, after a dance at the Lakeside Casino. I didn't want to think about what she told me that fateful night in Calgary so I repressed it from my mind. It was many years after she died that I thought about the sordid details, and how they surely must have affected her life. I have no doubt that this event scarred her for life and contributed to the breakdown of her mental health. I have a friend who went through a similar trial. She overcame her humiliation, married, and raised a family. Had mother married as well as my friend did, she might have weathered her storm with a better outcome. Although the perpetrator of this crime is no longer living, his family descendants are a respected Stratford name which I will never disgrace by a disclosure; especially now. I sometimes wonder though, what the offender had to say for himself when he met his Maker.

Inevitably my mother's recollection of the past would include the stories of her trials with my father. My father was a fast talker and a smooth operator. Finally, after telling me any number of hair-raising episodes, she got around to the days of her early romance when Bruce Sr. swept her off her feet.

"When your father was courting me, we would come in the house after a dance, and sit in the front room and neck. Eventually, we were having sex. I think Grandma knew, because she kept warning me not to marry Bruce. That's when we decided to elope, because Grandma didn't like your father, and wanted me to break off with him." (An incongruous admission indeed after all the blame mother had heaped on Grandma for not warning her about the dangers associated with men.)

This final story which mother told me in Calgary reveals how divorced from reality she had become. When mother started attending the Congregational Church back in 1940, she fell in love with the pastor, John McLeod. To quote her,

"The feeling was mutual. Believe me, when we shook hands the sparks flew. That's why I left the church and attended Memorial Baptist." Alas, mother has this capacity for misreading people. Ultimately it would lead her inward to conversations with nonexistent voices. This was still to come. (A few years later, exasperated with mother's problems, I stopped at London General Hospital after work to see if I could talk to a psychologist. Remarkably, I was allowed right in, with no waiting. I told the doctor about mother's history, carefully avoiding the sexual part. I would have been too embarrassed to reveal that. The kindly doctor I spoke with explained to me, that as a result of all the tragedy in mother's life, she had probably become schizophrenic. I now have a new word in my vocabulary to comprehend).

Sexual harassment and its murderous evil is, as of yet, unknown to me. I will learn about that later. In high school we are reading **Tess of the D'Urbervilles**; I see shades of mother's experience in **Tess**.* While many women have survived this kind of tragedy, and to their credit overcome it, in my experience, with mother's sensitive nature, she imploded under the strain. A divorce plus the death of friends, when friends were few, tipped the balance. I still wonder if she had not misread John McLeod, that with friends like the Spackmans, and others at the church who genuinely cared for her that she might have pulled through. Ah — the "if onlys" of life. I was still sufficiently naive to imagine, that I could somehow rescue mother from her

*In 1891 Thomas Hardy wrote his melodrama that shocked Victorian England. Tess suffered rape at the hands of a well-to-do gentleman who lured and lied Tess into a marriage by bribing her impoverished family with money. Her violation, unwanted pregnancy, the death of her baby, and her entanglement with Alec D'Urberville cheated her of her true love, Angel Clare. In a fit of self-destructive revenge, she murders Alec. Circumstances overwhelmed her innocent and purer nature. More sinned against than sinning, she dies for her crime.

illness. I never succeeded. There are two kinds of Schizophrenia, those who are totally incapacitated and those you can help. Mother fell into the latter category. Remarkably, mother, despite all her emotional liabilities, remarried, was widowed and remarried again.

Years later despite the difference in years, John and Rita McLeod became my friends. I now have every proof that I needed to dismiss mother's bizarre assessment. What John McLeod would have regarded as pastoral care, mother mistook for infatuation.* I now know that mother's emotional imbalance, which incorrectly misread people's ordinary attentions as hostile, also read into Pastor McLeod's friendliness a meaning that would not stand up to reasonable scrutiny. Those tumultuous days in Calgary that caused me so much anxiety, also became a window to understanding the complex nature of my mother's fragile personality.

Three weeks have gone by, and we are no closer to saving any money than when we started. Mother's part time employment is subsistence and no more. I decide on action — now! I tell mother I will sell my bicycle and my skates for whatever they bring and hitchhike home. Mother is terrified at my desperate plan. We decide together that hitchhiking across Canada in winter might not be so wise. I come up with a new plan. I will take the cash from the sale, and travel by bus (the cheapest way to go). When I get home, I'll find the money somehow to get mother home. I negotiate a sale at a local bicycle shop. The owner tells me I could do better, if I sold privately through a newspaper want ad. That would take time, and I am in no mood to wait. I take $27.00 for bike and skates. The next snag comes when I discover the only bus route is through the U.S.A. I also

*In 2007 I rediscovered an old letter mother had written to Wray Woods, her brother-in-law, alluded to in chapter five. Mother writes, "I fell hopelessly in love with the new minister, but I now know it was the Word of God I loved. He had a lovely wife who sang in the choir. His words were like pearls and I was glued to my seat." This delightful and recent discovery made me realize that mother, to her credit, in part, finally figured things out. The church and the christians in it are an imperfect lot, but those who discover this healing sheepfold are much better off.

discover I have only enough money to get to Chicago. I reason, "Chicago is further south than frozen Northern Ontario. If I get to Chicago, there's plenty of car traffic to Detroit. I will hitchhike home from Detroit." Once I cross the bridge to Windsor, I'm almost there. By faith, or was it desperation, I take the risk. I buy my ticket to Chicago, and tell mother my plan before she can object. The die is cast; I pack my suitcase, while mother makes up a supply of Deviled Ham sandwiches to last me for three days. I am off with no money in my pocket. I will drink water with my sandwiches. I will persevere till I'm home again.

That evening, I am reading a fairy tale about Camelot where life is serene and things are perfect. Turning to mother I say,

"You know what; Stratford is my Camelot!"

Chapter 36

Homeward Bound

Mother is choked up, and kisses me goodbye at the bus station. I tell her everything will be fine, and like a freshly broken racehorse determined to win, I board the bus. I give mother a triumphant wave. It was a gesture of assurance that mother's self imposed exile would soon be over. It is an exhilarating feeling, to know that in three days, by my calculations, I will be in Ontario. Scenes of Stratford fill my memory. Ontario Street lined with its fine old houses. The Jumbo ice cream parlour, with its 10 cent butterscotch sundaes; talking to my friends; and best of all, my beloved home on Brunswick Street.

It is Thursday November 28, 1946, and I am on my way to Winnipeg. From time to time, I chat with people who ask me where I'm going. When I tell them my story, they shake their heads and commend me for my pluck. The prairie landscape is draped in white snow and by the time we reach Regina it is dark. I sleep on the bus with my seat tilted back, and awaken Friday morning at Winnipeg. I change buses. We are heading south, and are soon in North Dakota. My sandwiches are disappearing faster than my allotment allows, but they are getting stale. That's when I meet my 'angel unaware.' As we approach nightfall, I am talking with a friendly gentleman. He has engaged me in conversation, and is amazed at my story. When the bus driver announces an hour wait for those who wish to buy their dinner at the restaurant, my 'angel' says to me,

"And what are you having for supper?" I explain to him the Deviled Ham sandwiches. He gives a little laugh, and invites me to have dinner with him. I explain,

"But I have no money."

My angel says, "I'll buy your dinner."

I need no second invitation. I thank him and order, what else — a hot chicken sandwich. We return to the bus and chat until we arrive at St.Cloud, which is his destination.

"Take care of yourself and arrive safe," my angel says.

"Thanks, I will."

Thus I am introduced to American generosity. I pass the second night on the bus and arrive at Minneapolis before midnight; by morning's light, we are approaching Chicago. We stop and start our way to the downtown Union Station. This is where my ticket runs out. I still have three of my now stale sandwiches. I am brimming with anticipation. Union Station is an enormous building with grand windows that give the feeling of being out-of-doors when in fact we are inside a sepulchral building thronging with people who are coming and going somewhere else.

Which way is east, I wonder? I'll need to ask someone who knows. It is then I see a desk that says 'Traveler's Aid,' manned by a matronly lady wearing a uniform. I remember mother saying, how, when in doubt ask the 'Traveler's Aid.' They will always help. I approach the woman and tell her what I plan to do. I ask her to give me directions to the highway that will get me to Detroit, so I can thumb my way home.

"How old are you?" she asks. I straighten to my full height and reply,

"Fifteen."

"It's against the law for a minor to hitchhike in Chicago," she sternly affirms. "You are talking to a police officer, and I'm taking you into my custody as of now!" (I have never heard of a woman being a police officer. I am surprised and wonder how I get out of this one).

"I didn't know that." I meekly reply. (I think, "I don't know, if I believe you. I have hitchhiked many times at home. It's not against the law in Ontario.")

"Where are you from?" she demands.

"Stratford, Ontario."

"Do you have any relatives there that could help you get home?" Her voice softens a bit.

"I don't understand the question," I tell her. The uniformed lady is blunt. She tells me that I have to get someone in my family to advance money to pay for my safe return to Canada on the train. My adventure is dashed; I was sure I could hitchhike my way home. I was innocent of the dangers of the downtown core of cities like Chicago and Detroit. Disappointed at my lack of cunning, and feeling like an unwanted alien facing the full weight of American jurisprudence, I confess—

"The only one in my family that could afford to send money for my return to Canada is Uncle Norman in Tillsonburg." The stern policewoman picks up the phone, and asks for information. I am shocked to hear her say,

"Can you give me the telephone number for Norman Gillatly in Tillsonburg." (She never even asked my permission.) I am humiliated: "What will uncle Norman think of me? He will be mad." I am astonished at how quickly connections can be made. She is talking to Uncle Norman, and explaining that a Canadian minor is illegally in the United States, and must be deported immediately. The conversation ends with the policewoman giving her name and saying,

"The money order be must made out to the City of Chicago Police". Uncle Norman, through the miracle of the telegraph system, is to wire $15.00 to cover the costs. He did just that. An hour later all transactions are completed and my officer is phoning Uncle Norm. (Telegrams, the mainstay of my era, ended in 1989 with the communications revolution.)

"Your nephew will be on the New York Central, and will get off at Aylmer, Ontario, at 2 A.M. Sunday morning." Then for the first time, her demeanor softens, and I hear her say,

"Thank you for being willing to take care of your nephew; I really appreciate it."

I am amazed at how easily it all came together. Tonight, I shall be on the New York Central, heading for Aylmer, just sixteen miles from Uncle Norm and Aunt Jean. The responsibility of having to hitchhike through Michigan in winter over unknown roads is gone. My spirit is lifted and I feel euphoric.

"You are free to explore Union Station," my police officer says, "but you must not leave the building. Can I trust you to do that?" I agree to the terms.

"Your train leaves at 6 o'clock; meet me here and I will buy you your supper." So for the second day in a row, I will have a decent meal. I ditch two stale sandwiches and down the last Devil's ham sandwich I have ever eaten.

Time goes fast at the Union Station. I especially enjoy watching the American soldiers. This is 1946 at the beginning of the cold war. There is plenty of military activity in the United States, and soldiers like to go home for weekend furloughs. At 5:00 P.M. my police officer and I rendezvous at the coffee shop and peruse over the menu. I am charmed by my policewoman. Behind that stern exterior is a soft heart after all. We chat leisurely over supper and I thank her for the meal.

"Don't thank me for your supper, thank your uncle. He paid for it. There was enough money left over, after I bought your ticket to handle that. Here's your change."

She gives me 35 cents, and escorts me to the train. Waving goodbye, she smiles and says,

"Good luck, you will be in Canada by midnight."

Half the passengers are soldiers, who are on their way home for weekend furlough. They are young men, who are full of enthusiasm and fun. I eavesdrop on their conversations, and laugh at their jokes. They like to smoke. The coach is blue with puffs of cigarette smoke sufficient to give everyone on board a good dose of cancer. I am so inspired that I determine to smoke myself. (I've already told you how that happened when I got ahead of my story.) The time goes quickly, and the occasional stop sees a few soldiers saying goodbye. Detroit virtually empties the coach. Passengers who are Buffalo bound are in short supply. I literally have the coach to myself. I miss the banter and actually feel a little lonely. At 2 P.M. the conductor shakes his drowsy passenger and says,

"This is your stop, sonny. Time to get off the train."

Aylmer is not exactly an exciting place. I am there with nobody but the stationmaster, who informs me that he is going home. He tells me the morning shift will arrive at 6 P.M. He stokes the potbellied stove and says,

"There will be less and less heat, as the night wears on. The morning staff will open the draft, and get the fire going."

I understand this quite well, as that's my job at our house in Stratford. I am reminded of those chilly mornings when I fire up the stove in the kitchen. I watch him as he pours the coal on the golden fire and remember Grandma's kitchen. I will see it soon. If I were home right now, I would have made two pieces of white toast from bread purchased fresh at Dorothy's Bakery. I would have toasted it golden brown with the long handled fork over the glowing coals before I stoked the fire. I would have smothered the toast in melted butter and eaten them with a hot cup of cocoa. Memories of Grandma's cooking flood my mind. Monday was hamburger patties and fried potatoes. Tuesday was always a pork chop and gravy over potatoes. Wednesday was scalloped potatoes and two slices of cooked ham. Thursday was roast beef with leftovers kept for Saturday. Friday was meatless with macaroni and cheese. Sunday was the feast with a pork roast or a stuffed chicken on alternating Sundays. Her weekly menu never varied, so I knew exactly what to salivate for in advance. Thoughts of home activate my longing and trigger the hunger pangs, which I wisely repress; "Tomorrow will be better."

I lay down on the wooden bench and try to sleep. I awaken every 15 minutes as the clock bongs its way through the night. At 6 o'clock the welcome sound of the day crew greets me. I am shivering by the stove, and glad to see them. I think, "Uncle Norm will be coming soon," He does not disappoint me. The car pulls up at seven. It is an anxious moment. Sheepish, I mutter,

"Sorry about the 15 dollars."

"Don't even think about it," replies Uncle Norm.

"I was only doing my duty — hop in and tell me all about it," he is chuckling as he puts my suitcase in the trunk. I tell him my story, chattering away about my great adventure. Years later, I realize that to be generous to someone who is poor has its own reward. Soon we are in Tillsonburg and my stomach is grumbling. Aunt Jean greets me, "Welcome traveler, I guess you've been on quite a journey." Aunt Jean gives me a hug and exclaims,

"Lordy child, you smell like a cigarette factory." I remember the train from Chicago; the soldiers and the air blue with smoke and explain. Aunt Jean hangs my coat outside on the line to air out. Next, she treats us all to a hearty breakfast. Bacon and eggs, a feast I'll never forget.

Uncle Norm tells me that since it is Sunday, we will drive to Stratford together. Uncle Norman puts my repacked suitcase into the trunk. I am wearing clean clothing that Aunt Jean has freshly ironed. Grandma, by miracle of the telephone, now knows the whole story. Since Uncle Norm always visits Grandma every second Sunday afternoon, the timing is impeccable. She awaits our arrival in expectant anticipation. I think, "Grandma's feast awaits us. I can hardly wait." As we make our way to Stratford, I tell Uncle Norm that my next challenge is to get mother home. On that topic, Uncle

Norm is noncommittal. I quickly understand that Norman has reached his philanthropic limits. I make no requests for mother.

Approaching the city of Stratford is exhilaration maximus. I am ecstatic with joy. Grinning from ear to ear, the familiar sights are wonderful. As we drive through Woodstock we turn north. Coming up HWY 59 we drive through Tavistock. The familiar facades of the village stores make me glad. Spontaneously, I break out laughing. Aunt Jean quips,

"Bruce, I think you're glad to be going home."

"Am I ever!"

When we reach highway 7, we turn left at Shakespeare. I relish the sight. Soon Kroehler's factory looms up on the right; in 1947 it was an imposing landmark (today it has been replaced by the Arden hotel). I am thrilled to be back. When we get to 'The Commons' I see the faces of kids I recognize, an experience I have been denied for five long weeks. Within minutes we pull into the driveway at 156 Brunswick Street.

"There's Pinkey Murphey," I exclaim. With my first glance at the home place, my spine tingles with the exhilaration. My eyes are wide with the sight.

"There it is; we're home!"

A knowing glance between Uncle Norm and Aunt Jean escapes my notice. They are both smiling as I quickly open my door. My feet are touching sacred ground.

I race to the back door and lift the latch. I can see Grandma through the window. She has been watching out for our arrival for the last hour. I can see her smile. Our eyes meet with mutual affection. I have missed her. Later I learn, not as much as she has been missing me.

"Hi Grandma, I'm back!" Grandma hugs me tight and wipes her tears away.

"I'm so glad to see you again."

"Me too, Grandma!" I add these words, "and I'm never going to go away again." Uncle Norman has carried my suitcase in while Aunt Jean has joined the tear wiping ceremonies. After my suitcase is deposited in my bedroom, I bound downstairs and quickly (very quickly) tell Grandma all about my adventures. Next, I exude,

"I'm going out to see Johnny."

Chapter 37

Stratford is still the best.

The kids are glad to see me. I am a celebrity for all of ten minutes.

"I can speak from experience," I say, "I have been to New York on the East, and to Vancouver on the West. I have seen a lot of territory in between, but of all I have seen, Stratford is still the best."

Monday, December 9, I wake early. Today I am actually looking forward to going to school. In fact, I am there early. I go to my homeroom slipping in behind my desk, unoccupied for five weeks. My homeroom teacher, Margaret Baldwin will arrive any minute. She is a tall, statuesque, middle aged woman. Her appearance is striking. She has platinum hair, streaked with gray, down to her shoulders. Her lipstick was always red contrasting with her hair. One by one the kids come in, and are startled to see me. I enjoy my brief notoriety. The reaction is always the same,

"Where have you been?" I revel in the disclosures, embellishing the story.

By the time the dozen or so early birds have come, Miss Baldwin arrives, papers in hand, examining them as she walks to her desk. I'm grinning from ear to ear, my eyes glued on her momentary distractions. At last she looks up and in astonishment blurts out,

"Well, look what the cat dragged in; where on earth have you been?" I walk to the front of the class, and give Miss Baldwin my carefully scripted note that Grandma has written. She looks at it and says,

"I think you need to get down to the office, and see the principal."

I cheerfully comply and walk into David Fuller's office. Mr. Fuller has a trademark; his left hand is paralyzed. He always wears a glove to cover the lifeless hand. He is also a lay preacher in the Brethren Assembly on Rebecca Street, where Uncle Frank and Aunt Marg Gillatly attend church. He knows me and he knows my mom. After a few perfunctory questions, he sighs, and sends me back to my classroom. I return to my class relieved and feeling great. What a contrast to the terrifying day when I attended that Calgary high school for a few hours; I am accepted and right where I belong.

My next big hurdle is Christmas exams. However, something even bigger, is also on my mind. How are we going to get mother home? Grandma has been thinking about this as well and explains that she has made some phone calls and has a plan. The insurance policy that mother borrowed against to get money to go west has matured. The bank loan can now be repaid. After the interest is taken care of, there is $50.00 to spare. Enough money to get mother home. She calls Mrs. Greenberg and asks for mother. We will send her the money as soon as the policy is processed. Mother, contrary to all she has said about leaving Stratford for good, is happy to hear her western exile is over. A subsequent phone call gratefully acknowledges the money has arrived. She has purchased a ticket on the CNR and will be home Sunday, December 15, at 8 P.M.

"What a shame;" Grandma says, "all these people keep calling for appointments to get their hair done, and I have to tell them your mother is in Alberta. There she is working for next to nothing, when she could be earning real money." I ponder this statement, and suddenly I get a brain wave.

"I know what to do!" I exclaim. "We will take appointments for customers anytime, provided they are willing to wait till December 16."

"You can't do that," says Grandma. "What if your mother is delayed?"

"We know when she's coming back," I insist. "We have to do it; we don't have enough money to run the house." I figure this is our chance to get some business for mom so she can earn extra money. After all, we need money to live! Calgary has not been without its lessons.

Grandma is adamant; she will have no part of such a hair brained idea (no pun intended). Just then the phone rings. I answer in my best business voice. Someone is on the line asking to speak to mother. She wants an appointment to get her hair done. My heart is racing. Grandma has disapproved of my plan, but I know I am right. I say to the lady,

"Mother is away just now, but she will be back on Monday, December 16. I can make an appointment for you then, if you are willing to wait." The customer agrees that the 16th is acceptable. I book her immediately. I march back into the kitchen where Grandma is doing the dishes, and tell her what I have done. Grandma grudgingly gives her approval.

"But I'm not booking any appointments for your mother; if you want to do this thing, you will have to return all the phonecalls." I agree to the terms.

The next day when I get home from school Grandma says,

"There's a phone number on the pad, a customer wants an appointment. I told her you would call her as soon as you are home." I smile the pleasure of the victor. Grandma is cooperating. She has come on side. She just won't admit it. I book mother's next appointment. This is Christmas; the ladies want to look their best, and mother has the reputation of being good at her craft. The prospect for business is good.

Meanwhile, I am facing my other crisis. Exams! I am cramming like mad. Math and French are my big ones. For French, Miss Baldwin has me stay after four; she explains to me what has to be learned. I take copious notes, and finally get out of school by five. Mr. Burnett is more accommodating. He invites me to come to his home after supper. I dutifully arrive at 7 P.M., and get a crash course in geometry. On this one, I do a little better. Outside of geography, geometry is my favourite subject. When Friday comes, I write my exams with reasonable assurance; I hope to do well.

As for the beauty parlour, my planning is as follows; mother will be home Sunday evening, December 15. I have her first appointment booked for the very next day. We are anxiously awaiting mother's return. The train arrives at 8 P.M. Time hangs heavy; where is she? By nine, we phone the station. Is there a lady waiting at the station? The stationmaster tells us there is nobody there.

"Mother isn't there." I say to Grandma, "She must have been delayed."

"What are you going to do about the Monday appointments?"

"I will reschedule them for Tuesday." I reply

"What if she doesn't come back tomorrow?" Grandma rejoins.

"That's a chance I have to take;" I resolutely affirm.

I phone the three ladies in question and tell them mother has been delayed for a day. She will arrive Monday night. One by one the customers agree to new appointments.

"She had better be here by Monday;" says Grandma, "or you are in big trouble."

"She will be here; I am sure of it," I say, my confidence a little shaken.

Monday evening we are anxiously watching out the window. Suddenly a car pulls up at 8:20 P.M.

"Grandma, it's a taxi, it must be mother!" I exclaim. "It's the good news we've been waiting for. Mother is home!"

When she comes through the door, she pays the cab driver 50 cents. He carries in her suitcases, thanks her, and leaves.

"That's the last 50 cents to my name," says mother.

I tell her she has a surprise waiting for her.

"What do you mean?" Mother asks. I show her the appointment book and explain what I have done. She is amazed and pleased. Tuesday she dons her white smock. In the next seven days, she makes a hundred dollars clear. That is five times her Calgary weekly wage. We have a good Christmas.

December 20th, we get our marks back. Mr. Burnett informs the class that his star pupil (me) gets 90%. For a brief moment, I am undeservedly enthroned with the gods. The class now gets a brief lecture on how it pays to work hard learning geometry. The truth is, I'm not as good as it appears. Mr. Burnett in his private tutoring had used the very questions that would be on the exam to get me caught up. I revel in my undeserved praise. Miss Baldwin brings me down to earth. In French, I get 57%, a failing grade. I show my displeasure at the poor marks, and Miss Baldwin says,

"Now see here Mr. Woods, what more can you expect? Or let's all take a five week holiday." Thus brought back to the world of reality, I still get to breathe a sigh of relief. I didn't contest Miss Baldwin's definition of my absence as a holiday, but I think to myself, "A holiday that I don't ever want to repeat." As an adult I will take other trips to Calgary and to Vancouver in much better circumstances and with satisfying results. This, however, is in the future. For the present, I think, "I will never leave Stratford again."

I make it through the fall semester without failing because my average is above 60%. January 1947 is a new day and I savour the joy of knowing I am home where I belong.

It is Christmas and I need spending money. I decide to apply at Tamblyn's Drug Store for a delivery job. Mr. Kells is the manager and gives me a job; I like him. He is an Army veteran living with his wife at the in-laws. For so many returning soldiers who are now married, there is no available housing. He anxiously awaits a new house being built on the north end of town. The government has been funding a building boom in houses all over Canada. Wartime housing is nearing completion. These small houses are readily identifiable to this very day anywhere in Canada. Their cookie cutter appearance is unmistakable. Somebody designs a mistake in Ottawa, and everybody pays for it. While those houses that remain may not look like much, at the time, they were a godsend. Stratford's allotment is located to the east of Mornington Road. Returning war veterans get first choice. Mr Kells is in that category; all others need not apply. He makes a prediction that surprises me. Those houses are so cheaply built they will be tomorrow's slums. I don't think it got quite that bad, but to this day you can easily pick out the wartime housing in any community across Canada.

At Tamblyn's, I get $4.00 per week, and 30 cents an hour if needed on Fridays. Money I desperately need to spend on the vices of my choice. It is there that I learn how to wrap Kotex, and do it quickly. All personal products are wrapped this way. It's called being discreet. (Years later when I wrap presents for our ten grandchildren, I always think about those days.) I have many jobs, but mostly I deliver orders all over Stratford on a Tamblyn's bike. I need to replace the bike I sold in Calgary. I know exactly where to buy it. I want my own bike (man sized)! Now that I'm a wage earner, I go to Whetlauffer's and buy my very own bicycle. It is a postwar CCM single sprocket bike complete with ball bearings, and costs $42.50. Prices have not changed in four years because Ottawa is still holding down inflation by wartime price controls. Its $2.50 down and a dollar a week, until it's paid for. At last, I can feel truly grown-up; I have my very own man-sized bike. My choice is between red and red, so I choose red.

One Friday night, I am working dusting the shelves. Edna Murray is on the counter. When I get to the cigarettes, I decide to steal a package of Player's Mild, and put it in my pocket. Edna glances down at me and says,

"What's that in your pocket?" Bold as brass, I reply,

"That's my wallet."

"A wallet doesn't have sharp corners on it; you've just scoffed a package of cigarettes." I protest and with a straight face, I lie, "That's my wallet."

"You are lying; you stole a package of cigarettes," Edna replies.

I am a lousy liar; I should have admitted the truth, and asked forgiveness. I don't. I stall and bluster, and finally talk my way through it, convincing myself that I pulled it off.

At the end of June, Mr. Kells, tells me my services will no longer be required. I was expecting that because Clarence Springer is my senior. He gets to work full time for the summer.

"Can I reapply in September?" I ask.

"You can apply again in September and — if I need you, I will hire you then." However, the problem is, he never needs me. He hires other boys instead of me. I pay a big price for those stolen cigarettes. Which 'shows tagoya' smoking is hazardous for your health in more ways than one. As Thumper the rabbit (of Bambi fame) says,

"If you can't say anything nice about a person, don't say anything at all." Concerning Mr. Kells, will you all now join me in a moment of silence –? (No I didn't.) As far as I know Mr. Kells lived to a ripe old age. My misfortunes are of my own making and from now on I'm as exemplary as a preacher's parable.

I finally get a job delivering newspapers. The work is harder and the pay is not as good. I grin and bear it, deciding to make the best of my situation. I'm not going to harbour an attitude. A little perk comes my way in the 1947 high school 'Collegian'. Editor Shirley Bradshaw is commenting on the kids in grade 10. There is a name list under the caption of 'Can You Imagine.' About ten kids out of more than one hundred are singled out for mention. The first reads as follows, "Can you imagine, Bruce Woods being shy." This cogent observation I take as a compliment. The following year I get honourable mention again. Mary Stortz, our French teacher, is asked to design the ideal grade 11 boy. Amongst several entries for a variety of talents and assets, my contribution to the ideal Grade 11 student is 'smile'. I take this in stride, but am revelling in a better discovery. At long last, I have mustered a whisker on my chin. I proudly show it to mother who promptly goes out and buys me a Schick razor. I faithfully shave every day whether I need it or not. Optimism sees the bright side of everything — even pessimism.

Chapter 38

Trying to fall in Love

As I have already informed you, Barry Knechtel gave up his paper route on Brunswick Street and I needed a job, so I take over the route starting September 1, 1947. It pays $4.00 a week, and introduces me to the paperboys. Al MacDonald I know and we talk. We arrange a football game to be played on a Saturday afternoon at the high school flats. It's our gang vs. Al's gang. Bev Crawford is their star ball carrier (remember the guy at Sea Cadets I had to box); he's good but we've got John Butler who is our best player. I am sure we will win. Too bad for the audience; it was such a good game and not one person to witness the champions. Not even the girls showed up. I can't remember who won the game, so I'm sure it must have been us. There goes my optimism again; I just remembered; it was them. Just as well nobody showed up for the game.

They say that lightning never strikes twice in the same place, but my best friend Jimmy Johnston gets struck twice in the same month and a third time six months later. First, with a bowling ball; second by love; and third with a broken heart. It all begins when I discover that a little extra income can be earned by setting up pins at the five-pin bowling alley on Ontario Street. I make a dollar for four hours work getting home around One A.M in the morning. I share this with Jim Johnston who soon follows suit.

Jim and I work together on separate lanes. The bowler has three chances to get fifteen points. Get a strike and you add another 10 points; if you get all the pins down in two bowls you add 5. Once all the pins are down, we scramble to set them up again for the next customer. One night a novice to the game imagines that even though one gets all the pins knocked over with two bowls, since he paid for three, he might just as well bowl the third ball down the lane even though there are no pins left. Poor Jim! Correctly assuming that the frame was over, Jim is on his feet head down setting up the pins for the next round. Of course, he doesn't see the third bowling ball bearing down and gets conked on the head. It knocks him out and gives him a slight concussion. He got over it quickly but, for an anxious day, we all felt pretty concerned for Jim. I even blamed myself for introducing Jim to the job. Once Jim was in the clear with no after affects, we had a great time ribbing Johnny for just about everything that went wrong; and, if nothing went wrong, us kids made something go wrong, just so we could tease Jimmy Johnston. The more sustained effect of the second lightning strike was when Jim fell in love. I remonstrated with Jim,

"Joan Morris is ruining my life."

The nerve of it all, just like that our friendship is down the tube. I should have known when I saw them together at the City Hall teen dance. Can that girl jitterbug! To boot, she's pretty and petite. Jim is smitten. Now I'm the wallflower. Every time I call on Jim to go someplace, he's busy. So I decide since all my friends are getting girls and going steady I will do the same. I have decided to fall in love. Something new has been added. I now have wavy hair. For some inexplicable reason it seemed to happen overnight. As I examine my hair in the mirror, Grandma catches me preening in front of my dresser.

"And just who are you practicing for?" She caught me flat footed preening! A little embarrassed, I reply,

"I'm the only kid that doesn't have a girlfriend." Grandma responds,

"Well don't be in hurry, there are plenty of fish in the sea."

I consider the prospects. Joan Johnston is too young; besides, her mother won't let her date until she's sixteen. I have to fall in love with somebody else, so who will it be? I decide to go right to the top and date the most beautiful girl in Stratford. Her name is Barbara Douglas. She is returning a book to the library. Good! A date and I don't have to spend any money. A perfect match for a guy who doesn't have any money to burn. We walk to the library and browse. On the way back to her house we hold hands. When we get to her back door, we kiss. After about a dozen kisses, I can't think of anything else to say or do, so I say good night and walk home, asking myself, "now why was I so bored?" Pan and Puck where are you when you're needed? Useless good-for-nothing gods! Always loafing when a little chemistry is in demand! Bad luck, maybe some other time.

John Beal is the friendliest guy in Stratford. He knows everybody by their first name and once he's met you he never forgets your name. He's the radio announcer at CJCS, our local radio station. Once I asked him how he enjoyed listening to my current favourite popular song, which happened to be, "Bongo Bongo Bongo, I don't want to leave the Congo, Oh no no no no no. Bingo bango bungo, I don 't want to leave the jungle, I refuse to go." I am about to discover the power of music to either inspire or drive you nuts.

"Bruce" he says, "When I got this job, I thought, wonderful. As disc jockey in charge, I can play all my favourite songs and get paid for it. Well kiddo, at the time, I didn't like classical music and, I supposed that I would always enjoy the popular stuff and endure the classical. But you know what? The more that I listened to the good stuff, the more I liked it, and the more I listened to the popular tunes, the more I got tired of them. As for your Bongo-Congo song, after you've played that thing 20 or 30 times, I tell you Bruce, it drives me crazy."

Now I have to tell him something to impress John that I too am a connoisseur of good music. I concur about the Congo song and tell him about my discovery of classical music when at long last I met my father in Toronto. Now he knows that I don't have a resident father and treats me like a kid brother, because John Beal was like that. It was no wonder that everyone liked John Beal. He invites me to his Saturday morning show when local talent is given an opportunity to perform. The next Saturday, I am at the CJCS studio, which has about 50 seats. The place is packed. Featured that morning is Janice Riddell. She is definitely pretty and we make eye contact right away. She poses and waits for the piano introduction. I have a flashback. Good thing mother didn't know about this, or I'd have been singing 'Robin in the Rain' for all the world to witness my demise. Janice sings well and judging by the clapping, the older audience obviously approves. I react to her singing voice. Classically trained and mature, her song doesn't appeal to me. When I get home, I tell mother about this cute girl who spoiled her song with her jiggely voice, and promptly decide that I will avoid the CJCS Saturday talent show from now on. A week later the phone rings and mother calls me,

"There's a girl phoning for you who says her name is Janice Riddell." I gasp and think, "Not the girl with the jigglely voice."

1947 Definitely not shy

1948 The dude

I have been indiscriminate as to whom I told that I didn't like her voice. Somebody squealed. I am in trouble.

"Hello Bruce, I noticed you at the radio station the other day, and thought it would be nice to get acquainted. I'm having a house party with several kids coming and wondered if you would like to come," says this friendly voice. I gasp the relief of the undiscovered guilty but Janice assumes it is only surprise. Grateful that no one has blown my cover, I accept her invitation. In later years, after I came to appreciate opera, I have wondered whatever became of Janice Riddell. Just now, I'm getting over the shock of this invitation and meekly acquiesce. After I hang up the phone I think, "A house party with Janice, but how could I ever fall in love with a jiggely singing voice like that?" The address is a house on St. Vincent Street. I think to myself, I know that street; it's where the rich people live. Mother tells me I ought to be nice to Janice. I tell her, I have no desire to be rich or to hang out with rich people. Amazing how poor people can boast about the virtues of the labouring class, and how glad they are that money means nothing, while their actions belie their behaviour. The house party comes and goes, and try as I might, I don't fall in love with Janice Riddell. However, I shamefully admit, I did admire the well-appointed house.

My next effort to fall in love is with a scholar by the name of Margaret Pogson, the smartest kid in her class. She is attractive and plays field for the Stratford Rotinettes ball team. She is now in grade eleven, but still comes to school in pigtails. "Aha," I think, "a prospect for mother's beauty salon." She lives near Aunt Elsie who knows the family well. I scheme and plot a meeting with Margaret. I propose to Aunt Elsie that if she approaches Margaret's mom for me, the deal would be a free permanent wave by mother's new student assistant. Of course that hairdresser-in-the-making is me. I have thought I ought to take advantage of my opportunity to learn the business. Here's my chance to learn under mother's supervision with Margaret as the beneficiary. No dice! Aunt Elsie is not going to risk her friendship with the Pogsons for some hair-brained (hmmn?) idea of mine. I put this out of my mind for now.

Then, Divine intervention takes place. Margaret phones for an appointment to have a permanent. No help needed from me. Indubitably, this has been ordained by heaven. Amazing, the Deity has overheard and I didn't even pray for it to happen. You can imagine how pleased I am to think that my stock rates that high in important places. The day arrives for Margaret's appointment and I am trying to figure out how to make this an occasion to be remembered. I decide on a sudden emergency for something that I've long since forgotten. I make a surprise appearance and mother frowns. I mutter some sort of apology for the interruption, and disappear as promptly as I came. Having botched my big opportunity, I decide I'm a terrible candidate for love and give up on the whole idea. Anyway, Margaret didn't have red hair so why did I even bother.

I am now in grade eleven and Miss Margaret MacGregor is our homeroom teacher. She is a Christian woman with high principles. I remember that because every time she looks at me, I am convicted for my wayward life (well, I was just as wayward as anybody I knew; surely that counts for something). In 1947, I have too much respect to mock in class, but in private I do. After all, machismo is universal! Boys will be boys, and all that bravado that parades itself as worth has not yet run its course. In other words, I am still a conceited jerk. As the girls would say, "Why do guys never seem to get it?" I'm afraid in those days, I qualified. Sometimes a guy is lucky enough to meet a girl with character who can stand up to him.

That's what eventually happened to me, but not just yet.

My Uncle Gordon's Elsie has three sisters. The two youngest are Alberta and Alice Deacon who are knockout beauties. They are identical twins. They are three years older than I am; definitely out of my league, but I love to watch their antics. They dress alike. They walk alike. They dance alike. When they sing songs and snap their fingers they do it in perfect time. They are fun to watch and they make me laugh with their stories. They know how to exploit their gift to the consternation of the guys. One time they went out on a double date and switched names to see if they could deceive their boyfriends. It went off without a hitch and the guys were none the wiser. We howled with laughter over that one. All this helps me envisage the ideal girl, if only I could find her. Alas, I conclude, I guess I'm having too much fun with my guy friends to fall in love with a girl.

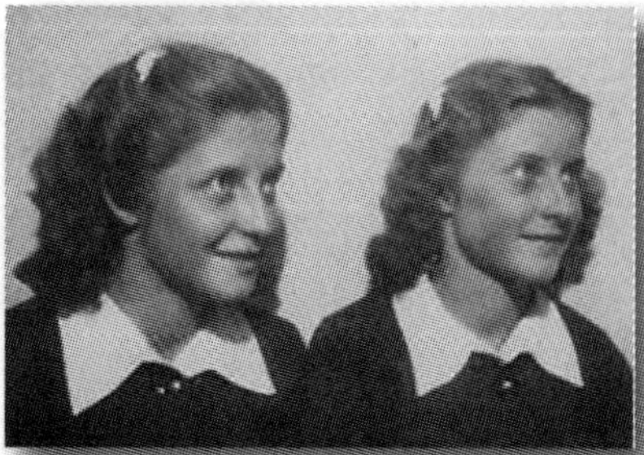

Alberta and Alice Deacon - identical twins

As for Jim, our friendship gets a new lease on life when Joan Morris dumps him for somebody else (Jim's third bolt of lightning). Just as well, he went on to marry Muriel Fountain and they raise a family of five children. I had the privilege of being Jim's best man at the wedding, but apart from that honour, I make no contribution to his well being worth mentioning. Meantime, my (well-grounded?) stable home keeps me content. If this surprises my reader, let me explain. First, I am having the time of my life with my friends and the things we do. Second, Grandma was always there. Through all the storms that surrounded her, she was wise. She was a faithful Christian; she was my role model. With all its shortcomings, for me, my home life is happy. My life is full. I feel secure. Unknown to me, my security will soon fall apart. I am to learn that familiar things like a house you have lived in and streets that you know and take for granted build a feeling of self-reliance and comfort; take them away, and your spirit is adrift. I am about to experience what mother must have felt when she left Camrose, Alberta.

Chapter 39

My Palace is Sold

The world I know is changing rapidly. For one thing, the government cancelled the bill enforcing wage and price controls. The first evidence of our world wildly out of control came through the six o'clock news. An upscale restaurant in Barrie has just doubled the price of a cup of coffee from five cents to ten cents.

"By the time you buy the coffee and pay someone to brew it, serve it, wash the cup and put a nickel in the till, you are past the line of profitability," says the radio announcer quoting the restaurant owner. We scoff at the radio report.

"Imagine, a dime for a cup of coffee! That's outrageous," says mother.

"People will just switch to tea," quips Grandma. "Nobody in their right mind will pay that kind of money for a cup of coffee." Such is the momentous wind of change that comes with the post war era. But this is only the beginning. Other winds are blowing that will tornado me to my own personal land of Oz. At the time it seemed traumatic and unnecessary. In retrospect, the things that happened proved to be a crucible for the better; certainly it was better for me. While I acknowledge my mother's love, I must also acknowledge her unfortunate disintegration.

Mother never denied me anything I wanted. Thankfully, her ability to indulge this very spoiled kid is coming to an end by the time I'm mature enough to face my trials and overcome them. At the age of sixteen when my world collapsed, I was given the opportunity to self-destruct. Instead, I chose to live. I had help. In the gospel of Luke there is a touching story of a widow and her dead son. Jesus interrupted the funeral procession by raising the dead boy to life. I feel a kinship with that boy; my experience will be similar. Without the 'Jesus Encounter', I would have been just as bad a marriage risk as my father.

Our family is about to face a crises that will send Grandma, mother and me in three different directions. To us it is traumatic, yet it pales before the real tragedy that came that fall. In retrospect the tragedy of 1947 is what happened to my friend Gunner Edwards.

He lives on the East Side of town, and often passes our house walking home. He stops to chat awhile. I wave him a goodbye. It is the last time I will see him alive. Stratford is playing a football game against Woodstock; however, we lose the game. The good news is that that evening there will be a dance at Stratford High. Barry Knechtel, Bob Hess and Gunner attend the dance. They are wallflowers, since none of them know how to dance. Donald 'Zeke' Hatfield (not his real name) and his brother take a shine to a new Buick sitting on the General Motors lot and decide to steal it. They visit the high school dance and invite Barry, Bob and Gunner out for a beer and a ride. Deciding that this might be more fun, they accept the invitation and Zeke shows them what a Buick can do.

Things go fine on a quick ride to St. Mary's, however the return drive turns deadly. Rounding a curve, Zeke loses control and drives into a cement wall. The speedometer stuck at 93 miles per hour. Bob's head is scalped when he hits the ashtray. Fortunately for him he was in the back seat. It will take 156 stitches to sew his head back together. Gunner was in the front. He went headfirst through the windshield and was killed on impact. In modern times he would have been spared by a seat belt. Zeke's brother went to jail. To their credit, the brothers finally re-established themselves in business. They set up (appropriately) an auto body shop in Stratford. He and his brother repair cars that are damaged in collisions. From time to time, I think back on that horrendous Friday. The tragedy engulfed the living as well as the dead. In retrospect, this was the real tragedy of 1947. However, having acknowledged this, I now turn the reader to mine.

On the home front, I imagine that things will somehow always be the same, but Grandma tells me she's worried. Mother has just told a customer to stop looking at her "that way." The startled lady was so upset, that she walked out of the parlour in tears. This is not the first time. Mother still imagines the world is against her. Things are clearly getting worse. As a result, the beauty parlour business is falling off dramatically.

There is nothing so important to a well-groomed woman as looking her best. Getting a good hairdresser does not come easy. That's why mother did so well in the hairdressing business. She did good work. However, there is a limit. It was common knowledge that mother had emotional problems. Nonetheless, women will put up with a few idiosyncrasies to get a good hairstyling. Thus, mother's business fared well even though people notice the odd behaviour. However, when mother imagines evil intent, and remonstrates with customers accordingly, a line is crossed. Her business is in sharp decline. As business gets worse, mother blames Grandma. Grandma's palsy gets worse. Things are clearly out of control. There are rumblings with the brothers.

A family pow-wow has to be held. Decisive action must be taken. Grandma's sons have had enough. Mother can no longer earn enough to keep the house going. That's one issue, but the other concern is Grandma's health. Our domestic arrangement is in disarray. Grandma is at the breaking point. Having decided in advance, without mother's knowledge, the sons (somewhat influenced by their wives) have made up their minds. Norman cannot come to the showdown, but Frank and Gordon convince him that they can handle things on their own. The brothers have chosen a day in November. They come after I have finished my paper route. Since they intend to accost mother with what they perceive as intolerable behaviour, the question is what to do about 'Brucie'. After some discussion they decide, now that I am sixteen, I must be present. The atmosphere is tense; mother is looking scared. Grandma is trembling. Very quickly the scene turns ugly. Years of pent up emotion explode into a scene that nobody really understands. The sons blame mother for everything that has gone wrong. Mother is in tears. Grandma is in shock. An ultimatum is given. Grandma and mother meekly accept.

The succession of events is rapid. The house is sold for $3500. Grandma will go to live with Frank and Margaret at 30 McLagan Drive. Margaret had decided that without even consulting Grandma. I have reservations. I am sure that arrangement won't last. I will live with Gordon and Elsie till I can finish grade 11; after that I will live with mother, wherever that turns out to be. Proceeds from the sale will be divided. Grandma gets $2200, mother gets $1300; from now on she will have to fend for herself. I will join her when she sorts herself out. Nobody really believes that mother can make anything go, but they wash their hands of her. It is swift. It is brutal. The issues are settled. I decide, that since I no longer play with toys that I will gather up my Dinky toy tanks, battleships, and airplanes and sell them to Jones Second Hand Store. I give him two six quart baskets of Dinky toys and he gives me a dollar. Today, I would gladly buy them back for twice the price that I received.

Now Aunt Margaret really gets involved. With Grandma coming to her house, she perceives herself as "in charge of things." She takes action without consultation. A quick real estate transaction takes place within the week. When Gordon finds out that a house worth $5000 (his estimate) was sold for $3500, he is livid. How quickly the family armistice has dissolved. Meanwhile Grandma lasted three weeks at McLagan Drive. In no time, Grandma and I are both living at uncle Gord's house. With Elsie and Gord and the two kids, that makes six people living in a two-bedroom house. It is left to Elsie to keep the peace. We are all in transition and nobody is quite sure just where they fit. Mother went to Rochester to find out all about the Harper Beauty Method that guarantees all comers that (provided they pay the fee) they can get rich quick. The domestic arrangement at Gord's house is testimony to the diplomacy of Aunt Elsie. There was a bribe. Gordon and Elsie were renting 475 Albert Street and the owner wants to sell. Grandma's money provides the $600 down payment (1/3 of the price) for the house, in exchange for lodging. She will also contribute for the food she eats. It's a good arrangement for everybody. I sleep on the couch till I finish grade eleven. In June of 1948, I move to London to live with mother who is struggling to set up a new business in rented quarters under the banner of the Harper Beauty Method.

The torch I have been carrying for Joan Johnston is laid aside. The deadline before she can date is still one year away (not till she's sixteen, her mother said). I know if Lucy Maude had been writing this story, Gilbert (I) and Anne (she) would have got together, but that's the stuff of fiction, I'm writing history. It's probably just as well. Bud Haveling has his eye on Joan Johnston, and he's an athlete. With that strikeout king, I wouldn't have had a chance.

I eventually marry the beautiful Joan Amy from Waterloo. The girl with the flaming auburn hair marries Bud who dies early of cancer leaving Joan Johnston, widowed at 35 with two daughters to care for. She remarries and is widowed again. She is an overcomer and her faith sustains her. She goes on to be one of Sarnia's leading citizens in local affairs. Her brother Jim (Johnny) took Muriel Fountain as his wife and as I have already told you, I was his best man at the wedding. John Butler, Archie Mulford's successor in the heroics of football, became a High School teacher. Royce Clark, who continually got himself into trouble with the ladies, became a career man in the Canadian Army. Vincent Schooley is a tragedy. Who would have thought this debonair, self-confident, happy-go-lucky, guy would die so young? He was killed at a railroad level crossing when a train demolished his car. Alan MacDonald pursued a career in the newspaper business. I have just completed my 50th year in the ministry, and divide my time between my acting career and preaching.

Joan Amy became my wife in 1951. She urged me to write this book and suggested the title.

Chapter 40

A New Beginning

When I packed my suitcase for London, I left part of my heart behind in Stratford. Meanwhile mother was vainly attempting to establish a beauty parlour advertised as the Harper method. It is a franchise affair operating out of Rochester, N.Y. that succeeds for the few, and bankrupts the many. Mother was in the latter category. My flirtations led me to Margaret Dennett, and a new round of friends in the city of London.

I fell for Margaret. I didn't even care that she was too religious. All I wanted to do is be with Margaret, even if that meant going to church. She was a gutsy kid who even at 16 was not afraid to stand up for what was right and challenge what was wrong. My relationship with Margaret didn't last very long, but Margaret pointed me in the right direction, for which I am forever grateful. As for the practical side of life, I had no difficulty finding work. I got a job in construction, a fact which illustrates how desperate employers can be for common labourers. Remember, I'm still the skinny kid. Those were the postwar years, when Canada couldn't find enough workers. No wonder immigration opportunities abounded. 'Displaced Persons' or 'DPs' (mostly Europeans) were everywhere. I got a job at Husband's Transport at the unheard of salary of 80 cents an hour. However, living with mother had its privations. I had only arrived a few days, when it was Sunday, with no food or money in the apartment. We managed breakfast and a stringent lunch, but there was nothing for supper. Mother had 25 cents to her name, so I made a proposal.

"Let's get four bus tickets, two for you and two for me." I said. "We'll hunt golf balls." We took the bus to the south end of Wortley Road, and found our way to the London Country Club. Walking into the rough, we began our search. Sure enough, after about two hours, we had a treasure trove of lost golf balls. Accosting a golfer leaving the course, I said,

"How would you like to buy some golf balls?" His reply to me was,

"Where did you find these?" I told him where, pointing to the rough.

"You know," says this golfer, "you're not supposed to do that; the country club has its own people who look for lost balls." To which, I reply,

"I didn't know that, but when you're hungry you do these things."

"What do you mean by that?" he grumbles.

I then tell him our circumstances. He softens and gives me all the loose change in his pocket, which amounted to $1.13. With two unused bus tickets, we make the return journey. Back at 80 Dundas Street where mother has her shop; our next problem is how to buy food. All the grocery stores in London are closed on Sunday. I take my cash and go to a local restaurant across the street, and explain my plight. The manager thinks it over and says,

"I can spare a dozen eggs and a loaf of bread, you can have them for the price I paid."

"Agreed!"

I take my groceries home, and we have scrambled eggs for supper. The next day mother has two appointments. We are eating again. Friday is payday, and together we manage a few more weeks. Unfortunately for the business, the handwriting is on the wall. Mother tells me she will sell her equipment and fend as best she can with what she can salvage. No longer able to cope with the public, she eventually took work caring for shut-ins with room and board provided. That's how she met her future husband. Her good fortune was my miracle. Even Jim Langford's untimely death didn't deter the miracle. After five more years of testing, another miracle. Sid Jones married my now widowed mother. Her three marriages included five years with Bruce Sr., three years with Jim Langford*, and ten years with Sid Jones. As things turned out, the last was the best of all. In a letter written to my Uncle Wray (recently ordained a Deacon and Lay Reader in the Anglican Church) a few years before her death, my Mother penned these words,

"All my life, I used to hate myself because I made so many mistakes, saying and doing the wrong thing and being so afraid of people — but I found out from the Bible that no one is perfect in this world, not until we reach heaven; then will we be made perfect like Christ and be satisfied in Him forever."

1953, Mom and Jim Langford, her seond husband

1963, Mom and Sid Jones, her third husband

When I read these words (written January 3, 1962, but hidden from my eyes until my Uncle Wray gave me the letter at my Mother's funeral in 1975), I was justifiable proud and moved with compassion. My only regret was her inability to put these concepts into practice for Grandma's sake. To Grandma's credit she understood her daughter's illness and held no bitterness. Mother's grip on reality was always tenuous and yet not quite over the cliff as the following quote from that same letter reveals.

*Mother was so preoccupied with her troubles real and imagined that she lacked the capacity to understand how deeply she had wounded her mother. After she had married Jim Langford, mother made her peace with Grandma. Grandma did not live to know that soon mother would be a widow.

She died assuming that her unfortunate daughter was cared for. Her faith was rewarded. Mother married Sid Jones who provided a home and income. Grandma enjoyed living at Uncle Gordon's house because Aunt Elsie took good care of her and treated her with respect. There would be no nursing home for Grandma. I visited her as often as I could. Right up to the last, we had wonderful times together. I was twenty-four when she died.

"I fell hopelessly in love with the new minister, but I know now it was the Word of God that I loved. His words were like pearls and I was glued to my seat. I didn't want Bruce Jr. to be like me. So I gave him singing lessons and he sang solos in the (music) Festivals and at concerts when he was only 4 years old." In actual fact, I was 10 years old when I took music lessons and I never sang at concerts; I did sing at three music festivals and the story of how I bombed out has already been told. Mother's letter reveals how wishful thinking and reality can get a bit tangled up. It also reveals her complete commitment to see her son succeed and I honour her for that.

My father's fate stands in commiserate contrast. He decided to go into the aluminium window business, which after World War II had become big business. My father was a super salesman but not a good business manager. He was smart enough to build a business making good money, but quickly, as the business grew, he found himself in troubled waters. He was well over his head in new orders and deeply in debt. In attempting to challenge the Corporates, he took in a wealthy partner who cleaned him out. When his partner fled the country, he also emptied the bank account. With the exception of the house my father lost everything he had worked for. Dad tried to resurrect the old Capital Rock Wool Company but with limited success.

My father eventually sold his house and bought a rundown mansion on the corner of Dixie Road and Dundas Street in Mississauga. A smart move to be sure. The property included two acres. It would have been a gold mine, if he had waited a little longer to sell to some developer. However 'when poverty walks through the door love flies out the window'. There are domestic rumblings and quarrels. Dad should have looked within himself and admitted he was in the wrong. Instead, he lost his head and left Phyllis for Sharon Sullivan (not her real name), a woman much younger than himself. The affair lasted 18 months. With his tail between his legs he contritely returned to Phyllis who magnanimously took him back. That's when he discovered he had cancer. Trying to opt out of the hectic life, he and Phyllis agreed to sell the property (prematurely, as things turned out). Together they would look for something up north, but sadly Phyllis had a car accident that laid her up in hospital for months. That's when Dad found his dream. A marina was for sale on Lake Simcoe.

With Phyllis in hospital, the hand of prudence was unavailable for a second opinion. Bruce pleaded with Phyllis to trust his judgement. He was afraid his deal of a lifetime would be snapped up by somebody else. To accommodate Bruce Sr., Phyllis agreed. Lake Simcoe had high water that year due to the unusual rains. This deceit of nature had hidden the real condition of the marina. The following year the water level returned to normal. The shallow waters told a frightening story. The marina was inaccessible by all but the smallest of boats. To put it plainly, Bruce had been taken. Ultimately, cancer claimed a very embittered man. When my father died, the bank seized his Cadillac and foreclosed on the marina. Payments on both were in arrears. Bruce Sr. died penniless. Before he died, I was at his bedside saying,

"Dad you never ever went to church or had much faith in God. Remember the thief on the cross beside Jesus. He was a lot like you, yet in his dying gasp, he turned to Jesus and said, 'Remember me when you come into your kingdom'. To which Jesus replied, 'This day shalt thou be with me in Paradise. Dad, you can say that prayer right now." I thought Dad's reply was so touching; he said,

"Phyllis too!" I replied,

"Phyllis too."

But now I am 15 years ahead of my story. So, let's return to my circumstances in 1948. When mother vacated her quarters, I strike out on my own. I live with my new friend George McBride, for a few weeks, while his folks are away on vacation. The McBrides definitely are not religious, just as Margaret's parents are not religious. However Margaret, who in contrast to her family is a devout Christian, goes to the Wortley Road Baptist church with me in tow. I look upon it as a date. Margaret and I are now going steady. I am now bouncing between Margaret the Christian and George the Agnostic. Who will win this battle for my soul? The subject of religion is now a daily discussion with George and me. We will pool our ignorance for hours, and come to some remarkably firm conclusions about the Bible, and the folly of being a Christian. I never cease to be amazed at the authority of the illiterate. George and I are now philosophers. Not bad for two guys who have never really seriously picked up a book on philosophy, or read the Bible for ourselves. The discussion ends abruptly with the return of George's parents. Meanwhile, I move into Art and Margaret Sadler's boarding house on Wortley Road, two blocks south of the Baptist Church. My guardian angel brings a full report to Gabriel and is amazed to see his boss pleased and chuckling to himself. It's so out of character with the otherwise abstemious archangel he is used to. Naturally, to be polite, he laughed too and wondered if Gabriel knew something about our subject (me) that he wasn't telling.

Thinking about my discussions with George, and attending church with Margaret is an interesting contrast. The question being; is this Christianity stuff really true. It occurs to me that perhaps, I ought to read the Bible for myself, and see what it really says. I do just that, beginning with Genesis, the first book of the Old Testament.

Now if you wanted to write a meaningful report that would establish the equality of the sexes, the dignity of work, and in the treatise demolish idolatry, discredit astrology, undermine mythology, liberate people from enslaving legends, and set forth a worthy Creator/God in 800 words, how would you write it? Just to complicate things, the story must capture the minds of both, the savage and the erudite, the young and the old. What would you say? How would you write it? The first chapter of Genesis does exactly that.

I am a lover of history. As I read on, I enjoy the story of the origins of the Hebrew race. I am not even finished reading Genesis, when I make a life altering decision. I think to myself, "This book tells the truth." Sorry George, you lose the argument. I've made up my mind. Becoming a Christian is the only choice I can possibly make (there is pandemonium on Olympus, the gods are in disarray over one that slipped through their fingers). So I gave up smoking and cussing. I went to church for every meeting. If they would have let me in, I would have gone to the Women's Missionary Society (All I would have had to have done is show them how I throw a baseball). I also decided that I definitely wanted to be a minister. Yes, it really happened. It was that turning point that Jesus called being 'born again'.

Thank you Mr. McIntee for inviting me to church; you didn't know it, but your persistence stirred old feelings that could not be forgotten. Thank you Charles Michie; I don't remember anything you taught me in Sunday school, but there must have been something deposited in my brain that Mr. McIntee's invitation to church stirred up. Thank you Helen Westurn; your confrontation with me on a Toronto streetcar eventually paid off. Thank you Margaret Dennett, who had the guts to confront a wayward kid with a high standard of Christian morality. Thank you Grandma for reading to me Hurlbut's story of The Bible, you planted good seed that eventually took root and grew. And last of all, but certainly not least, thank you mother for loving me unconditionally. You imagined when you died that you left no legacy of worth. You left me wealthy. Because you loved me, I have been able to love.

It all starts in the cradle. You had a perilous existence, but considering the rapids and the hidden shoals of the river of life, you did fine. When tragedy overtakes a life, a comeback is hard. Compound the tragedy and the mind collapses under the strain. Yet mother, somehow through it all, you survived. You actually attain the stature of the heroine who overcomes, and passes that heritage on. You sacrificed yourself that I might attain a better life. Is not this the true Christian example?

Furthermore, you evangelized me. I don't think you realized how well you did the job. This spoiled kid finally got it straightened out. I discovered the greatest love of all. The love of God!

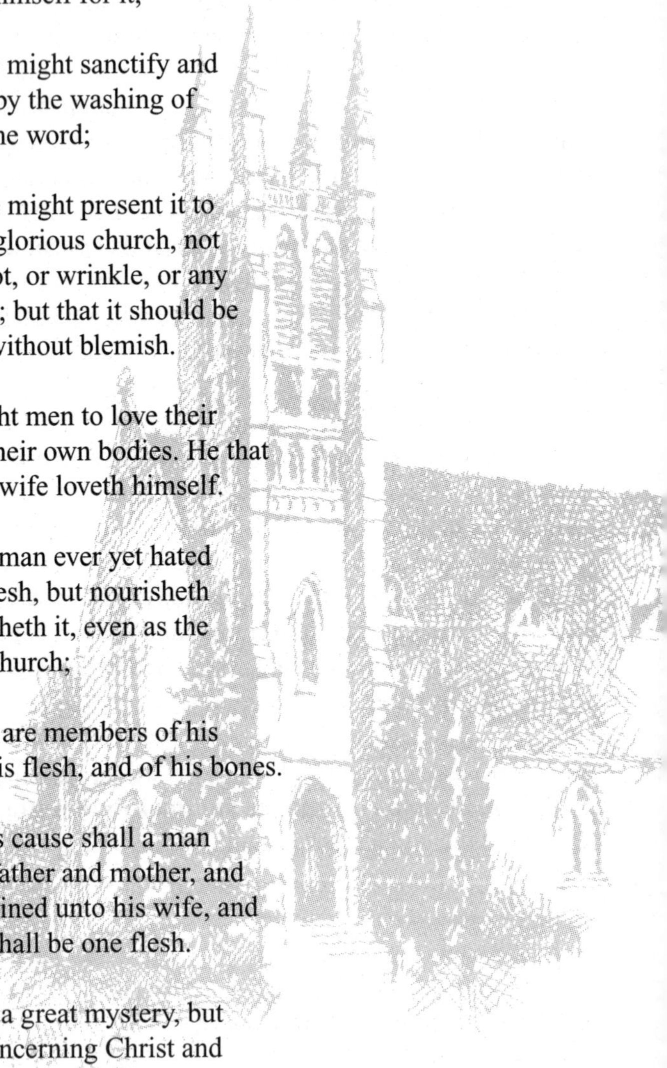

25 Husbands love your wives,
even as Christ also loved the church,
and gave himself for it,

26 That he might sanctify and
cleanse it by the washing of
water by the word;

27 That he might present it to
himself a glorious church, not
having spot, or wrinkle, or any
such thing; but that it should be
holy and without blemish.

28 So ought men to love their
wives as their own bodies. He that
loveth his wife loveth himself.

29 For no man ever yet hated
his own flesh, but nourisheth
and cherisheth it, even as the
Lord the church;

30 For we are members of his
body, of his flesh, and of his bones.

31 For this cause shall a man
leave his father and mother, and
shall be joined unto his wife, and
they two shall be one flesh.

31 This is a great mystery, but
I speak concerning Christ and
the church.

Ephesians 5:25 – 31, The Bible, King James Version

About the Author

Bruce Woods is a retired minister who spent 37 years in the Baptist Church. He spent the first sixteen years of his life in Stratford before he moved to London, Ontario. He received his B.A. from Western University and his M. Th. from Dallas Theological Seminary. He is married to Joan Amy of Waterloo with four children and ten grandchildren. At his wife's prompting (she also suggested the title) he has written his memoirs of his early years growing up in Stratford. Rev. Woods has been a contributor of many articles to his denominational magazine 'The Evangelical Baptist'. He was in Vancouver from 1966-1972 where he participated in the 1971 Centennial producing the re-enactment of the coming of John Morton, Vancouver's first settler for CBC Television. He is also the playwright of two 'one man' dramas 'David and Bathsheba' and 'James a Skeptic Believes', which he regularly performs in both Canada and the United States. He has lived in Hamilton, Ontario for the last 35 years where he has pastored three different churches. He was the founder of Hamilton Baptist Non-Profit homes for low-income families. Active in local ministerial affairs, he was a co-founder of the Hamilton Theological Society, teacher of the downtown Business Luncheon for Men and Women and co-chaired with Mayor Bob Morrow the Millennial Christian Festival. From time to time, he has been interviewed by Crossroads TV. for 'One Hundred Huntley Street', The Hamilton Magazine as well as The Hamilton Spectator. He presently holds his credentials with the Congregational Christian Churches of Canada.

If you would like to communicate with Bruce A. Woods you may contact him at

167 Fallingbrook Dr.
Ancaster, Ontario L9G 1E7
E-Mail brjwoods @ sympatico.ca
Phone 905-648-1589
Web Page: www.between two women.net